'A very personal story and a ve[...] his life, from Spain where he was [...] es, is not only a physical journey [...] His feelings and views about the exploitation of a[...] arly those that are raised and killed to be eaten, are powerfully and poignantly described. Those who have already started to tread the vegan path will find it profoundly reassuring. Those with different views will, nonetheless, have their eyes opened to a new way of thinking. After all, there can never be too much compassion and kindness in the world.'

Virginia McKenna OBE,
co-founder of Born Free Foundation

'An incredibly comprehensive guide to what it means to be an ethical vegan, from its historical origins to the practicalities of everyday modern life. Jordi's court case means that the beliefs of ethical vegans, quite rightly, have to be respected. A book like this is really helpful for anyone who wants to understand why.'

Kerry McCarthy MP

'A personal journey and one of the most important stories in veganism today. Jordi Casamitjana's *Ethical Vegan* dives into the deep past of our relationship with animals, from Buddhist ethics to Taoist wisdom to the latest social and cognitive science. He explores what it means to live ethically alongside non-human beings. I loved this book for its generous telling of his legal battle to win recognition for veganism in the workplace, its wide ranging sources, and the way in which Casamitjana pinpoints what we need to do now to make the world better for animals, including us humans.'

Dr Alex Lockwood,
academic and author

'With Jordi Casamitjana's lucid storytelling interspersed with ancient wisdom and empirical evidence, this book can illuminate our understanding of what it means to be vegan in much the way Yuval Noah Harare's *Sapiens* explained what it is to be a modern human. As informative as it is incisive, as inspiring as it is inviting, this book will become one of the stand-out pieces of literature in the animal liberation movement. A must read whether you are vegan, vegetarian or otherwise!'

Joel 'Jay Brave' Bravette,
sustainability champion and trustee of The Vegan Society
and Made In Hackney youth ambassador

JORDI
CASAMITJANA

ETHICAL
VEGAN

A PERSONAL
and POLITICAL
JOURNEY
to CHANGE
THE
WORLD

To all the wasps, and their fellow earthlings

Contents

Preface

The guy who did the vegan thing

I like birds. I like all animals, actually.

Other than humans, birds are the most common vertebrates you encounter if you live in a city, like me. Sadly, though, most people ignore them as if they were nobodies. Many don't know the difference between a coot and a moorhen. They are both chubby black waterfowl commonly found in the parks' ponds, but the top of the moorhen's beak is red, and the coot's is white. I used to mix their names up, but their feet help me to remember – moorhens' feet are similar to those of laying hens, while coots' are more webbed and closer to those of ducks.

As a ritual, every time I see any of them, I quietly tell myself their name. I was doing just that, relaxing on a bench by the pond of my local park, when a bearded jogger passed by me. He looked at my black beanie with the word 'vegan' distinctively printed on it, did a double-take, and slowed down. I knew what was going to happen next.

He stopped, hesitated for a couple of seconds, and while approaching me said: 'Are you the guy?' I said nothing at first. 'Are you the guy that did the thing, about the vegan thing?' he said with a quiet voice coloured with a touch of embarrassment. Reassuring him, I nodded and smiled, 'Yes, I am the guy.'

How did I end up in this position? How on earth did this middle-aged man end up with his white-bearded face invading most devices and newspapers (for a few days) and become 'that guy'? How on earth did a single email sent to a few charity workers end up making history and changing the lives of hundreds of thousands of people overnight? How on earth did this idea, simultaneously cooked up in the Aegean Sea and the Kingdom of Magadha thousands of years ago, end up being such a fast-growing cultural trend, which in turn may become one of the last hopes of humanity?

I feel I am at the intersection of three different stories which define ethical veganism. Yes, ethical veganism, not just 'veganism'. This recognised philosophical belief is no less important than Christianity, democracy or socialism. Not just a diet; not just an opinion, nor a trend. This compelling force makes me dispose of banknotes, reject fruit-and-nut mixes, walk with my eyes fixed on the floor, talk to strangers mesmerised by the sight of modern servitude, and feed a daring mosquito with my blood. This is a 21st-century revolution which began more than twenty centuries ago.

If you are a human considering becoming an earthling, a meat-eater considering becoming a vegetarian, a plant-eater considering becoming a vegan, or simply want to learn about the foundations of veganism, this book may be for you. This book asks three fundamental questions, explores three universal ideas and tells three intertwined stories. It looks way back into the ancient past, pays close attention to the dynamic present and dreams away into the hopeful future. It will take you on a journey as personal as it is global, as contemporary as it is timeless. And it tells of identity, truth and rightness.

The most revolutionary ideology brought to life.

1.

The Most Powerful
Idea Ever Conceived

Who am I?

My first story is about my personal journey of identity, which made me become an ethical vegan, and it begins in a hospital in Barcelona. One of the first things I must have seen when I popped out into this world was the lens of an 8mm cine camera. My father was a cameraman and had his own small film production company, and many experiences from my beginnings were immortalised in celluloid. My parents must have been quite happy to meet me. After my entrance – or exit, I should say – they found out I was male (this was pre-ultrasound), which must have pleased them as it would work well with my older sister. However, either that day or perhaps a couple of days later, they discovered an aspect of me I had no idea I possessed. They discovered my name. They discovered my name was Jordi; that I was Jordi.

But Jordi is not on my birth certificate. When my parents had already met me and knew it was my name, they had to deal with something most Catalan parents had to face in the mid-1960s: the Spanish State ... and at that time this meant the Spaniard Francisco Franco. He was a fascist general – an actual fascist rather than someone who acts fascistically – who won the Spanish Civil War in 1939, and since then had led an authoritarian regime which heavily oppressed any other culture not belonging to his pure Catholic-Spanish elite. Therefore, Catalans, Basques and other nations in the Iberian Peninsula administered under Spain were oppressed and persecuted by Franco's minions.

Any symbol of the Catalan culture was made illegal. This included traditional music and costumes, newspapers, radio, accounts of Catalan history in schools, the Catalan language (you were not allowed to use it in public), and also, of course, all Catalan names. My parents would have been arrested if they had written my name on my birth certificate ... and so would the clerks if they had allowed them to do so. They had to write the Spanish version of it instead – which I will not mention here as, for predictable reasons, I passionately hate it.

Franco died of old age in 1975, when I was eleven. I remember fascism well. I remember being yelled at in the street, 'Speak Christian!', for being caught speaking Catalan. I remember the police storming my local church as an informer had told them there was an unlawful gathering inside. I remember attending guitar lessons, learning forbidden Catalan songs, while one of us had to be by the window checking nobody would pass by and hear us. I remember how terrified I was of the police – all Spaniards, all moustached, all aggressive – who we called 'the grey people' on account of their dull uniforms. I remember being the victim of twenty muggings in a single year and not been able to report them because ... well, you know why. Afraid of the outside world and with a perfect bullies' target look – short, glasses, helmet-style haircut and overdressed – I seriously considered what I could do when I grew up that did not require me to go out at all.

I was born Jordi, a boy from a well-defined culture and nation, and my parents expected I would join their ethnic group as 'one of them' ... but the world told me: 'No, you are not Jordi. No, you are not Catalan. No, you don't belong to the people of your family ... of your neighbours, of your friends.' The first crystallisation of my identity, my first individual basic right, my first expression of personhood, the first consequence of my thought, was denied to me. The essential question – 'who am I?' – was challenged from the beginning.

My parents taught me to resist. They found schools for me where teachers dared to teach me in Catalan. They kept a forbidden traditional Catalan hat hidden in a wardrobe that I could clandestinely put on for a few minutes once a year or so. They never allowed anyone to call me other than by my real name. I never let 'the grey people' tell me who I was, or who I wasn't.

Many years later, I did it. In 2019, while already in Britain, I filled in the papers – I got the witnesses, I got the declarant, I got the solicitor – and I officially changed my first name to Jordi by enrolled deed poll. However, that name isn't on my hat, on my jacket or my T-shirt. Through my life, I had discovered a new identity to add to my first one, one that feels more authentic, more complete. My first story takes you through my journey to that discovery – a soul-changing destination.

What is this?

At the end of 2016, I was living alone in a one-bedroom studio flat in south London, not far from where the silent film actor Charles Chaplin grew up. It was very small and in quite a state of disrepair, but I put up with it for more than ten years because the landlord never increased my rent. It was on the first floor above a convenience store in quite a busy road, but luckily it had double glazing so the noise was tolerable (which helped a bit with the temperature as the electric storage heater wasn't very good). My living room doubled as a kitchen, and over the years it had accumulated a lot of stuff (books, CDs, old VHS tapes, work files, all sorts of electronic devices and small figurines of animals). All the flats I lived in since I moved to the UK had an air of temporal residence rather than a home. For instance, rather than decorating with framed paintings or pictures, I used posters badly stuck with pins or tape (in my living room I had one of a photo of planet Earth, a reproduction of a 17th-century world map, a tree of life diagram with the major biological groups and a poster of Shania Twain singing 'Man! I Feel Like A Woman'). A kind of man cave, I suppose.

I was in my fifties but I had lived in so many places throughout my life that I think I'd lost my sense of 'home', and everywhere I stayed felt like a temporary en-suite room of an imaginary old hotel with an absentee receptionist. I didn't mind. I was quite happy just to have a place where I could lock the door and let myself loose in the ravines of my imagination, or someone else's. But somewhere inside me, a voice urging me to 'settle' nagged me now and then, and with age it became more difficult to silence, especially because in the last few months my new job forced me to use public transport, which I had been lucky enough to avoid in my three previous positions.

On the 17 December 2016, around the time I was seriously considering whether I should move somewhere 'nicer', I received an email titled 'Important information from your employer about workplace pensions'. I was expecting this, as three months had passed since I was employed by the animal protection charity, and the office manager told me that by this time my work pension would kick in. The email said:

> The government has introduced laws aimed at getting more people to save for their retirement. Simply put, employers have to enrol eligible jobholders automatically into a qualifying pension scheme if they're not already in one … You don't need to do anything because you'll be automatically enrolled into your employer's pension scheme, which is provided on 01 Dec 2016.

We all are born in a readymade world. It's all there, well, most of it. People born before us left it there, ready for us – where we can go, what we can wear, what we should eat, what we could do. The possibilities are not endless. They are very limited, and depending on your gender, class, colour or ethnicity, they may be even more limited. But part of the 'introductory package' of this world is the idea that everything is done for us – we shouldn't be worried, everything has been sorted out. Therefore, when you receive an introductory pack of a new pension fund, the temptation is to assume everything is fine, taken care of.

I don't buy it, though. Many of us, vegans with whom I share my philosophical belief, don't buy it. We don't accept what is offered to us at face value, because more often than not it will not be what we can have, what we should have. When someone offers anything to us, we always mentally ask the question **'what is this?'** What is it made of? How was it made? Who is going to profit from it? What is the truth behind it? We look, we check, we dig, and we learn such truths, and when I did all that with the new pension fund I had been enrolled into, I found something I did not like, something I could not accept. I discovered it was investing in companies that test on animals and damage the environment; companies I would consider highly 'unethical'. This discovery made at the end of 2016 marks the beginning of my second story, which led to a series of events culminating with a substantial change in the way vegans are treated by the establishment – a paradigm-changing resolution.

What should I do?

Ideas don't come out of the blue – not even the blue comes out of the blue. There is always a natural context behind everything, even behind the apparent colour of the sky. The third strand to this shared journey originated thousands of years ago. It's the story of how the idea of ethical veganism came about. For me, it comes from an impulse that is very old, very ancient. It existed long before anybody was capable of having an idea. And that impulse is called biological altruism.

Life on this planet started about four billion years ago, just after the Earth cooled down sufficiently. A few self-replicating molecules became better at it by getting more complex and by using the matter and energy around them more efficiently. Very soon, they began competing with others, as they were all trying to use the same limited resources and those who found a more efficient way to use them multiplied in higher numbers. Every time something changed in the environment, some molecules which may not have been dominant before got a chance to 'win' now, as they were better 'adapted' to the new circumstances. Welcome to biological evolution by natural selection. It all began with some molecules competing with each other in order to replicate more, and it never stopped, leading to all the current biodiversity on our planet.

Looking at it less scientifically, life sprouted with the concept of selfishness – 'Me, me, me' – which translates into: 'I want everything, I want it all.' However, if this has been the basic tune of biological evolution for millions of years, time has had a very interesting effect on the overall final melody. Life has become more and more complex, and the way it expresses the tune has become more elaborate.

Biologists have a term for this called 'levels of organisation'. This means structures in Nature, with things at higher levels being composed of things at the lower level. Typical levels of organisation we find go from the subatomic level to the atomic, molecular, cellular, histological, organismal, populational, ecosystemic, biospheric, planetary, to the galactic level – and we could keep going.

Although the idea of dividing living beings into 'levels' is quite old (Aristotle was talking about it in the 4th century BCE) this was often done more for reasons of 'hierarchy' (who is supposed to be superior to whom – with humans always crowned at the top) rather than to describe different degrees of complexity. The roots of the contemporary notion of biological levels of organisation are more recent and were formulated by the 'organicist biologists' of the early to mid-20th century, such as Joseph Woodger, Ludwig von Bertalanffy or Joseph Needham. They proposed a sort of middle-ground solution to a debate between two opposite approaches in biology that was discussed at the time: the 'mechanists', who stated biological phenomena were 'nothing over and above' their physicochemical components, and the 'neovitalists', who stated biological phenomena must involve non-physical forces or entities (God, Dharma, 'energy', etc.). 'Organicists' devised quite an elegant truce between them: it is the increase of the level of organisation which creates the illusion there must be something other than molecules interacting, but there isn't anything else. Those external forces are not real, but the effect of an increasing level of organisation.

In a way, when you observe a higher level, you kind of forget to regard the lower levels and instead begin to see new properties of the system. For example, if you look at the forest, you might cease to look at the trees, which might make you conclude that woods have 'magical' properties you had not seen before in trees alone – but they haven't. It's an illusion. When you were looking at trees alone, you did not notice how they interacted with each other, with the symbiotic fungus in the ground, with the plants around them and with the rest of wildlife living with them. And with ourselves, we see humanity as a collective group of human organisms that does amazing things, and we forget each that each organism alone also does amazing things … and we forget each organism is only an array of amazing cells also doing amazing things, and so on. Every time we look at a higher level of organisation in a system, we tend to forget the levels below, and that is when we seek 'external' explanations of how the system works, because it seems easier than looking down a level.

I remember when I first grasped this idea in 1981, five years after Franco had died of natural causes, marking the end of forty years of oppression. I was sitting in a very crowded lecture room in the annexe of the main red building of the Faculty of Biology of the University of Barcelona. Here I was, finally, fulfilling my destiny. I was going to become a zoologist after the degree I had just started. In school, I only had good grades in life sciences (I collected insects, seashells and minerals, you see), and when I heard about the biology degree, I knew it would be for me.

When I was a child a Spanish documentary maker, Dr Felix Rodriguez de la Fuente, was always on TV. He was our equivalent of David Attenborough, and just like Sir David he had such a distinctive way of speaking that he was often the target of keen impersonators. He was particularly partial to wolves, and his documentaries about them fascinated me.

Did you know the concept of 'alpha male' was first coined after studying wolves? The term was first used in 1947 by Rudolf Schenkel of the University of Basel, who based his findings on researching the behaviour of captive grey wolves (*Canis lupus*). It means one male is the 'boss' of the pack, and not only makes the most important life decisions for the group but also dominates all the other individuals physically and reproductively. This view of grey wolf pack dynamics was popularised in 1970 by David Mech in his book *The Wolf*, which must have influenced Dr de la Fuente, as he started filming his documentaries with wolves a few years later. However, because David Mech's research was mainly in captive populations with unrelated individuals, he eventually found the concept of an alpha male may have been an erroneous interpretation of incomplete data. He formally disavowed this terminology in 1999. Now we know a pack is usually a family consisting of a breeding pair, who are equally dominant, and their offspring of previous years.

The first animals I developed a huge bond with were a kind of modified wolves: dogs. First Nuska, a light brown short-haired nimble mongrel, I don't know which mix of breeds she came from, and Nit, a purebred German shepherd who was the only fully black puppy in the litter ('Nit' is Catalan for 'night'). My first experiences of love and grief came from my relationship with them, especially from their tragic deaths. Nuska died being run over by a car when we were on holiday when I must have been nine or so, and in my late teens I had to put Nit down as she was suffering from a painful disease – it was one of the most dramatic, soul-crushing moments in my life. I consider them my siblings, actually. I was not their father; we all were fathered by my parents. I was not their owner, we all were owned by my parents. We were equals. Brothers and sisters in a common struggle.

I spent a long time with them away from humans, often having naps with them under the table. I got closer to them than to most people I knew, and they trusted me as one of their own. They kept appearing in my dreams many years after their departure, trying to fill the void they left behind. They were both wolves at heart, I could see it. I could see them trapped in the wrong place, as I felt I also was. I could see their identity being messed up by others, as mine also was. They told me how to handle the situation better than any person has ever taught me. They taught me how to handle people. They taught me how to survive.

Although they both revered my father, I now realise that if they saw him as the alpha male, this must have been for the same reason the first studies of wolves arrived at the same erroneous conclusion. We were all captive, in a way. Captive in an urban world with no hills to howl at the moon from. Captive in a genetic and cultural mistake designed by those who do not know reality and Nature. We all were living in unnatural settings trying to cope in the best way we could. We all were trapped in this hostile world without an instruction manual. Everyone was telling us who we were supposed to be and what we were supposed to do. We all had our muzzles and leashes to wear, and we all like to run in the fields of freedom.

After watching as a child Dr de la Fuente's documentaries titled *El Hombre y la Tierra* (Man and Earth), showing him in the proximity of wild Iberian wolves, I wanted to become him, but I did not know how. I wanted to do what he did. I wanted to go to the 'wild' and observe animals in Nature, without interfering with their lives. I wanted to learn from them; I wanted to commune with them. This idea was far more appealing to me than any profession that involved being around people – because, in my experience, humans were quite dangerous creatures who seemed to have a problem with my existence. I was sure wolves would not share such an attitude, as Nuska and Nit had told me.

In Catalonia, there was not a separate degree in zoology; instead it was a specialisation of the five-year biology degree (the first three years were the same for everyone, and then you specialised in either fundamental biology, botany or zoology). Within zoology, there was a new discipline which fitted even more what I wanted to be: ethology, the comparative study of animal behaviour in the wild (popularised when three ethologists, Konrad Lorenz, Niko Tinbergen and Karl von Frisch, won the 1973 Nobel Prize). But it hadn't been long since General Franco had died, and the still powerful Catholic Church objected to the teaching of ethology – according to them it profanely placed humans and animals 'at the same low level' – and none of the universities in Catalonia had a degree in it at that time. So I had no other choice but to enrol on my general zoology degree and teach myself ethology with any book I could find. My academic journey was all set up and ready to go, and it began in that crowded lecture room in the annexe of the Faculty of Biology at the University of Barcelona.

I had heard of the concept of 'levels of organisation' at school, but I had not grasped its true significance before I started my degree and read *The Selfish Gene* by Oxford professor Richard Dawkins (the 1976 bestseller which popularised ideas developed during the 1960s by W.D. Hamilton). This book allowed me to see things from a point of view I had never considered before and helped me to make sense of it all. It is the view of the 'gene', the view of the entity at the lowest level of the system, rather than the view of the organism or the group. Lower than organ, lower than tissue and lower than cell – so low most people forget they exist.

One of the most interesting aspects of this view is that what we observe in Nature makes more sense if we see organisms as the way genes reproduce, rather than genes as the way organisms store and pass information to others. Let's look at fungi, for example. When we see a mushroom in the woods, we tend to think we have seen the 'organism' mushroom, but in fact we have only seen the reproductive organ of a much bigger organism which is spreading in the soil all around it, in the form of microscopic filaments called mycelia. We can understand better how fungi work if we see the organism as the mycelia not normally visible to us, which, once a year, reproduces by 'erecting' some visible mushrooms.

In Richard Dawkins' book we have that word again: 'selfish'. This word has its counterpart, though. From the gene-centred view, the more that individual organisms are genetically related, the more sense it makes for them to behave selflessly with each other, as this will help the genes they all share – what counts is the genes replicating, it doesn't matter in which organisms they do it. It's no longer 'me, me, me'; we now also find 'we, we, we'.

Here comes the interesting thing about this. A selfish molecule may become a selfish gene, but when a selfish gene starts to reproduce in groups of genes within an organism, the selfishness becomes co-operation. To survive, it is in the interest of the selfish gene to help all the genes of the organism where it lives to survive too. If the organism dies and doesn't reproduce, all genes die with it. By moving up the level of organisation from gene to organism, we can now see a new property emerging: 'altruism'.

We use the term altruism in everyday life as 'the disinterested and selfless concern for the well-being of others', but when W.D. Hamilton developed this concept within biology in the 1960s he meant 'the behaviour by an individual which increases the fitness of another individual while decreasing the fitness of the actor'. Altruistic behaviours appear most obviously in kin relationships, such as in parenting, but may also be evident among wider social groups. These behaviours allow individuals to increase the success of their genes (more copies of them surviving and multiplying) by helping relatives who share those genes too. Hamilton created a formula predicting that the more genes are shared between two individuals, the more altruistic behaviour you should see between them. There is abundant evidence that proves this theory, and the most spectacular example of it can be found in the behaviour of social insects, the subject of my PhD studies.

The last two years of my biology degree were on zoology. At that time I had already been learning off-campus about ethology thanks to Dr Enric Alonso de Medina, who was trained by the famous Oxford ethologist Desmond Morris (who specialised in human ethology, and who in 1967 wrote his first bestseller, *The Naked Ape*). Dr Alonso de Medina taught it 'unofficially' in lectures from his home and other venues, which were popular as they had this air of 'forbidden truth'.

That was the early 1980s, and I was still living with my parents in a modest seventh-floor apartment in a Barcelona quarter called El Guinardó – very close to the famous Park Güell where I used to play as a child, unaware that Gaudí's architectural marvel would be the obligatory stop of any tourist for years to come. Although I thought my looks were modern enough – round Lennon glasses and small ponytail styling what essentially was a 'mullet' – I continued being an introvert more interested in Luke Skywalker's recent fatherhood news than with partying or dating.

By the fourth year of my studies, I had to start doing proper research. I had to choose a zoological subject and write a dissertation about it. I thought I could do a little bit more than that. I could find some animals 'in the wild' and conduct a field study to add to my dissertation. Which interesting animal could I found in the middle of a cosmopolitan city, though? I loved Hamilton's theories, but also the work of E.O. Wilson, which coined the term 'sociobiology' (a field of biology which aims to explain social behaviour in terms of evolution). Wilson, who started his career studying ants, used sociobiology and evolutionary principles to study the behaviour of social insects, and then to understand the social behaviour of other animals, including humans – it was fascinating stuff. Therefore I thought I should also choose a social insect as my first subject of study. I consulted Dr Alonso de Medina and he suggested I could try social wasps, as very few people had studied them (on account of their danger and lack of commercial value), and he had found a small nest of the wasp *Polistes omissus* in a brick structure in the campus. This type of wasp doesn't build very big nests, and it does not cover them with a paper wall. The nest's cells are visible from the outside and therefore the wasp's behaviour can be easily observed. Perfect, I thought.

What happened the first day I approached that nest changed my life. It was located in a big field inside a two-metre-tall rectangular structure which functioned as an air ventilation chimney of an underground parking facility. It was halfway from my faculty to the university canteen, where I often ate as it was cheap – a very convenient location indeed. The structure was not built properly, and the bricks had exposed holes perfect for holding nests inside. I took my notebook and approached the chimney with some trepidation. About ten metres from it I could already see some wasps flying in and out of one hole. I slowed down, and stopped. As I could not see anything from there I took a few steps forward. Then I did the same again, creeping closer and closer to the hole. Then I saw her.

I already knew who she was. I had read about *Polistes* before approaching the nest, and I knew that to protect it the colony's workers take turns as guards. They stay by the entrance of the nest and look out for danger. If they perceive any, they open their wings slightly while releasing an alarm pheromone the other wasps can smell. If the danger increases the guards dash out and try to sting the creature threatening the colony, leaving the alarm pheromone in the 'target', and then all the wasps know who to sting. The more they manage to sting the target, the stronger the pheromone 'smell', as it is in all the stings. I knew that if I approached and they stung me I had to run away fast, as they would chase me for some time. When I saw the guard at the entrance (clearly distinctive from the others as she was looking out and checking everyone flying in) I was paralysed by fear.

But how on earth I could become an ethologist if I froze every time I approached a dangerous animal? I had to pull myself together. I had to draw strength from somewhere and overcome the instinct to run away, which had been imprinted in my behavioural repertoire through evolution (the sight of black and yellow in animals, a pattern called 'aposematic', causes an instinctive reaction of 'danger'). I needed to move a bit closer to be able to study the nest, and I moved slowly using my notebook as a shield to protect the bottom half of my face. That is when she saw me.

The guard moved abruptly and faced me right on. The front of the *Polistes* head is quite flat, and when seen from the front the two big kidney-shaped compound eyes look like two elongated 'alien-style' eyes – quite scary if you have never seen them before. In other words, as opposed to ants and bees, these wasps seem to have a distinctive face. The guard turned her head and squared her face with mine. My heart was pumping fast and adrenaline circulated in my bloodstream. My pupils contracted and became fixated on her face. She vigorously moved her antenna trying to smell me, looking at me from head to toe. Her wings gradually opened. They opened twenty degrees or so ... and then she closed them, her body relaxed, and she resumed her task of checking traffic as if I was no longer there.

This one-inch individual had seen me, she knew I was a dangerous human as she had encountered them before, but she judged me, and judged me correctly. She assessed my behaviour and concluded I was not dangerous ... because it was true, I wasn't dangerous. I had no intention to harm her or her family, and she could read all that in me. She could read me better than I could read her. She treated me better than other humans had treated me.

My heart kept pumping for quite some time, but not because of the feeling of imminent danger any longer, but because I witnessed an interspecific interaction that taught me something very profound. These tiny creatures everybody hates, everybody kills at the first opportunity, were not that different to us. In fact, they seemed even cleverer than us. Most people look upon themselves as superior beings, and look at the rest of animals as commodities they can exploit or destroy at will. My urge to become an animal protectionist was sparked that day. I concluded that there was something fundamentally wrong in the way we treat other animals, and that animals needed to be protected from humans. And the ecological behaviour of wasp of the genus *Polistes* became the subject of my PhD studies, which for ten years justified my new nickname: 'the wasp man'.

* * *

According to Hamilton, it is not surprising *Polistes* live in colonies and protect all their members even at the risk of their own life. This is because they are 'haplodiploids', like ants and bees.

There are three ways in which genetic material is passed to the next generation. 'Aploids' share all the genes, which is not always useful, as mixing genes from parents would give you more diversity and make you fitter to survive. All vertebrates are 'diploids', who share half of their genes. This is by far the most common type, where offspring have half of their genes from their father and a half from their mother. Finally there are 'haplodiploids', where most offspring share 75 per cent of the genes – this type is not common, but includes Hymenoptera, an order of insects composed of ants, bees and wasps.

In haplodiploid animals, a female produces daughters by mixing her genes (from her eggs) with the genes of the father (from the sperm). After mating, she keeps it in a reservoir of sperm and releases it gradually to fertilise the eggs, but when she runs out she can produce full individuals from her eggs alone, and these individuals will be male. So females have 50 per cent of genes from each parent, but males only have genes from the mother. Also, if an insect colony has only one queen, and she has only mated once (the standard), then the relatedness between all female workers in a nest is 75 per cent.

Therefore, according to Hamilton's rule, in haplodiploid animals you should find societies in which individuals are more altruistic with each other to the point of often risking their lives to save any of their siblings, as most of the members of these societies would be 'sisters' who share more genes than sisters in other species.

This is precisely what we find. The most sophisticated social species on the planet with the highest level of altruistic behaviour are found in ants, bees and wasps, which are all haplodiploid. The colonies of these insects are mostly composed of females.

Here comes a fascinating thought, though. Why did the guard of the nest I studied not raise the alarm, if her interest was protecting all her sisters? Why did she not do it when anybody approached, no matter who they were? Why did she have to 'judge' each situation and decide when to do it? It's because raising the alarm is also costly for her sisters. Some wasps might die by coming out and trying to sting me. It's important to be measured and judge well.

Helping each other even if you aren't even the same species can have an evolutionary benefit. 'Mutualism' is when different species help each other regularly. A classic example can be found in the Ocellaris clownfish who dwells among the tentacles of Ritteri sea anemones. The anemone eats from the leftovers of the fish's meals, and in turn the stinging tentacles protect the clownfish from its predators.

Genes may be selfish but they co-operate when it benefits them in the long term. Selfish genes working together within social species tend to create altruistic behaviour with the members of their society as this is ultimately good for them. However, individuals in these societies may sometimes also behave altruistically to individuals of other societies, even if they belong to another species, because some of their genes may still be in these other species, and the risk of paying a negative price for being hostile may be too high.

It may be beneficial for the individual to help others in need even if this is at some cost to themselves, as the favour may be returned in the future. This is known in evolutionary biology as 'reciprocal altruism', a concept first developed by the sociobiologist Robert Trivers in the 1970s. An example of this is the warning call many species of birds or mammals produce when they detect a predator, which exposes them, increasing their chances of been targeted by the hunter, but may help others to escape, including other species too.

Another example is the vampire bat. When they return to their sheltering caves after a feeding expedition, where they sucked the blood of other mammals (hence their name), they sacrifice their own food by regurgitating some of the blood they found and giving it to their 'friends'. As this difficult-to-find food is the only thing they can eat, without this sharing many would become undernourished. There is also the red-winged blackbird (*Agelaius phoeniceus*) found in North and Central America. The males help to defend the neighbours' nests, even if this leaves their own nest temporarily exposed. Memory is helpful to survive. It allows you to remember generosity and kindness, and to 'pay it back'.

Many years after the publication of *The Selfish Gene*, Richard Dawkins said he could see the title might have given an inadequate impression of its contents, and in retrospect he thought it would be better titled The Immortal Gene. I think he is right. The genes alone may behave selfishly, but when you look at the higher level of organisation where these genes reside, at the individual, societal and population level, we see the selfishness diluted, and altruism and respect now appear as evolutionary positive attributes. Because many of the genes are shared by many species, and they don't die but they get together with other genes and keep replicating in different organisms and species, immortality is what characterises them, not selfishness.

Think about it. The first-ever gene managing to replicate successfully in the first living cell may still be in all of us, in all living beings on this planet. In all animals, in all plants, in all fungi, in all bacteria. This gene, and all its primordial 'friends', has been replicating and multiplying for billions of years. While organisms die and species evolve, these genes have always been here. They are the common denominator of any earthling.

Somewhere sometime, early humans who might have had profound encounters with an altruistic animal as I had with the wasp probably had similar revelations and must have articulated their experiences to others and expressed them with a simple new idea. Perhaps this idea was later passed from person to person, from generation to generation. Perhaps at one point it became part of a belief, creed or dogma. Perhaps it was discussed in different parts of the world and then spread to new lands and minds. What happened to this idea over thousands of years is the third story I tell in this book.

Three stories, three questions, three ideas. First we ask, 'Who am I?' and the answer 'I am me' deepens as we grow in a quest for true identity which never ends. Second, 'What is this?' The first consequence of sentience is to 'seek the truth of the world around us'. This questioning urge, this need for truth colours every act and can take us to extraordinary places – for me a single email seeking the truth about a pension policy grew into a ground-breaking court case which revealed to the world a reality most people knew very little about.

The third idea is the most important because it is no longer about me, but about us, about everyone, about everything. The answer to the question **'What should I do?'** This idea is strong because it is both positive and negative. This idea is useful because it's universal. This idea is powerful because it is simple.

This idea is: **'Do no harm'**.

DO NO HARM

LEVELS OF
ORGANISATION

RELATIONSHIP
STRATEGIES

Galaxies
Planet-systems
Biospheres
Ecosystems
Populations

Organisms

Organs

Cells

Genes

Molecules

Atoms

BIOLOGICAL

Altruistic

Increasing the
fitness of another
while decreasing
the fitness
of the actor

Selfish

Be the fittest
and replicating
more at the
expenses of
others

2.

The History of Being Kind

I didn't make history, history made me.

Contrary to what some grumpy people prone to use terms such as 'millennials' believe, veganism is not a modern phenomenon, and it has existed in one form or another for centuries. This is how it all began.

One word, *ahimsa*

Is there a simple word for the idea of 'do no harm'? Yes, *ahimsa*. It comes from the Sanskrit root *hiṃs*, which means 'to strike'. *Hiṃsā* means 'wish to injure or harm', and *a-hiṃsā* is the opposite of this. As far as we know, this word was already in use in the ancient kingdom of Magadha, in Northern India, hundreds of years before the Common Era.

Magadha was situated in what is now the southern part of the Indian state of Bihar, in the area between the cities of Patna and Calcutta, south of the River Ganges. At the time of the kingdom's creation, about 600 BCE, the region must have been full of the highly venomous king cobras, the powerful Indian rhinoceros, the huge (and bluish) nilgai antelopes, the punk-looking Indian boars (with a mane which runs in a crest along its back from its head to lower body) and the majestic Bengal tiger. Most interestingly, although we now associate tigers with Asia and lions with Africa, at that time the Asiatic lion (with moderate mane growth at the top of the head making the males ears always visible) and the Bengal

21

tiger would have roamed that land together, while the practically blind Ganges river dolphin, now considered among the most endangered mammals of the region, would have been a common sight in the big rivers. Being in the north, it would not have been as hot as we tend to imagine the Indian climate, but during the monsoon season from June to September the rain would fall hard, making the climate very humid. When there is plenty of rain and lots of fertile land due to the sediment brought by the many rivers from the Himalayas, civilisation can prosper and kingdoms can grow. It was around this area that the first domesticated chickens were bred from the red junglefowl (which still exist today) about 8,000 years ago.

Between 2000 and 1200 BCE the Aryan peoples from Persia (now normally called Indo-Iranian people as the Nazis misappropriated this term) entered north-western India through today's Pakistan, moving eastwards up to Magadha. They followed the Vedic religion, a complex animistic (nature-worshipping) religion with many male gods and a strong ancestor worship component, which included elaborate animal sacrifices, of horses, cattle and sometimes humans, performed to ask for gods' favours.

Why animal sacrifices, though? Human's capacity to empathise with others is innate, and as we have seen in the previous chapter, biological evolution also favours respect and altruism beyond the immediate family, especially in social species with good memories. In the Palaeolithic period, humans had been living for hundreds of thousands of years as what the author Daniel Quinn calls 'leavers' in his 1992 novel *Ishmael*, only taking from Nature what they needed. However, about 10,000 years ago, in the Neolithic period, most people became the patriarchal 'takers', conquering and mastering the environment, selfishly taking everything they could find and believing themselves to be the pinnacle of creation.

The agricultural revolution had begun, and with it goats, sheep and cattle became domesticated. The natural empathy towards other creatures must have been set aside, as animals became now 'property', no longer equal beings trying to survive in a hostile world. For the first time, a sentient being had become the 'owner' of another. In early 'taker' civilisations, hierarchies of beings were established both within their societies (kings, emperors, pharaohs and other 'superior' people grabbing all the power) and in their mythology (religions now had gods in hierarchical systems too). When facing droughts, floods or plagues, people must have thought that offering the 'inferior' beings they 'owned' in sacrifice to their scary gods would appease them and stop all their calamities … and the senseless killing began.

V

When I was 'the wasp man' in Catalonia, in my early twenties, I witnessed a lot of senseless killing. I was doing my PhD on *Polistes* wasps' behaviour and Dr Enric Alonso de Medina was directing it. Enric, an eloquent young lecturer with remarkable body-language-reading skills and a flair for challenging orthodoxy, and who had lived in London for eight years, continued being the 'rebel' who was teaching ethology unofficially off-campus. Apart from lectures, he organised field trips to different parts of Catalonia, and I went along to assist him. We wandered through the wilderness and looked for wildlife, and then talked about what we found. I would walk ahead of him and when I spotted an animal of interest I discreetly pointed it out. By the time he arrived with his cloud of students, he had smoothly changed subject to the behaviour of the animal I found, as if everything had been planned. I became quite good at it. I could identify most birds by song and most insects by sight.

Particularly satisfying were the one-week courses we ran in the Pyrenees during summer, as the fauna was very diverse and reliable. I always felt that, ecologically speaking, Europe meets Africa in the Pyrenees. You find species from both continents, especially in some strategically located valleys. Enric had been going there for years and had found some amazing treasures we could show to the students.

On one of these trips I experienced something I would never forget. It was on the south coast of Catalonia, on a sandy beach on a very hot day, and we had found some amazing antlions, predatory insects of the family Myrmeleontidae, whose larva bury themselves in a pit of sand and catch distracted ants by throwing sand at them to make them fall in. After such a good discovery, we had a lunch break and I wandered off, trying to find the wasp nests I had already located on previous trips. I found one on a large cactus – an ideal place for wasps. When I was in the middle of counting the number of nest's cells, I heard a horrible sound. It sounded familiar, but it was far too loud and continuous. It was the scream of an animal in great pain, and it chilled my soul. I did not know what to do, but eventually I headed in the direction of the sound, somewhere behind another dune. The sound faded before I arrived, and I saw a man walking away with something in his hand which looked like a hammer.

I realised what had happened, and I stopped. I thought there was nothing I could do – it was obviously too late. That man was an 'owner'. He was an owner of another sentient being, and he lived in a culture where owners of other sentient beings were allowed to dispose of them in any way they see fit. Yes, laws regulated how, but those who wanted to cut corners could go to discreet places to dispose of their property without any witnesses, or to skin them to sell their fur, or to cut them in pieces to sell their flesh, or to offer them to someone as a gift. It could have been any animal because millions were being executed in similar ways around the globe at that same time. That one, though, happened to be an unwanted old dog.

V

When all ancient civilisations and religions began exploiting animals and sacrificing them to their gods, I have no doubt there would have been people who had their empathy intact and knew this was wrong. They must have been horrified at the screams they heard as I had been behind that dune. I was a coward that day because I did nothing, but 2,500 years ago the bravest of people must have challenged such traditions publicly. We know some Sramanic monks certainly did – these monks travelled around Magadha and renounced home, possessions and the established old Vedic religion. Mahavira was one of them.

Brahmin priests of the kingdom of Magadha had a ritual of not eating animal flesh before sacrificing an animal as part of the common Vedic tradition, somehow showing a certain element of 'guilt' for what they were about to do. Mahavira must have seen this and taken it to the next level: why sacrifice them at all? As a Sramanic monk, he was not bound to the Vedic religion and he could publicly challenge it. At that time, even some traditionalist Brahmins may not have disagreed with him entirely, as the ancient text Upanishads suggests.

Mahavira, this ex-prince who became an itinerant monk begging for his food, and who had walked naked because he didn't replace the rag he wore when it fell off, later became 'enlightened' and taught crowds of followers. In his lectures he talked about *ahimsa*. He said every soul can be supreme and in every living being he saw the same spirit he had. He saw the greatness in every ordinary being, and therefore we should avoid hurting any other creature. Although this is framed in a religious context with supreme beings, spirits and purity, in essence he was teaching the core message of today's veganism, five centuries before the Common Era.

Where did he learn about *ahimsa*? Many say the word had existed for many generations before him (even thousands of years before) because he did not 'invent' any of the philosophies he was teaching. We'll never know, but Mahavira and all the teachers before him already had a good understanding of how *ahimsa* is a principle which should be followed in everyday life. They taught that the Vedic religion should be replaced by one which had *ahimsa* as its major tenet. A religion that, arguably, already existed in Magadha before the Aryans came to India from Persia and brought with them the Vedas. Mahavira's was one of the oldest religions and we can still find millions of people following it. This ancient religion is called Jainism (also known as Jain Dharma).

Followers of Jainism are called Jains, and their ideas come from twenty-four Sramana monks known as Tirthankaras, the twenty-fourth being Mahavira. Through the centuries Jains have built temples which show images of these 'saints'. In fact, in the north-west London borough of Harrow, there is a temple dedicated to Mahavira, with a typical statue of him sitting with wide shoulders in the lotus position while meditating, his hands together resting palm up under his belly, and completely naked (this is one of the ways to distinguish Jain statues from those from Buddhism).

For Jains, mammals, birds and fish are all five-sensed beings, invertebrates have two or three senses and plants only have one sense. Jains try to avoid hurting all living beings, but the more senses they believe they have, the more important it is to prevent their suffering. In a way, Jains can also be seen as early environmentalists, as they tried to exploit the living environment as little as possible. Devout Jains take five main vows: *ahimsā* (non-violence), *satya* (truth), *asteya* (not stealing), *brahmacharya* (celibacy or chastity or sexual continence) and *aparigraha* (non-possessiveness). And the first vow means, in practice, living a vegetarian lifestyle which avoids harm to all animals but allows the consumption of milk – therefore Jainism is the first known example of a cultural ideology using the concept of vegetarianism, the antecedent of veganism.

The first Jains I ever met were in one of the London Vegans monthly talks in Holborn I have been attending since 2010. Nishma and Mahersh Shah are a lovely Jain couple who run a UK vegan catering company called Shambhu's, which often serves delicious food at vegan festivals and events such as these talks. They both have dark hair, brown skin, gentle features, and a very calm and polite demeanour. Nishma, who is a Kenyan-born Indian, also runs vegan cookery classes – I love her award-winning vegan cheesecakes. Although most Jains are vegetarian, Nishma and Mahersh are actually vegan, being founding members of the Jain Vegans Working Group. In an interview on Femalefirst.com, Nishma said:

> My childhood and early teens were in a lacto-vegetarian Jain family environment in Kenya, and actually, we didn't consume cheese or eggs. Nor did we buy leather products or own any animal products. I was made aware of the principle of *ahimsa* (compassion, reverence and non-violence to all life forms) from a very young age and to be mindful of the finite resources our Earth can offer.

Mahavira was a contemporary of another important historical figure, another Sramana monk, and one you most likely have heard of: Prince Siddhartha Gautama, more popularly known as the Buddha. Born in Lumbinī (right under the Himalayas in present-day Nepal), after renouncing his family who had given him a sheltered comfortable life (it is said he was married and had a son), Siddhartha Gautama discovered how much suffering other people endured outside his palace, and began travelling south in the search of enlightenment, learning from different Sramana teachers following different philosophies. He started with the northern India capital city Rajgir (the first capital of the kingdom of Magadha), and there he met a Braham teacher with whom he underwent an 'extreme fast' which involved not eating any animal at all. He broke the fast and moved on to the next teacher. He met vegetarian Jain teachers and learnt about *ahimsa*. He also met the Ājīvikas, a vanished religion (although it lasted 2,000 years) whose commitment to vegetarianism lay somewhere between the Buddhists and the Jains. Makkhali Gośāla was their main teacher, and he was a disciple of Mahavira who later went on to create his own religion – he also followed the idea of complete renunciation, including nakedness.

In his early travels, Siddhartha Gautama was exposed to many philosophies which used the concept of *ahimsa* in different ways. He ended up in a place now called Bodhgaya, in north-east India. There, he sat cross-legged by a fig tree (known as the Bodhi Tree, the direct descendant of which can still be seen in the same spot) and, after some meditation, it is said he reached enlightenment and became 'the Buddha', which actually means the enlightened one. From that moment on he taught his view of the world and how to escape the suffering of the cycle of reincarnation (his dharma) for forty-five years. The new religion of Buddhism had begun.

He taught a spiritual path including ethical training and meditation such as *jhana* and mindfulness, and he also criticised the animal sacrifices of Brahmin priests, because *ahimsa* is an important concept within Buddhism. The Buddha initially taught people not to consciously kill any living being, including insects. However, what mattered was the intention, so you could eat a dead animal if you did not intend to kill it. Therefore, Buddhism, although sharing with Jainism the desire of not doing any harm to other sentient beings, was a more pragmatic religion less concerned about what people eat. If a monk was given flesh of an animal not killed for him, he could eat it. Buddhism presented itself as a 'middle way' between those who lived a life of opulence eating everything and those who lived an ascetic life rejecting everything.

It's not surprising it caught on – it had the perfect PR hook, I would say.

It did not take long for Jains and Buddhists to publicly argue about who best interpreted the concept of *ahimsa*. Buddhists sometimes portrayed Jains as 'extremists' – sounds familiar? And then a century after the Buddha's death (possibly around 400 BCE in Kushinagar, in the Indian state of Uttar Pradesh, not that far from where he grew up), Buddhism split in two: Theravāda and Mahāyāna.

The Theravāda school is more focused on personal salvation from the endless cycle of suffering, death and rebirth to attain Buddhahood and reach 'Nirvana', and it says people can eat meat if they have not seen, heard or suspected it was particularly acquired for them (they claim that the Buddha ate part of a pig in his last meal). On the other side, the Mahāyāna school is also concerned with the salvation of 'other' beings – for them those about to reach Nirvana should wait and stick around helping others to attain it too, and meat should never be eaten (they claim that pig wasn't what the Buddha ate in his last meal, but some sort of mushroom pigs eat). Today most Theravāda monks (found in Burma, Sri Lanka and most of Indochina) are not vegetarians but Mahāyāna monks (found in China, Japan, Mongolia, Vietnam and Korea) should be.

V

Most people wrongly assume all Buddhists are vegetarian. Equally, most people would assume that staff working in animal protection organisations are at least vegetarian, but often they are not. However, my expectations on this issue were high when I was employed by an anti-hunting animal welfare organisation in August 2016 – which will remain unnamed by me because it doesn't matter which one it was, and I don't want to give them any unwelcome publicity. I assumed most staff would be vegetarian, as I knew the CEO was, and on my first day at the office I was enthusiastically greeted by Laura, the friendly office manager, a committed ethical vegan like myself who was always busy collecting stuff for animal sanctuaries. Because she organised all purchases, none of the toiletries were tested on animals, and all the food provided by the organisation was vegan. Even all the food at the office Christmas party was vegan (which had allowed me to attend after many years avoiding them, as I could not be in a celebrative mood in the same room where the remains or secretions of an animal were being consumed). I felt quite at home.

This is why three months later, when I discovered the pension I had been auto-enrolled on was investing in companies which test on animals and damage the environment, I could not believe my eyes. Surely this would be against most staff's wishes, and also against the charity's purpose. Besides, I had worked in the same organisation from 2004 to 2007 as the hunting campaigner, and at that time it had a pension fund with the term 'ethical' in its title. Why did they change it to this 'non-ethical' fund? When did they change it? Did the staff know about this? Did the CEO know about this? As an ethical vegan I could not let this one go, as a percentage of my salary would be invested in such companies, as well as a percentage of my colleagues' salaries and indeed a percentage of the donations from vegan donors.

This was a big problem, and one I had to solve. It was my duty. The first thing I had to do was to tell management about my discovery, and in January 2017, the same day I found out, I sent an email to the CEO, the chief operations officer (COO) and the head of finance telling them what I had found, hoping there would be a very innocent explanation.

It was around that time that I finally decided to move to a better flat. I thought that it would be a good opportunity to get rid of a lot of my stuff, and as I had some savings I was prepared to pay a bit more. However, I did not want to go far because, after all these years, I'd become quite fond of the area. It was close enough to the city centre so I could easily walk there, it had three nice parks close by where I could read and observe wildlife, and although it could not be compared with Hackney, Camden or Kensington regarding the number of vegan eateries, it was getting better.

The entire South Bank area of London had undergone a spectacular transformation since I first arrived in the early 1990s, and the pedestrian walk by the river from Tower Bridge to Westminster Bridge was lovely. I spent many hours promenading there and making magic with my camera from the light playing with the funny-shaped buildings, the capricious curvaceous river and old relics of history strategically landscaped in an organic way that only time could have designed. I loved the city. I loved the Cockney foxes coming out at night with their busy walks. I loved the lush parks, the quirky corners, the majestic structures. I loved the cacophony of languages reverberating through the tunnels and bridges. I loved the warmth of the anonymous Londoner, who would not talk to you but would come to your aid without prejudice. I loved London.

Above all, though, I wanted a garden. If not, I wanted an allotment. If not, a yard. If not, a balcony. I wanted a place where I could grow some plants, and I could use them to feed myself and the local wildlife who had been displaced by these noisy scary stinking littering pretentious primates. I wanted a bit of earth of my own where I could grow life. It didn't need to be big. It was time to go online and look for a home.

V

Ancient empires come and go

By now you could be forgiven in thinking the story of veganism began in India. After all, Mahavira, the Buddha and even the Upanishadic Brahmins who all used the concept of *ahimsa* come from there. This is not quite true; veganism was also sprouting independently in other parts of the world more or less at the same time.

In the 6th century BCE, when the Celtic Britons became the dominant culture in the British Islands and in Central America the Olmec civilisation began to decline, Greek civilisation had spread all around the Mediterranean. Because they wrote prolifically, we know a lot about them. They had a complex religious system with many gods and many religions. Among their religious practices, as in the Vedic religion of the East, they also sacrificed animals – and they also ritualised such killing in a way that suggests they may have felt a bit guilty. One of those who did not like the killing was Pythagoras.

Mostly known these days for his mathematical theorems, Pythagoras was from the island of Samos in the eastern Aegean Sea, a good location to learn about the East as it belonged to Persia when he was born. Pythagoras became the leader of a kind of cult in a Greek city called Croton on the southern tip of today's Italy, following many new ideas most Greeks would have considered extreme. One was the belief in reincarnation (he used the concept of 'transmigration' to explain how souls move between animals and humans), and because of this they avoided meat and eggs because they did not want to eat anyone who could have been a human before. His cult became more and more influential, and when other Greeks saw it as a threat he eventually had to flee from Croton and he died in exile, but the Pythagoreans continued until the middle of the 5th century.

Pythagoras and his followers were not the only vegetarians in ancient Greece. It is thought the mythological Orpheus and his followers, the Orphics, were vegetarian, and Plato talked about Orphism to describe the peaceful diet of the golden age of an innocent and pure world, whose inhabitants were subsisting entirely on things inanimate and abstaining wholly from animate beings. Epicurus, a Greek philosopher who thought the world was made of atoms and who rejected supernatural beliefs, also encouraged vegetarianism because he thought eating meat was decadent and unnecessary. He believed the greatest good was to seek modest, sustainable pleasure through knowledge and limiting desires, advocating for a simple life.

V

During my PhD studies, my encounters with animals gradually pushed me to become a more ethical person. The wasp guard had taught me about how animals, no matter which, were far more similar to us than we all thought, and witnessing a dog being beaten to death by his 'owner' had taught me how much animals, even those supposedly more loved, were suffering unnecessarily. In both experiences, I had been a passive observer. Was my inaction in the case of the dog a tacit endorsement of such injustices? Was there anything I could do to remove some of the blame we share collectively for the way we treat our fellow earthlings? Was there anything that could realistically be done? Was there anything I, an insignificant student, could realistically do?

All these thoughts bothered me and began affecting the way I conducted my research. The sources of data of my thesis on the ecological behaviour of *Polistes* were threefold: wild nests I found all around the country, nests built in the experimental fields of the faculty and nests I took to my tiny flat to observe more closely. For the latter (and also some wasps at the faculty), I marked each individual with a code of enamel paint on their thorax, so I could identify them (each would then be assigned a letter for the paint colour and a number for the pattern of spots. For instance, the most extraordinary wasp I ever met was V5, 'v' being the first letter of *vert* – green in Catalan). To apply the marks, I had to capture the wasps using a butterfly net or a glass container and place them in a device I had built to immobilise them. They were obviously in distress when I was doing this, and it bothered me.

Insistent guilt about some of my research was growing, and to compensate I began 'rescuing' wasps in peril. Every time I heard about a wasp nest that was going to be destroyed, I intervened to try to prevent it. As I was now known throughout Catalonia as 'the wasp man', sometimes the police would take me to particularly problematic nests they had been alerted about – by then Catalonia had its own police force and I did not need to deal with the 'grey people' any more. I remember one particularly enormous nest which expanded more than a metre wide. It belonged to another species, the German wasp (*Vespula germanica*), and it was found in a small village inside a garage after the family returned from a long holiday. Fully geared up with a beekeeping suit, I removed the entire nest and I took it to the experimental fields of my faculty, where the colony of more than 10,000 individuals was allowed to live in freedom until the end of its life cycle (in temperate latitudes most wasps die in winter and only hibernating future queens survive).

I became a 'conscientious objector' – conscription was still practised in Spain – and I was rescuing thousands of animals from certain death, but that was not enough. My guilt was too strong, and I felt some of my research was now 'tainted' with some questionable practices. My personal life was not going well either. My long-term relationship with a musicologist ended, and it was difficult for me to survive and carry on with my research as I had not received a grant for my PhD (who is going to give anything to a study of wasps?), and I had to work in all sort of jobs to pay the rent on my tiny flat in Barcelona's Gothic Quarter, which I'd moved into when I finished my bachelor's degree. For a few months, when I could not find any work, I was only eating a baguette each weekday and a proper meal at my parents' on Sundays – at one point I only weighed 52kg.

In 1993, when I was quite close to completing my PhD thesis and gaining my doctorate, cemented from then on into the often cruel world of academia, I decided to leave. To leave my PhD studies, to leave my flat, to leave my city, to leave my country and to leave all the possessions I had, other than what I could carry in a rucksack on my front and another on my back. I had to go somewhere else where I could use my scientific background to dedicate my life to protecting animals.

I had no idea where to go other than to head north, and I didn't have that much money. I wrote several letters to family and friends saying goodbye, and on an overcast mild day in mid-June, I posted them on my way to Barcelona's Sant Andreu Comtal train station. From there I took a train to Portbou, the very last station in Catalonia before France. I was nervous all the way there. I was jumping into an uncertain future with no parachute, but I knew it was the right thing to do. I felt the pressure in my stomach, my shoulders and my head. It felt almost as if I was going to explode. In a travel diary I began that day, I wrote:

> I am alone in my compartment with my two backpacks. It's almost raining. I left my old life behind. It's difficult to write on a running train but the moment is too important to lose. It's the beginning of my new life, in other countries, other languages, other people and perhaps other ideas.

When I arrived at Portbou I changed tracks as the French railway gauge is different. I took a train to Cerbère, in the French part of Catalonia (the Catalan countries, where Catalan is spoken, stretch into France, Andorra and even Italy). When we crossed the border I felt all the pressure leaving my body, and as a newborn baby I started to breathe. 'It's going to be OK,' I thought. 'As long as I don't look back and keep moving forward, it's going to be OK.' I was somehow being reborn into a new identity I was yet to discover, and it felt exciting and liberating.

V

Back in the Ancient East, someone who also made a dramatic change to a more ethical life was going to make a lot of difference to many animals. An Indian ruler of the 3rd century BCE, when Buddhism and Jainism were already flourishing, became one of the most important leaders in history advocating vegetarianism and animal protection. His name was Ashoka, and he is often depicted with long hair and a tall jewelled turban. Born sometime in the late 4th century BCE into the Maurya dynasty of northern India, it is said he was disliked by his father, King Bindusara, because of his short stature and rough skin, and as a consequence he left his kingdom when he was still a prince. When he managed to suppress a rebellion against his father at Takshashila with an impressive army of elephants, horses and infantry but without actually killing anyone, he regained the favour of the king. His career as a conqueror began, and it continued when he was crowned, after he'd outperformed his older brother, the heir.

His thirst for power and land made him a violent ruthless ruler deserving of the title of Chandashoka ('Ashoka the Fierce'). He successfully conquered all the country's neighbours and his empire kept growing and growing, covering almost the entire Indian subcontinent, from the cold Hindu Kush (the mountain range that stretches through present-day Afghanistan, home of the acrobatic Siberian ibex, the imposing brown bear and the shy snow leopard) in the west, to the wet Bay of Bengal (in present-day Bangladesh, home of the fitful hoolock gibbon, the surprising estuarine crocodile and the gregarious Indian skimmers) in the east, to the hot dry tropical forest of the Deccan Plateau (in the present-day Indian state of Karnataka, home of the iconic blackbuck, the strong water buffalo and the insectivorous sloth bear) in the south. He became the most powerful man on Earth.

However, after one of his biggest battles in Kalinga (the eastern coastal region between the Mahanadi and the Godavari rivers) where many people were massacred, he had a crisis of conscience and converted to Buddhism. He realised the goals of his actions did not justify the means, and conquering through violence was wrong. From then on he was known as Dhammashoka ('Ashoka the Righteous').

Because he was the supreme ruler of his empire, he was able to impose his new beliefs on his subjects. What he did is truly amazing. He created animal hospitals (possibly the first in history), enacted laws to protect species and habitats (including off seasons for hunting), banned animal slaughter, forbade feeding animals to other animals and opposed the use of animals as food. He drastically reduced the killing of animals for cooking in his kitchen. One of his edicts says:

> Formerly, in the kitchen of Beloved-of-the-Gods, King Piyadasi, many hundreds of thousands of animals were killed every day to make curry. But now, with the writing of this Dharma Edict, only three creatures – two peacocks and a deer – are killed, and the deer not always. And in time, even these three creatures shall not be killed.

Alas, everything changed after his death. His empire crumbled (as most tend to do), and all his animal protection laws vanished. Eating animals become the norm again and animal sacrifices resumed. Imagine how different the world would be today if his descendants had kept *ahimsa* an integral part of policymaking. However, he left an important legacy: he made Buddhism an institutionalised religion that would end up spread around the entire East.

Jains, Pythagoreans and Mahāyāna Buddhists were milk-consuming vegetarians, but were there any groups of vegetarians that did not eat eggs or dairy products (what we call 'dietary vegans' today) in those ancient times? Yes, there were, and to find them we need to move to the Middle East. Several centuries before the Common Era a new ethnic monotheistic religion developed among the ancient Hebrews. It was characterised by a belief in one transcendent God who, according to its most sacred scriptures (later called the Bible), revealed himself to Abraham, Moses and the Hebrew prophets. It was Judaism, a religion still followed by 14.5 to 17.4 million people today. Around 1 BCE the Roman Empire conquered the land where the Hebrews lived, and near the Empire's second city, Alexandria (in today's Egypt), the Roman soldiers found a curious group of people who did not eat any animal products, including milk and eggs. They were ascetic monks and nuns from the two Jewish sects called Essenes and Therapeutae, and they avoided all animal food because they thought it was self-indulgent. A description of the Essenes from the text *Quod Omnis Probus Liber* includes:

> ... they live in villages, avoiding all cities on account of the lawlessness of those that inhabit them. Some of these men cultivate the soil, others live by peaceful arts and so benefit themselves and all their neighbours. They do not lay up treasures of gold or silver for themselves, judging contentment and frugality the great riches. With them are no makers of arms or of military engines and no one is occupied with anything connected with war. They all avoid commerce and navigation, thinking that these employments make

for covetousness. They possess no slaves, holding all men to be free and all are expected to aid one another as real (gnesiois) brethren.

The main distinction between the Therapeutae and the Essenes is that the latter were anti-intellectual, while the main objective of the former was 'wisdom'. Both sects' main argument was that, according to the Old Testament, Adam and Eve lived a vegan lifestyle in the Garden of Eden.

Moving further west, to the city of Kyrenian, on the northern coast of Cyprus, a bearded curly-haired priest of the Greek God Apollo wrote this about animals in the late 1st century CE: 'for the sake of a little flesh we deprive them of sun, of light, of the duration of life to which they are entitled by birth and being'.

His name was Plutarch, and he did not eat any meat. He described humans as badly equipped to eat meat as we don't have any of the claws and fangs meat-eating animals possess. He was the first person to use 'science' rather than religion to justify vegetarianism and became very influential to future vegetarians.

For instance, a century later, inspired by Plutarch and the Pythagoreans, another bearded Greek philosopher named Porphyry wrote this very vegan message:

> If, however, some one should, nevertheless, think it is unjust to destroy brutes, such a one should neither use milk, nor wool, nor sheep, nor honey. For, as you injure a man by taking from him his garments, thus, also, you injure a sheep by shearing it. For the wool which you take from it is its vestment. Milk, likewise, was not produced for you, but for the young of the animal that has it. The bee also collects honey as food for itself; which you, by taking away, administer to your own pleasure.

Porphyry belonged to the mystical Neoplatonists, who claim meat-eating impedes communing with the divine (although they may have fallen short of becoming vegan).

We can find some more dietary vegan groups in the 3rd century CE, where a new religion with dietary vegan priests emerged around Persia from the Jewish mythology of the Gnostics. Manicheans were very important for a while: they followed their leader, Mani, who was born in the capital of Mesopotamia, and who probably was very influenced by the Jains.

As is often the case with these religious leaders, Mani came from a rich family and was educated to be a monk/priest, this time of a cult following a Jewish–Christian ascetic called Elchasi. He did not like it, and left and created his own religion. He went straight to King Shapur I and told him he was the next prophet and brought with him a book of Jewish–Christian mythology as his credentials. The king believed him and his religion became official.

Manicheanism was an interesting religion based on an eternal cosmic struggle between good and evil. They believed that during this battle, bits of 'good' become trapped in the living matter we see in our world, and to be freed back to this battle, only the Manichean Elect (the top priests) could liberate them in their 'pure' bodies and rituals. These priests had to be so pure that not only could they never lie but they could never be violent against anyone else, including animals. These Elect were definitively vegetarian, and very likely also vegan.

Before Christianity established itself in the forms we find today, there were many other forms and interpretations of the life and teaching of Jesus Christ. In the 2nd century, the Ebionites, reminiscent of the Essenes, were vegetarian Jewish Christians who believed Jesus was vegetarian. In the 3rd century Manicheans and Christians were now competing with each other, but they were not yet the dominant religions in Persia, which eventually got rid of them both. The same thing happened in the Roman Empire, where the emperor Diocletian tried to get rid of both at the turn of the 4th century. However, the next emperor, Constantine, converted to Christianity, and Christian persecution ceased. Since then, the dominant orthodoxy systematically got rid of the 'heretical' ascetic Christians and their 'extremism' (including their vegetarian tendencies).

Because of Christianity (and especially St Augustine, who was an ex-Manichean who converted to Christianity and ended up hating vegetarians), vegetarianism lost much momentum in the West, but further east it was still going strong. In the first millennium of the Common Era, vegetarianism became mainstream in India, as the mixing of Brahmins, Jain and Buddhist traditions led to what we call today Hinduism (although this is an umbrella term which covers all sorts of religions in India, and which the people we call Hindus do not always use). Debates on whether to eat meat or not didn't stop, and animal sacrifices had not disappeared, but over time most Brahmins became vegetarian as they saw it as purity – and also as a high-status quality.

When the worship of three Hindi gods, Shiva, Brahma and Vishnu, became very prominent, this helped the vegetarian cause, as the latter god (often represented with light blue skin and four arms), also called the 'protector', was said to support not eating meat, and some of their followers became vegetarians. However, there still were all sorts of tensions between Jains, Buddhist and Hindus.

In the 2nd and 3rd century, Mahāyāna Buddhism, the more ritualistic, more mythological, and more pro-vegetarian form of Buddhism, expanded. A Mahāyāna text called the Laṅkāvatāra Sūtra mentions more than twenty reasons why the Buddha could not have condoned meat-eating in any circumstance. At that time, Mahāyāna Buddhism was already well established in China (while Theravāda Buddhism expanded in South-East Asia), but it had to face the followers of the Confucian philosophy opposing monasticism. When shaven Buddhist monks not eating animals came along, a real cultural clash occurred as Confucius' teachings forbade the harming of your own body, including cutting your hair.

Buddhism in China also had to face Taoism, an organised religion possibly founded around 500 BCE by Lao Tzu (a curator at the Royal Library in the state of Chu), which had reacted against the official religion of the empire involving many animal sacrifices. Taoism, which still exists today, believes in the harmony of all things, and some Taoist religious orders encourage vegetarianism to minimise harm because they consider all life forms are sentient. However, Taoism does not advocate rigid rituals and they don't go as far as prohibiting eating meat (except beef, which seems to be banned in most Taoist lineages). Therefore, Buddhism and Taoism had some common ground. (In fact, it seems that tofu, the vegan staple made from soya beans, was created by the Taoist Prince Liú Ān in the Han dynasty between 179 and 122 BCE.)

Both Confucianism and Taoism draw from the ancient Chinese philosophical concept of Yin and Yang. It predicates all things exist as inseparable opposites, such as female–male or dark–light. Taoists favour Yin (feminine, passive, dark, soft, old, etc.) while Confucianists favour Yang (masculine, active, light, hard, young, etc.). In this context, the concept of *ahimsa* feels very Yin, and hence Mahāyāna Buddhists would have clashed less with the Taoists. Taoists influenced Buddhism in China, and later in Japan, transforming it into Zen Buddhism (which emphasises self-restraint, meditation, and insight into the nature of mind and things). *Ahimsa* kept expanding in all directions.

The big gap of the dark Middle Ages

A woman with her hair covered was meditating on a mountain close to the Iraqi city of Basra when wild animals gathered around her and stared at her in wonder. A wise old preacher approached her and the animals ran away. Surprised, he said: 'The animals fled when they saw me. Why did they stay with you?' She asked in return, 'What did you eat today?' The wise man replied, 'Meat and bread.' She then said, 'When you have eaten meat, why should they not flee?' This woman was Hazrat Rabia, a Sufi mystic, possibly the single most influential ascetic woman of Islamic history, and this story makes many think she was a vegetarian.

From the 7th century we have Islam, the religion of the new Arab prophet Muhammad, and many orders of ascetic devout spiritual Muslims tracing most of their precepts from Muhammad's cousin Ali are called Sufi mystics. Many of these did not eat meat as a step towards spiritual growth and even abstained from taking any kind of animal product while in training. Hazrat Rabia was one of the most influential ones.

After the death of her father and famine striking Basra, she went into the desert to pray and live in semi-seclusion. There she developed the doctrine of Divine Love known as *Ishq-e-Haqeeqi*, a model of mutual love between God and all the beings of creation. She wrote:

> O Lord, if I worship You because of Fear of Hell, then burn me in Hell; If I worship You because I desire Paradise, then exclude me from Paradise; But if I worship You for Yourself alone, then deny me not your Eternal Beauty.

Keeping the idea of *ahimsa* evolving and expanding in the Middle Ages wasn't easy. The big gap of the Medieval period, covering from the 5th to the 15th century, was later labelled the 'Dark Ages' because of the cultural and economic deterioration that took place in Western Europe. In that environment ideological progress was severely handicapped. Nevertheless, *ahimsa* and vegetarianism survived and somehow kept going in the West, mostly through

Muslims such as Hazrat Rabia. Although the compassion side of Islam did not develop into avoiding eating meat in the dominant communities, there are always rebels who see through orthodox religious dictates. For instance, Abu Hatim, a single preacher with an *ahimsa*-like message, created around the year 906 a whole community in southern Iraq called al-Baqliyyah (a.k.a. 'the Greengrocers') where animal slaughter was forbidden. In Basra, a clandestine esoteric Arab group called the Brethren of Purity (*Ikhwan al-Safa*) wrote in the 8th or 10th century a fable titled 'The Case of the Animals versus Man Before the King of the Jinn' about other animals putting humanity on trial – which somehow must have inspired my first novel, which manifested my veganism.

Remember the Manichaeans and their vegan priests with their sanctity of life beliefs? Although they vanished in the West, they survived in the East a bit longer, because Islam at that time was quite tolerant of other religions. However, in 750 a new Islamic regime which was much less tolerance of religious diversity took over and began persecuting the Manichaeans. By the 10th century, they fled from southern Iraq and ended up in the Uighur Steppe Empire, in central Asia, where luckily for them their religion was adopted by the king, and they managed to hold on there for a while even after the king died. In the 840s the emperor of China took over Uighur and banned foreign religions including Buddhism and Manichaeanism, but one Elect managed to escape to the south of China and re-established his religion there. By the end of the 9th century, Confucianism, Buddhism and Taoism became the established religions in Imperial China, and Manichaeanism still existed as a minor sect. However, by the 12th and 13th centuries, they were seen by the establishment as 'Vegetarian Demon Worshippers', and eventually the Elects disappeared.

We also find full-on vegans in the middle of the Golden Age of the Islamic civilisation. Abul'ala Al-Ma'arri was one of the greatest non-religious poets of the early 11th century. He was blind from a young age due to smallpox, and he was living in self-imposed ascetic reclusion in Ma'arra but becoming a major public figure, as people came to listen to his lectures. Ma'arra was a 'proper' vegan and lived well until his eighties writing many poems about avoiding all animal products. This is an excerpt from one of his most inspiring unequivocal vegan poems, which should be framed in all modern ethical vegans' bedrooms:

> You are diseased in understanding and religion.
> Come to me, that you may hear something of sound
>   truth.
> Do not unjustly eat fish the water has given up,
> And do not desire as food the flesh of slaughtered
>   animals,
> Or the white milk of mothers who intended its pure
>   draught
> for their young, not noble ladies.
> And do not grieve the unsuspecting birds by taking
>   eggs;
> for injustice is the worst of crimes.
> And spare the honey which the bees get industriously
> from the flowers of fragrant plants;
> For they did not store it that it might belong to others,
> Nor did they gather it for bounty and gifts.
> I washed my hands of all this; and wish that I
> Perceived my way before my hair went grey!

Many vegans today would be very surprised to realise these words were written many centuries ago by an Islamic poet from Syria. The sentiment sounds so contemporary, so 'relevant' to the cause, which they probably associate more with modern Western values.

V

My bosses were also very surprised when in January 2017 I sent them the email telling them what I had found regarding the default pension fund of the charity. They had no explanation for why the current fund was so 'unethical'. From 2015, there was a legal requirement for all companies to choose a default pension, and management at that time (which had since changed) must have altered the fund without checking where the money would be invested. 'Not to worry,' my bosses told me, they would sort this out. The COO wrote back to let me know they were doing a review of all financial investments, and they would change the fund.

I had no reason to believe this would not happen, but as I had lived long enough to know often things take longer than anticipated, I wrote back requesting my contributions (6 per cent of my salary) should not be paid into the fund while they were sorting the problem out, as I did not want a single penny invested in vivisection. They agreed, and then I asked management to notify all staff of my discovery, allowing them to request the same if they so wished. As I suspected, nobody at the charity was aware of the fact their pension fund was investing in such companies.

I wonder how many people have the same level of ignorance about their pension fund, especially if it was chosen by their employers. How many people are aware of what happens around them, with the products they buy, with the services they order? We seem more inclined to use most of our brain capacity in fantasy worlds with elaborate characters and rules which do not resemble reality in TV, books and games, and by the time we need to consider the things other people offer to us in real life, the choices available in front of us, we don't feel we have the energy or the knowledge to make an informed decision. We choose what everyone else chooses and we don't ask questions, and others who see us making our choices also end up choosing what we choose. Multiply this by 7.8 billion people, and you have a status quo where billions of animals are tortured because most people did not bother to ask the question: 'Is this really necessary?'

I began to feel a bit anxious when months passed and I heard no more news about it. Eventually, I decided to investigate further and contact the pension provider directly to ask. They told me I still was enrolled in the 'unethical' pension fund, and contributions to it had been made on my behalf by my employer. I was shocked – that was terrible. Despite my early awareness, my precautions and my due diligence, I had failed to stop contributing economically to vivisection companies, something irrefutably against my ethical veganism! How could this have happened? I had been very clear about my request to stop my contributions, and I had been reassured it would be done; and yet, it wasn't done, and rats, mice, beagles or monkeys would have been injected toxic substances partially paid for by me.

Surprise was again the reaction of my bosses when I notified them of my 'second' discovery. They apologised and told me it would be sorted out and my contributions would cease. Can you imagine what happened next? Yes, it was the same story. I checked again; I discovered my contributions had not been stopped yet and now surpassed more than £1,000; they apologised again. I checked again, and again. I seemed to be trapped in a Groundhog Day loop.

In October 2017, though, ten months after I discovered the pension problem, it seemed the vicious circle could be broken. The COO, operating now as interim CEO, sent an email to all staff stating a new ethical fund had been found. All staff pension funds would be switched to this one unless anyone did not want that change to happen, in which case could they communicate this to her by the end of November. Would it happen? Would the change be finally made and my contributions moved to the new fund? I only had to wait until December to find out.

Other things were changing at the office that made my work

there more difficult. With the CEO temporarily out of commission for health reasons, and new senior management recruited, the organisation was no longer as vegan-friendly as it used to be. Those running it now were meat-eaters, and Laura, the vegan office manager, left and was replaced by another meat-eater who began introducing animal products in the office's meals. That boosted the confidence of some staff members who seemed to have a problem with veganism, and they became more vocal about it. I felt the organisation was gradually slipping away from its core values.

However, my frustration with the work situation was compensated for by my happiness caused by my new home. In April 2017 I had moved to a one-bedroom flat with a separate kitchen and a washing machine (I didn't have one in my previous flat and had to go to the laundrette). It was in a much quieter area but still in the same borough, even closer to my local parks. It was bigger, in an older building, but with a fully refurbished interior in which everything seemed to work to perfection. I had more space because I had got rid of a lot of stuff when I moved, and more light too due to the numerous Edwardian-style windows. After twenty-four years, this felt like a proper home. No more posters, then. Time to frame some of my photos (the owl monkey from Panama, the donkeys from Mexico, the wasp from Barcelona, the Boston glass building and a famous lecture I gave at Plymouth University – more of which in chapter 3) and hang them in prominent places.

Above all, though, it had a backyard. Mind you, a shared yard with other tenants, but as I was on the ground floor and I had a door that led directly to it, I could very much take 'ownership'. Crucially, it had a raised area with soil in it. I could grow my veg and have my tiny orchard there. My dream of growing some of my own food without harming any animals could become a reality now. Yes, I had to pay twice the rent I was paying before, but I had a stable job after all, so if I cut down on my expenses I could just afford it.

V

Back in the Christian West of the Middle Ages, there were still itinerant ascetics who did not accept the status quo, and who put to shame orthodox Christian monks who increasingly relaxed their dietary restrictions for convenience. For that, and other rebellious tendencies, they were labelled as heretics. There were two main dualist heretical movements, the Bogomils and the Cathars. They believed in two gods, one good, for spiritual things, and the other bad, for physical things; they did not believe in Hell; and they lived ascetic lives (including abstinence from meat and milk, which they considered 'bad' products of sex). Naturally, they were severely persecuted by the orthodox Roman Catholic Church, whose members became suspicious of any monk looking "a bit pale" (often these were forced to eat meat to test if their paleness was due to being vegetarian).

In India, from the 9th century, Buddhism began to disappear, and in the 11th and 12th centuries Islam joined the subcontinent, which eventually helped to see Buddhism off completely. By the 14th century, most of the 'heretical' religions were gone, and today's major religions settled in their most orthodox forms, as we know them today. Islam, though, did not eliminate vegetarianism in India. By the late Middle Ages, many Sufis in India were vegetarian, not only because of asceticism but also because of *ahimsa*. An example is Hamidu'd-Din Nagori, the 13th-century Sufi who preached vegetarianism to his followers in the New Delhi Sultanate.

Sikhism (the fourth Dharmic religion) originated in the 15th century in the Punjab region in northern India, and is based on the revelation of Guru Nanak. It's still a strong monotheistic casteless religion. Sikhs are easily recognisable because they often wear a turban, called *dastār*, and men often have beards. Although mainstream Sikhism allows meat-eating, it serves vegetarian communal meals to be inclusive. I have a friend called Navjeet with whom I do vegan street outreach in London, and he is a vegan Sikh. He told me about Los Angeles-based Sikh-American couple Ravi and Jacquie Singh, who run a project called Share A Meal, which gives free vegan burritos to the homeless. Navjeet said that giving free food to those in need is an important part of his religion, which stresses the concept of sharing, or *Vaṇḍ Chakkō*.

Sikhs in India started in the north-west, but in the north-east Vishnu worshippers continued to promote vegetarianism. In the early 16th century, a movement called Bengal Vaishnavism began, and for them Vishnu (the 'preserver' god) became incarnated into Krishna (the god of compassion, tenderness and love). That is where the well-known chanting and dancing Hare Krishna communities come from – a.k.a. the International Society for Krishna Consciousness, founded by A.C. Bhaktivedanta Swami Prabhupada in 1966 – which can be seen in most modern Western cities, and who are vegetarians because they follow the idea of *ahimsa*. (Unfortunately, they still use ghee in many of their dishes – as I have personally experienced when I stayed in one of their temples in Ecuador during my anti-bullfighting tours in the mid-2000s.)

Despite the difficulties of the medieval world, it appears there were many people, from many religions, who still advocated for abstinence from flesh, often in very hostile environments. It seems that *ahimsa* kept shining even in the darkest periods of history.

Someone turned the light on

Between the 16th and 17th century a big cultural change occurred in Europe which marked the end of the Middle Ages and the beginning of the Renaissance, which preceded the period known as the Enlightenment (some argue we are still part of it). The main philosophies around this period are centred in the concept of humanism (where humans, rather than the old gods, moved to centre stage) and the rediscovery of classical Greek philosophy – the perfect opportunity to get old Pythagoras, Orpheus and Epicurus (with his 'simple life' philosophy that included vegetarianism) back into fashion.

In Italy, among the famous artists Michelangelo, Botticelli and Tintoretto, we find one of the most celebrated vegetarians: Leonardo da Vinci – he was perhaps one of the first animal liberation activists on account of his reported fondness of freeing birds from cages – but in 17th-century France very fruitful intellectual developments were brewing: the 'Republic of Letters'. This was a network of philosophers, poets, scientists, naturalists, and so on, intellectuals who detached themselves from the dogma of the Church and 'the establishment'. One of their members was the scientist Pierre Gassendi, often portrayed with a timid gentle face, short hair with a receding hairline, wearing modest black robes and a small white collar – the fashion of the time. He was an advocate of Epicureanism and he objected to the views of Descartes, another colleague of their 'republic', about non-human animals being only irrational 'machines' with no feelings. Gassendi supported vegetarianism because he thought it was healthier and it was the 'natural' thing to do if you were a human. He based it on the study of human teeth compared to the teeth of other animals.

So far we have seen abstinence from eating meat as justified by *ahimsa*, purity, reincarnation, status or religious reasons, but with Gassendi we find 'health' reasons as the new justification. In the 17th century in India, physicians prescribed vegetarian food as a therapy to combat diseases, and it did not take long for the medical profession all over Europe to begin treating with vegetarian diets those suffering from illnesses perceived to be lifestyle-related. In the 18th century, many of Gassendi's ideas went back to France through English philosophers and writers such as John Locke (who believed animals have feelings and unnecessary cruelty towards them was morally wrong), Jeremy Bentham (who argued it was the ability to suffer that should be the benchmark of how we treat other beings) and Margaret Cavendish (who condemned humans for believing all animals were made specifically for their benefit).

In England, we had a revolution going on, which led to a civil war, the beheading of King Charles I in 1649, and the first English Republic led by Oliver Cromwell. Under his government, animal protection laws were passed as he disliked blood sports. The new Republic was fertile soil for 'radicals' to flourish, including those with 'unorthodox' diets.

One of them was Roger Crab, a Baptist priest from Buckinghamshire, who had fought in the parliamentary army and survived a serious head wound. He preached that it was a sin to eat any animal or drink alcohol. In 1641 he ceased eating meat, dairy and eggs, and in 1652, dressed in sackcloth, he became a pacifist vegan hermit in Ickenham, west of London. As the Jewish Essenes did centuries earlier, he kept referring to the Biblical Adam and Eve as the proof he was right. According to him, Noah's permission to eat flesh was a temporary measure to allow plants to grow after the flood. He wrote at the beginning of his autobiography the following:

> The English Hermite, or, Wonder of this Age. Being a relation of the life of Roger Crab, living neer Uxbridge, taken from his own mouth, shewing his strange reserved and unparallel'd kind of life, who counteth it a sin against his body and soule to eate any sort of flesh, fish, or living creature, or to drinke any wine, ale, or beere. He can live with three farthings a week. His constant food is roots and hearbs, as cabbage, turneps, carrets, dock-leaves, and grasse; also bread and bran, without butter or cheese: his cloathing is sack-cloath. He left the Army, and

kept a shop at Chesham, and hath now left off that, and sold a considerable estate to give to the poore, shewing his reasons from the Scripture, Mark.10.21. Jer.35.

He was repeatedly imprisoned for his views against the king and government and was accused of witchcraft by the vicar of Uxbridge. He died at the age of sixty-four, which wasn't bad as the average lifespan then was under forty.

Back in France, Voltaire was the epitome of the thinker of the 18th century, and one of the key figures of the Enlightenment, the European intellectual and philosophical movement based on reason and the evidence of the senses. He tried a vegetable diet when he was young as it had been prescribed to him by a doctor, and when he was an old man he wrote supporting vegetarianism – although he still ate meat. The famous Geneva-born writer Jean-Jacques Rousseau, Voltaire's main rival and the man who inspired the French Revolution, went even further. Although he wasn't a real vegetarian himself – possibly he was what today we would call flexitarian – he advocated children should be fed only a vegetable diet. He thought civilisation corrupts our 'nature' (Voltaire thought the opposite), and wrote novels inspired by the ideas of Plutarch and Gassendi, suggesting humans are not natural meat-eaters. Bernardin Saint-Pierre, Rousseau's disciple who was also a botanist, went even further; he was an actual vegetarian, writing more about the idea of humans being herbivores.

During the French Revolution of 1789, the revolutionaries who were vegetarian were the most radical, as they were also feminists and anti-slavery – what we would call today 'intersectionals'. Unfortunately, many of these were guillotined after the Republic was proclaimed in September 1792, as part of the bloody persecution during the dictatorship imposed by the Committee of Public Safety during what is now called the Reign of Terror.

V

When in the early summer of 1993 I left Catalonia with a bag on my front and a bag on my back, France was naturally the first country I came to. I would look at the atlas I brought with me, choose a nearby destination where I could sleep in a youth hostel, and take a bus or train there. Initially, the mild weather was quite pleasant, and between petanque-playing southern villagers and chicly dressed northern visitors, I squeezed my way through Occitanie. Everywhere I went I took notes in my diary (in precarious French) about things that drew my attention, from the wildlife I encountered around the pine trees and fennel fields, to the way passionate young couples sat on public benches during the long evenings with gentle breezes (often in more elaborate embraces than I was accustomed to). I also recorded everything I bought to have some control of my expenses (my earliest entry was eight francs for a *crêpe de sucre*).

The first place I stayed for some time was the Camargue, a natural reserve located south of Arles, between the Mediterranean Sea and the two arms of the Rhône delta. I had heard about it before due to its reputation for been very rich in fauna – as a zoologist I had to have a look, and I wasn't disappointed. I spent some time in the wilderness there, among the feral ponies, the coypus (big beaver-size rodents) and the many birds. At that time I still remembered most of the scientific names of common plants and animals, and I wrote down every time a saw one. I wrote '*Un possible Circus aeruginosus a dix metres, Fantasitique!!*' when I saw a western marsh harrier, and '*Incroyable, un triangle volant de Phoenicopterus ruber avec 182 oiseaux volant sur la mer*' when I saw my first pink flamingos flying (they have been breeding there naturally for centuries, but since 1972 an artificial island specifically created for them has helped them breed more).

After a while, I felt quite lonely (I wrote: 'Two people have been nice to me. They are the first, but I hope not the last. One was a dog, the other was a cat.'), and I thought it would be better if I travelled to big cosmopolitan cities where I would have better chances to find a proper life – and a job. I found my way to Paris, a city I knew quite well as it was the first foreign city I had visited, on a school trip when I was a teenager. Then I moved north to Belgium, but an incident with a group of neo-Nazis who chased me down an Antwerp street (I must have looked like the perfect target with my scruffy beard and very long hair) put me off the entire country, so I tried the Netherlands. After a couple of nights of being forced to sleep rough around Amsterdam's central railway station, I realised this country would not do either, so I moved to Hamburg, in Germany. I found the language too difficult, so I moved to Denmark, yet people seemed unfriendly to foreigners there.

In every country I visited I paid attention to particular behaviours to give me an idea of what it would be like to live there. For instance, the distance between people in a queue would tell me how outgoing they were (bigger distance: less outgoing), which interestingly seemed to correlate with latitude. I also measured the distance between a person and a pigeon before the latter flew away, as shorter distances suggested to me people were more animal-friendly (as they would chase them less often and the pigeons would be less scared of them). I used these and other factors to assess my chances of becoming an animal protectionist and a scientist in any of these countries. In retrospect, I think I was subconsciously sabotaging my chances because, deep down, what I wanted to be was British.

I always had a strong affinity with British culture. My favourite scientists were British (Charles Darwin, Richard Dawkins, Desmond Morris and Stephen Hawking), so were my favourite musicians, filmmakers and comedians. I was an Anglophile, I guess.

In Denmark, I had already run out of cash, and the country did not feel right for me. Lying down in a corner of Copenhagen's

City Hall Square during a relatively sunny afternoon, I had to decide my next move. I had two options: continue going north into Sweden or go west to the UK. It was an easy decision. I used my credit card to buy a coach ticket to London. I arrived there around 7 p.m. – the best time in early autumn, as the sun is low and the warm colours are always more welcoming. I walked a bit through the streets and I saw a pub. I looked through the glass window to find the TV was on, showing the ITV evening news. The presenter was Trevor McDonald, the well-respected, seasoned journalist. Right there and then, I knew this was the right country for me. I decided this was going to be my new home. I concluded it while watching a primetime TV presenter who happened not to be white. This must be a tolerant country, I thought.

V

At the end of the 18th century, at the time of the French Revolution, Britain may have been less tolerant. All the 'radicals' were also rounded up and imprisoned as George III's men did not fancy losing their sovereign's head as had happened to his counterpart across the channel, but as they were often kept together at the Old Bailey and Newgate prisons, they were able to share more ideas and to develop a network which, finally, we can call 'vegetarianism'. From these prisons, the first anthologies of pro-vegetarian writing were published. Part of this network was Dr William Lambe, who prescribed distilled water and a vegan diet.

This network reached the New World too. In Deerfield, Massachusetts, British-born William Dorrell ran a religious cult (the Dorrelites) whose members were vegetarian, did not use animal products for clothes and did not use animals for work – a step closer to our modern concept of ethical veganism.

The Romantics in England also experimented with vegetarianism. In 1812, poet Percy Bysshe Shelley moved to the house of Harriet de Boinville, in Bracknell, and there he lived a vegan lifestyle like everyone else in the house. He would go on to write about how humans would recover their peaceful nature if they abandoned meat-eating. In 1816 Mary Shelley, another Romantic and Percy Bysshe Shelley's second wife, wrote her novel *Frankenstein*, in which the monster is a gentle vegan – a fact which is ignored in the Hollywood versions of her book.

It seems that in the 19th century, Christianity once again allowed some vegetarianism on its fringes, and even some veganism. In Surrey in 1838, the teetotal James Pierrepont Greaves founded a vegan utopian community (which mostly ate raw food) initially called Alcott House but later called the Concordium (and his followers Concordites). Also, the anti-alcohol preacher Sylvester Graham created his own vegan 'Grahamite' diet composed of simple vegetables without spices, which was later used to fight against cholera.

These Christian churches and communes used different degrees of vegetarianism and veganism, but they were still religious groups. However, in September 1847, members of these main English vegetarian groups gathered together in Northwood Villa, in Kent, home of the Hydrotherapy Institute. There they created the first official Vegetarian Society, no longer directly linked to any particular church. Reverend Joseph Brotherton, the Salford MP, became chair of this new society and stated:

> It will be found, that abstinence from the flesh of animals is in accordance with every right principle, with justice, mercy, temperance, and health; while it will prevent cruelty, disease, and misery.

– note how 'cruelty', and therefore *ahimsa*, is already there, if as a secondary reason. Three years later the American Vegetarian Society was founded in a convention held in New York called by

William Metcalfe, an English preacher who in 1817 had started a vegetarian church in Philadelphia.

After many centuries of distilling the idea of not consuming certain animal products for one reason or another, we are now beginning to zoom in on the idea itself, regardless of the 'reasons'. You could now be described as a 'vegetarian', and people would know 'what' it meant without necessarily knowing the 'why'. Not quite ethical veganism yet, but getting closer.

V

In January 2018, I also thought I was getting closer to solving the pension problem I'd discovered a year earlier. In fact, I assumed it had been solved, as by the previous December the charity's staff were all to have been moved to a new 'ethical' fund. However, there was a potential problem. The interim CEO who had sent the email had now left the charity, and as the actual CEO was still ill, a new managing director was hired to help relieve some of the pressure and allow the CEO to gradually return (although in the end he did not return and the MD ended up replacing him).

I assumed he would have been informed about the pension issue, as I had been constantly reminding other senior staff members during all this time. Everyone was saying the solution had been found, and it was just a matter of finalising everything, which took a bit longer due to the high turnover of senior staff. Therefore, when I met the new MD to discuss the issue, I expected the same sort of reassuring message. I did not get it. Instead, the MD said the change to the ethical fund had not occurred, and it may not at all, as the acting CEO who dealt with it had done things wrong. He said I should not worry as he would look into it and find a solution. I was worried, though. Most staff would have assumed by now that their pension fund was finally ethical; they did not know the change had never happened.

Nevertheless, I decided to wait and give the new MD a chance to sort it out.

The 16th of February 2018 was a cloudy day – a bit chilly, but not too bad. Because it was a Friday, I did not go to our main office to work, but to an office space in central London staff were allowed to use. It had become part of my routine to work there on Fridays, I could walk there so it helped me save some commuting costs. It was a spacious room and the view was impressive – it was right by the river and you could see Big Ben. I was there by myself most of the time. I used my work laptop, which we were allowed to take home, which I placed on a raised desk so I could work standing. (I had worked that way for the last five years on the advice of a chiropractor.)

At 13:55, while I was sipping an almost cold tea with soya milk in my black Sherlock mug, I received an email from the MD that was addressed to all staff. It was about the pension issue and was supposed to clarify the situation, but it did not. It did not tell staff what was going on; it did not tell them what I knew. That upset me, but it had a link to the pension provider website, which perhaps would help. I thought the best thing to do was to relax, have a fresh warm cup of tea and a peanut butter bar from my emergency food drawer, and check the link after a while. About an hour later, after realising that going to the link was even more confusing, I clicked the 'reply to all' button and I asked the MD for clarification. This led to an email conversation with him that made me believe he was interpreting the pension problem as only affecting my pension fund, not a problem for my vegan colleagues, or the organisation as a whole.

I had asked the MD to tell staff what was going on with the pension a few days earlier, but this email only made things more confused. It also became clear that he would not send any further clarifying message as he claimed what he was allowed to say was limited, but it appeared each member staff who wanted an ethical fund had to contact the pension provider and request the change themselves.

I walked home as usual, and in the evening I went to the pension provider's website to switch my fund, but I couldn't find straight away the 'ethical fund' the MD had sent around that day as the 'alternative' to the current default fund. After looking for a while, I found it, but I also found eight more funds with the label 'ethical' in them. Some of them were less financially risky than the one suggested by management. The staff did not know this. I knew the bulk change to an ethical fund had not happened, and now I knew there were actually nine ethical funds to choose from. I had to inform staff, but I had to be careful how I did it, as the MD had advised me not to step into the role of a financial adviser as I wasn't qualified.

After working for hours on the issue with the information I had found, at 58 minutes past midnight I sent an email to all staff, with a disclaimer clarifying I was not a financial adviser and the email was not sent on behalf of management or the charity. In it, I included all the information about the nine ethical funds I had found, and how to change to them if they wished to do so. Crucially, I did not specify which I had chosen myself as I understood recommending particular tailored financial products is what financial advisers do.

At that time I thought I had saved the day and I could spend the weekend relaxing and going to the Vegan Festival organised by the Farplace Animal Rescue at the Oval. Staff would finally know their fund had not been switched to an ethical fund as they had been told, and they would now know how to do it themselves. I expected most staff would make the switch, they would find a suitable ethical fund with a financial risk they were happy to take, and because of it hundreds of thousands of pounds that otherwise would continue to be invested in animal testing would now be re-directed to more ethical companies. A win for everyone.

I was wrong. There would not be congratulations for having solved the pension problem. On the contrary, two days later, after finishing an induction meeting with a new employee during what seemed a normal working day, I was handed a letter from HR inviting me to a disciplinary hearing for 'failure to follow reasonable management instructions'. My jaw dropped and stayed there for some time. I read it and re-read it all over again, unable to process what the consultant who gave it to me was saying. It felt as if the world had collapsed under me.

V

In history, you also often see this sort of unexpected 'turn for the worse'. With the creation of vegetarian societies in the mid-19th century, things were looking good for vegetarians, who were now more organised, free from religion, and able to expand, but as we have constantly seen in this chapter, just when things look good a big political change occurs which sets things back. In America, it was the civil war between 1861 and 1865, which not only killed many people but also 'killed' the American Vegetarian Society, as in many respects it sacrificed itself to fight against slavery – many church folk and 'people of conscience' were galvanised around this important issue that took priority over any other cause – understandably, considering the big political progress President Lincoln was offering. The other big political upheaval was colonialism, messing up things for the vegetarians of the East.

In Britain, at a time when men with large mutton-chop sideburns and moustaches started wearing top hats (upper class) or bowler hats (middle class), and women with high, dressed hair, with complicated twists and rolls at the back, started wearing domed bell-shaped skirts supported by crinoline petticoats with horsehair in them, vegetarianism was also in decline. During the beginning of the Imperial Victorian era many radical causes were generally in decline, but many pioneering brave women kept the concept of *ahimsa* alive.

When in 1880 Anna Kingsford, a thirty-four-year-old women's rights activist from Stratford, Essex, graduated as a medical doctor from the Ecole de Médecine of Paris, it was a big deal. Women were not allowed to practise medicine in the UK, and this is why she had to study overseas. However, she achieved far more than a 'forbidden' degree: she did it without having experimented on a single animal. Paris at that time was the centre of advancement in the study of physiology, mostly as a result of experiments on animals, particularly dogs, conducted without anaesthetic. But Anna Kingsford was a leading anti-vivisectionist and a prominent member of the recently founded Society for the Protection of Animals Liable to Vivisection, the world's first organisation opposed to animal research. She was also a vegetarian (obviously for *ahimsa* reasons) and founded the Food Reform Society, which promoted abstinence from animal flesh.

In her pro-vegetarian book *The Perfect Way in Diet: A Treatise Advocating a Return to the Natural and Ancient Food of Our Race* she concluded:

> And if, for the vindication of the views advanced in these pages it be necessary or helpful to adduce authority, they have as advocates such a mighty array of names ancient and modern as no other school which the world has yet seen can boast. To these illustrious names of men who have thought as I think, and whose disciple no one need be ashamed to be, I make appeal; to Pythagoras and Gautama Buddha, to Socrates, Seneca, and Plutarch, to Porphyry, and Apollonius of Tyana, to Origen, Chrysostom, and Francis Assisi, to Gassendi, Gleizes, and Shelley – in

short, to all the most serious and luminous minds of the ancient and modern world. For with all these the first essential step towards perfectionment, whether of the individual or of the community, was so to regulate life that its sustenance should involve no shock to the moral conscience. The doctrine, which is that of the modern school of abstainers from flesh, was that of the Magi who initiated Daniel; of the Therapeuts, who drew their origin and their knowledge from Egyptian adepts; of the Buddhists, an expression of whose beautiful teaching is prefixed to this essay; of the Nazarites, who counted Jesus among their number; of the Essenes, who produced his friend and companion, John the Baptist; of the Ebionites and Recluses; of the exponents of the Christian 'Gnosis,' who kept alive and bequeathed to us through the Neo-Platonists that spirit of understanding, that 'seeing eye' and 'hearing ear' possible only in their completeness to men of pure heart and life.

Dr Kingsford sadly died at the young age of forty-one, but she wasn't alone. Another important vegetarian woman was Annie Besant (1847–1933), a prominent socialist women's rights activist, and in 1898, Frances Power Cobbe founded the British Union Against Vivisection by uniting five different anti-vivisection societies. All these pioneering women helped to rekindle the vegetarian movement at the turn of the century, at the very time when the suffragette movement began.

The British vegetarian society had not disappeared as happened in America and soon it expanded again. In 1902 Dr Josiah Oldfield founded the Fruitarian Society, a little-known clear precursor of the Vegan Society. Dugald Semple, a Scottish fruitarian, stated in 1907:

By fruitarianism is meant a dietary consisting chiefly
of nuts and fruits. Cooked cereals and vegetables are
not necessarily excluded, although the exclusion of all
cooked foods, should means and knowledge permit,
will lead to better results. For this dietary it will be
noticed that not only is flesh and meat omitted, but
also the animal products milk and eggs. The use of
these products by vegetarians has long been one of
the chief objections to vegetarianism, especially in
medical circles.

A young Indian law student called Mohandas Gandhi (yes, the
very man you are thinking of, later called Mahatma, which means
'venerable') became an executive of the London branch of the
Vegetarian Society. He first became vegetarian in India, promising
this to his mother before a Jain monk in the coastal state of Gujarat,
but when he moved to England he fully embraced the concept
after meeting members of the vegetarian and fruitarian societies.
He left Britain for South Africa before the start of the First World
War, and after returning to India and becoming a politician he
ended up becoming one of the most famous vegetarians on the
entire globe, and, of course, the man behind the independence of
India by non-violent civil disobedience tactics. A man who when
travelling through countries, cultures and professions must have
asked 'Who I am?', and when seeing what the British were doing
to his motherland must have also asked 'What is this?', and when
devising the strategies to change what was wrong must have also
asked 'What should we do?' A man who by answering all these
questions became an inspiration to many avant-garde activists all
over the world.

The busy century which brought us veganism
In 1892, on the way to the busy 20th century, Henry Stephens

Salt, a vegetarian, anti-vivisectionist, socialist and Eton-educated pacifist son of a British army colonel, wrote the following in his book *Animals' Rights: Considered in Relation to Social Progress*:

> Even the leading advocates of animal rights seem to have shrunk from basing their claim on the only argument which can ultimately be held to be a really sufficient one – the assertion that animals, as well as men, though, of course, to a far less extent than men, are possessed of a distinctive individuality, and, therefore, are in justice entitled to live their lives with a due measure of that 'restricted freedom'.

His work set up the philosophy of 'animal rights' separate from the ideas of vegetarianism, a new concept which for decades would ride alongside veganism, and many would see as synonymous with it. Animal rights is the idea that non-human animals are entitled to the possession of their existence, and that their most basic interests should be afforded the same consideration as similar interests of humans. In other words, it challenges the notion that non-human animals are objects, property, goods or commodities, and ultimately aims to change behaviours and laws to acknowledge the 'personhood' of non-human animals.

At the turn of the 20th century, vegetarianism continued to develop separately from the emerging concept of animal rights. For instance, in Germany, a new 'fitness' movement about returning 'back to Nature' became very popular: Lebensreform. Clearly health-oriented, it had plenty of fresh-air exercising, sunbathing, avoiding tobacco and alcohol, and of course, eating only fresh plants. A group of them lived in a commune near Berlin called Vegetarische Obstbau-Kolonie Eden (Vegetarian Orchard Settlement Eden). The health claims of a vegetarian diet went now from curing diseases to making people fitter, stronger and faster than meat-eaters. During the Second World War, this movement ended up high-jacked by the far right and became associated with the Nazis. Hitler ordered all vegetarian societies to join him, but they chose to close instead.

In the early 20th century, anarchism also doubled with vegetarianism in anti-capitalist Paris's anarchist communes. One of its best-known members was Louis Rimbault, who advocated for a vegan diet without spices, and started the *végétalisme* movement there. He ended up setting up a vegan nudist commune at Bascon – since then, *végétalien* is still French for vegan.

It was not all about health and politics, though. In Russia, the illustrious novelist Leo Tolstoy (1828–1910) became a vegetarian not to become fit or rebel against the establishment, but for ethical reasons, and to get closer to an ascetic life. He wrote:

> His first act of abstinence is from animal food, because, not to mention the excitement of the passions produced by such food, it is simply immoral, as it requires an act contrary to moral feeling – killing – and is called forth only by greed and gluttony.

V

When I first arrived in the UK in 1993 after having failed to settle in other countries, I also had to adopt a relative quasi-ascetic life, but not by choice. I had no money, I could not speak English, and I had nobody to call a friend. I knew the UK would become my home, but to all intents and purposes, I was truly homeless. I had a backpacker's guide to Europe, though, and I read the UK section to see if there was any good advice about how to settle there. I found something promising. It said the best way to find cheap accommodation was advertising on the notice board of the London Students' Union.

When I went to the address I discovered the union had moved, but there was a telephone number in the book, and I rang it. Someone picked up the phone but said this was no longer their number and they could give me the new one. The only moment of hopelessness I experienced as an immigrant in the UK happened right there. Due to my very precarious knowledge of English, when I wrote down the number I realised I did not understand one of the digits. I asked the person on the phone to repeat it, but still didn't understand. I hung up and felt desperation. How would I survive in this country if I could not understand basic numbers? How could I find a place to stay if I could not even find the place to put an advert looking for a flat-share? I felt I was not going to make it, and I had nothing to fall back on, as I had deliberately severed all connections with my past life to accelerate adaptation to my new future.

I then noticed a difference between the telephone number of the book and the number I tried to write down. The one in the book had an extra digit. I realised what had happened. The person on the phone had given me a double-digit – such as 'double three' or 'double seven' – and I did not know at the time this is how the Brits give two consecutive identical digits when dictating a telephone number. There was hope, after all. I only needed to try all combinations of double digits. It worked. I got the right number, I got the new address of the Students' Union, now in Holborn, I went there, I found the board, I saw an ad from an Andalusian student looking for a flatmate, I rang, and I found my first – but not the last – accommodation in south London.

I soon integrated into the world of immigrants in London, which helped me to survive. Fellow immigrants taught me which temp agencies I should enrol with, and I did all sorts of low-paid jobs (delivering leaflets, washing up in kitchens, setting up stadiums for concerts ...). My other job was to learn English and learn it fast. I had a very comprehensive plan for that. First, we set up a rule in our shared flat to not speak any language other than English. Second, we had the TV on all the time with subtitles. Third, every week I would go to the free Natural History Museum and read all the text in the displays' signs, taking notes about any word I did not understand. It worked well, and I did learn very fast.

I spent two years doing this all winter, and in summer I hitchhiked all over the UK – sleeping in a tent in the countryside – trying to find a job as a zoologist. I moved to many different flats during my time in London, and for a few months I even lived in a squat without paying rent – anarchist style – as the landlord had disappeared. One of the jobs I did in London for a few quid was to help a woodwork teacher I had befriended on a Russell Square bench to build some new workshop tables in his school. Little did I know then the serendipitous significance of that short-term occupation (which I had been totally unqualified to attempt).

V

During the Second World War, another woodwork teacher made history for all vegans. On a Sunday in November 1944 (possibly the 5th), five months before the war in Europe ended, a woodwork teacher called Donald Watson from Yorkshire, and his wife, Dorothy Morgan, met with colleague Elsie (Sally) Shrigley and three other members of the Vegetarian Society in a central London veggie café called The Attic Club. The purpose of the meeting was to discuss their objection to the consumption of milk and eggs, which would inevitably lead to the creation of a separate group. They had already tried to form a subgroup within the Vegetarian Society for those opposing the use of dairy products, but when they were refused a section about it in the magazine they realised they had to split. That was the beginning of the Vegan Society.

As we have seen, through different eras and cultures many people have attempted to avoid the use of animal products for all sorts of reasons and with all kinds of caveats and exceptions, and then the vegetarian societies were created to develop the abstinence from animal products as an idea in itself, without linking it to religion or status. But such societies still promoted the use of some animal products, and their approach was very 'health' oriented – *ahimsa* was only a secondary reason. Donald Watson (also a conscientious objector and vegetarian since the age of fourteen) and his colleagues were aware they had to make the final step.

Watson's group were only another bunch of vegans joining the many who had abstained from all animal products over the centuries (such as ascetic hermits, the Elite Manichaeans, Abul 'ala Al-Ma'arri, the Concordites, Roger Crab, the *végétalien* anarchists and the fruitarians) but none of them had a well-defined secular simple term they could use to describe how different they were from vegetarians who avoided some animal products but consumed others. Someone had to create that term, and Morgan, Watson and Shrigley, after consulting the members of their new society, chose the term 'vegan'.

By the end of 1945, after the war had ended, the Vegan Society was properly constituted, with Watson as its secretary, treasurer, auditor and banker – and the society is still going strong today. In 1947, Dugald Semple became its chairman, incorporating fruitarians into the vegan family. In 1949, Leslie J. Cross, Watson's successor, suggested the following definition of veganism: 'The principle of the emancipation of animals from exploitation by man', later clarified as: 'to seek an end to the use of animals by man for food, commodities, work, hunting, vivisection, and by all other uses involving exploitation of animal life by man'. A 100 per cent *ahimsa* definition.

By the 1950s, however, some vegans were becoming ill, and some prominent members of the society died. Dr C.V. Pink, vice-president of the society, investigated patients whose health deteriorated after following this diet for a period of five to fifteen years (of course, many members had been vegan long before the society existed). The problem was identified as a deficit of the vitamin B12. This vitamin is absent in the modern vegan diet as it comes from bacteria no longer found on well-washed vegetables or in the meat of animals who eat contaminated plants. Today it is added to the feed of livestock as since the beginning of factory farming the animals no longer eat such contaminated plants (so, most meat-eaters get B12 from fortified meat).

Luckily, vitamin B12 had been isolated in 1948, and it could be produced in a lab brewing bacteria. In 1952 Dr C.V. Pink and Dr Frank Wokes used it with great success to treat vegan patients. The Vegan Society began to market B12-fortified soya milk as an alternative to cow's milk, and over the years many other companies have developed other types of fortified plant-based milk. Now, fortified foods or the use of vitamin supplements have eliminated the B12 deficit problem.

Many national vegan societies began to be founded all around the globe. Germany's was founded in 1953 and India's in 1957. In 1948 Catherine Nimmo and Robin Abramowicz founded a local vegan society in California, but they disbanded it to join the American Vegan Society created on 1 November 1960 by H. Jay Dinshah in Malaga, New Jersey. This time, finally, *ahimsa* was the main reason given for veganism, and this was even the title of the American Vegan Society's magazine. People trying not to harm others, including cows and chickens, in any way, now had a name and a growing international community that was separate from religion. Veganism was finally a real movement.

The revolution of modern times

The hell that is factory farming and biomedical research expanded considerably from the late 1960s. In 1966, the US, the UK and other industrialised nations began the factory farming of beef, dairy cattle and pigs. Intensive animal farming is a type of intensive agriculture designed to maximise production while minimising costs, and therefore keeps livestock at high stocking densities at large scale. Because of it, agricultural production across the globe doubled between 1950 and 1965 and doubled again by 1975. The price, predictably, was paid by the animals, whose lives had been reduced to mere 'production' machines, far from what they are biologically and psychologically capable of coping with. In factory farms, animals are crammed together in barren pens, crates or cages, which prevents normal behaviour. This intense confinement makes them grow very fast (as they don't use energy for moving) and makes them very susceptible to diseases, for which they have to be given many antibiotics. Factory farming is also highly unsustainable as it is dependent on large quantities of grain-based feed, water and energy. Today, around two in every three farm animals are factory farmed, which means over 50 billion animals every year worldwide.

Vivisection had been developed in the 19th century, but in the mid-20th century biomedical research and animal testing became an industry, and the numbers of animals involved rocketed. Toxicology and metabolic testing become compulsory for new drugs in many countries, but animals were used not only to test new chemicals but also to test all sorts of procedures, including military and aeronautical. Dogs (mostly beagles) have been used to test tobacco products, cats in neurological research, primates (mostly rhesus monkeys and chimps) for all sorts of tests (from space vehicles to vaccines), rabbits in cosmetic tests and rodents (guinea pigs, mice and rats) in many studies of genetic diseases. The amount of suffering these animals have to endure is difficult to imagine, which is helped by the great secrecy of the biomedical research industry. Currently, there may be as many as 100 million vertebrates experimented on around the globe every year.

Since the 1960s, humanity was imprisoning, torturing and killing so many animals at a massively increasing rate that those who cared about animal suffering had more reason to speak out. From the early 1980s, the animal-rights movement and the vegan movement became closely entangled, as those who subscribed to 'animal rightism' (against all exploitation) were invariably vegan, while many who alternatively subscribed to 'animal welfareism' (against animal suffering but not against exploitation itself) were not yet. Since then the philosophical concepts of animal rights and *ahimsa* fused to create a transformative socio-political movement aimed to end systemic speciesism.

Animal-rights organisations which promoted veganism, such as Animal Aid founded by Jean Pink in the UK in 1977, or People for the Ethical Treatment of Animals (PETA) founded by Ingrid Newkirk and Alex Pacheco in the USA in 1980, began to rival the big animal welfare organisations, such as the RSPCA, the World Society for the Protection of Animals (now called World Animal Protection) or the Humane Society of the United States, which did not promote it. Animal rightism moved from 'extreme' fringe grassroots groups towards mainstream animal protection, as campaigning and lobbying became more professional. PETA was the first animal-rights organisation that did well-publicised undercover investigations of biomedical labs, and their 1981 exposé of the Institute for Behavioural Research (known as the Silver Spring monkeys case) became a model that many others imitated. This ground-breaking investigation led to the first arrest and criminal conviction of a US animal experimenter for cruelty to animals, and the first confiscation of abused animals from a laboratory.

It was in the late 1980s when we begin to see the term 'ethical' added to vegan. For instance, in Paul R. Amato's 1989 book titled *The New Vegetarians: Promoting Health and Protecting Life* we find this sentence: 'If you're a health vegan, people can say "I don't eat much read meat anymore". But if you are an ethical vegan, they would have to say, "I don't do much killing."' The 1996 book by Christine H. Beard titled *Become a Vegetarian in Five Easy Steps!* states an ethical vegan is 'a person who is a strict dietary vegan and who also avoids animal products in non-food items'.

In the 1990s and the early 2000s, veganism and animal-rights philosophies became more popular and consolidated themselves in distinctive factions often driven by different schools of ethics. On one side, 'deontological ethics' determines rightness from both the acts and the rules or duties the person doing the act is trying to fulfil, and in consequence identifies actions as intrinsically good or bad. One of the more influential animal-rights philosophers advocating this approach was the American Tom Regan, who argued animals possess value as 'subjects-of-a-life' because they have beliefs, desires, memory and the ability to initiate action in pursuit of goals. On the other side, we have 'utilitarian ethics', which believes the proper course of action is the one that maximises a positive effect. A utilitarian can suddenly switch behaviour if the numbers no longer support it. They could also 'sacrifice' a minority for the benefit of the majority. The most influential animal-rights utilitarian is the Australian Peter Singer, who argues the principle 'the greatest good of the greatest number' should be applied to other animals, as the boundary between human and 'animal' is arbitrary.

New organisations were created with the main aim to promote veganism, such as the Farm Animal Rights Movement co-founded in 1981 by Dr Alex Hershaft in the US, Vegan Outreach founded in 1993 by Jack Norris and Kevin Gallagher in the US, Viva! founded in 1994 by Juliet Gellatley in the UK, The Humane League founded in 2005 by Nick Cooney in the US, Veganuary founded in 2014 by Jane Land and Matthew Glover in the UK (who later founded the Million Dollar Vegan campaign) and Go Vegan World founded in 2015 by Sandra Higgins in Ireland. Later on, others were created to promote plant-based food without actually directly promoting veganism, such as the Good Food Institute founded in 2016 by Bruce Friedrich in the US, and ProVeg International founded in 2017 by Tobias Leenaert, Dr Melanie Joy and Sebastian Joy in Germany.

It is only in 2017 that we find a specifically 'vegan' law passed which directly and explicitly progressed the veganism cause. In 2015 the Portuguese Vegetarian Society (Associação Vegetariana Portuguesa) successfully gathered more than 15,000 signatures of citizens asking for vegetarian options (including vegan options) be made compulsory in catering of public bodies (such as prisons, public school canteens, universities and public hospitals), and on 3 March 2017, the Portuguese Assembly passed a law making their demands a reality.

Anarchism as a political movement had always relied on direct action outside the law, and when the animal-rights movement began mixing with these ideologies and tactics, UK groups such as the Animal Liberation Front (ALF), founded in 1976, or Stop Huntingdon Animal Cruelty (SHAC), founded in 1999, became the archetypal embodiment of radical militant animal-rights activism, and the inspiration of many other animal liberation groups. Several activists of these groups ended up in prison for their illegal activities (mostly destruction of property of the vivisection industry, or intimidation tactics, as these groups reject physical violence against people). In 1998 Barry Horne, while serving an eight-year sentence for planting incendiary devices in stores which sold fur coats and leather products, engaged in a sixty-eight-day hunger strike to persuade the British government to hold a public inquiry into animal testing. He died three years later while he was on another hunger strike, becoming one of the first martyrs of the movement.

Besides direct action, another manifestation of ethical veganism is public outreach. Proselytising through education to increase the number of vegans in the population and move veganism towards mainstream society – so real sustainable political changes can be made which significantly address the huge problem of animal exploitation – has become part of modern veganism. However, educating others to become vegan was already considered an important dimension of veganism by the pioneers of the Vegan Society. Fay Henderson, one of the women who attended the founding meeting at The Attic Club and credited by sociologist Matthew Cole for being responsible for the 'consciousness raising model for vegan activism', wrote:

> It is our duty to recognise the obligation we owe to these creatures and to understand all that is involved in the consumption and use of their live and dead products. Only thus shall we be properly equipped to decide our own attitude to the question and explain the case to others who may be interested but who have not given the matter serious thought.

In the last ten years or so vegan outreach has evolved with increasingly efficient and sophisticated methods. Advances in audio-visual technology was one of the key drivers in this evolution, as it can show vividly the reality of animal exploitation. In 2005 the American Shaun Monson produced a documentary, *Earthlings*, narrated by the actor and animal-rights activist Joaquin Phoenix (vegan since he was three years old). This showed, with very graphic images, the reality of humanity's use of other animals as pets, food, clothing, entertainment and scientific research. It became the 'must show' documentary among the vegan movement, and I have no doubt it was responsible for many people becoming vegan.

On 14 February 2015, British sisters Jane and Phoebe Frampton decided to go out on the streets and show clips of the documentary *Earthlings* on portable devices to passer-by, while wearing masks to prevent their faces drawing attention away from the screens. They called this The Earthlings Experience, and soon activists all over the world created their own groups and repeated the events. Other activists created their own events in their own style, sometimes with signs, sometimes with vegan food, with different types of masks, with virtual reality headsets, and so on.

Those who became vegan after chatting with any of these activists often became activists themselves, persuading more people to do the same, and as every year it is easier to argue for veganism, and it is also logistically easier to be vegan due to the increase in vegan-friendly options, the number of vegans keeps growing.

Today everyone is talking about veganism, which has been branded as one of the fastest-growing trends of this century. However, still billions of animals suffer because of humans, and the more vegans there are, the more people are unhappy about this. It does feel like a peaceful but relentlessly growing revolution destined to change the world through persuasion, common sense, compassion and respect.

Sally Shrigley and Donald Watson weren't religious leaders or statespeople. They weren't eminent scientists or philosophers. They weren't aristocrats or revolutionaries. They were modest people who, with their equally modest friends (none of them well-off patrons), took it upon themselves to make *ahimsa*, the most powerful idea ever conceived, an available concept to everyone, from any race, culture, nation, religion, gender or status. It worked because they created a simple, coherent, straightforward organisation, definition and name. With it, a transformative socio-political movement sprang up which may end up saving the world.

A 21st-century revolution that started more than twenty centuries ago.

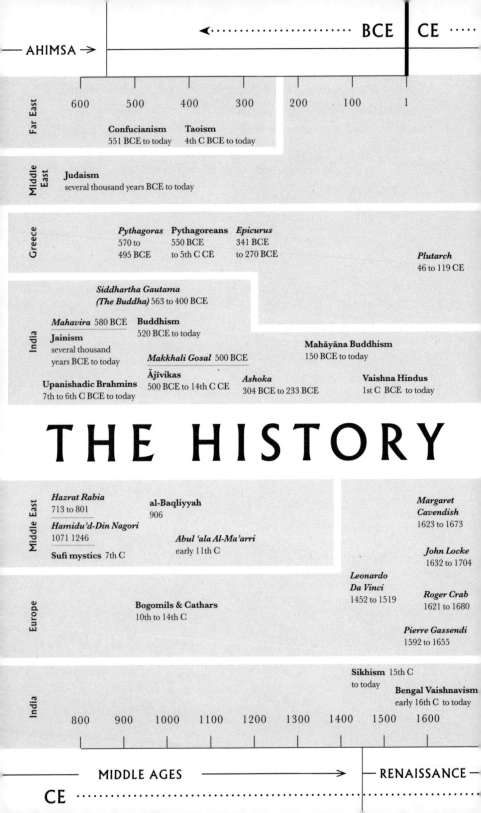

AHIMSA →

BCE | CE

Far East

600   500   400   300   200   100   1

Confucianism **Taoism**
551 BCE to today 4th C BCE to today

Middle East

Judaism
several thousand years BCE to today

Greece

Pythagoras *Pythagoreans* *Epicurus*
570 to   550 BCE   341 BCE
495 BCE   to 5th C CE   to 270 BCE

Plutarch
46 to 119 CE

India

Siddhartha Gautama
(The Buddha) 563 to 400 BCE

Mahavira 580 BCE   **Buddhism**
                       520 BCE to today

Jainism
several thousand
years BCE to today

Makkhali Gosal 500 BCE

Mahāyāna Buddhism
150 BCE to today

Upanishadic Brahmins   **Ājīvikas**   *Ashoka*   **Vaishna Hindus**
7th to 6th C BCE to today   500 BCE to 14th C CE   304 BCE to 233 BCE   1st C BCE to today

THE HISTORY

Middle East

Hazrat Rabia   **al-Baqliyyah**
713 to 801   906

Hamidu'd-Din Nagori
1071 1246   *Abul 'ala Al-Ma'arri*
                      early 11th C
Sufi mystics 7th C

Margaret
Cavendish
1623 to 1673

John Locke
1632 to 1704

Europe

Bogomils & Cathars
10th to 14th C

Leonardo
Da Vinci
1452 to 1519

Roger Crab
1621 to 1680

Pierre Gassendi
1592 to 1655

India

Sikhism 15th C
to today

Bengal Vaishnavism
early 16th C to today

800   900   1000   1100   1200   1300   1400   1500   1600

MIDDLE AGES →   — RENAISSANCE —

CE

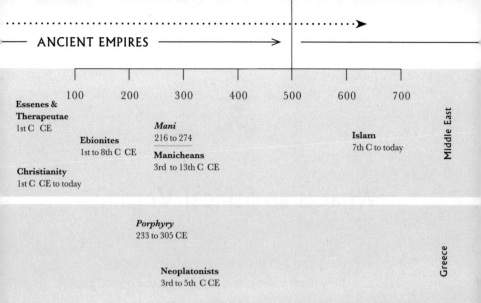

ANCIENT EMPIRES

100 200 300 400 500 600 700

Middle East

Essenes & Therapeutae
1st C CE

Mani
216 to 274

Islam
7th C to today

Ebionites
1st to 8th C CE

Manicheans
3rd to 13th C CE

Christianity
1st C CE to today

Greece

Porphyry
233 to 305 CE

Neoplatonists
3rd to 5th C CE

India

Vegetarian Brahmins
1st C CE to today

OF BEING KIND

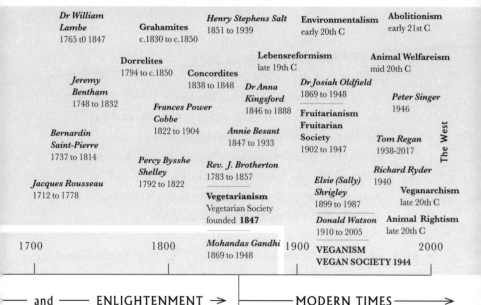

Dr William Lambe
1765 t0 1847

Grahamites
c.1830 to c.1850

Henry Stephens Salt
1851 to 1939

Environmentalism
early 20th C

Abolitionism
early 21st C

Dorrelites
1794 to c.1850

Concordites
1838 to 1848

Lebensreformism
late 19th C

Animal Welfareism
mid 20th C

Jeremy Bentham
1748 to 1832

Frances Power Cobbe
1822 to 1904

Dr Anna Kingsford
1846 to 1888

Dr Josiah Oldfield
1869 to 1948

Peter Singer
1946

Bernardin Saint-Pierre
1737 to 1814

Fruitarianism Fruitarian Society
1902 to 1947

Annie Besant
1847 to 1933

Tom Regan
1938-2017

Percy Bysshe Shelley
1792 to 1822

Rev. J. Brotherton
1783 to 1857

Richard Ryder
1940

Jacques Rousseau
1712 to 1778

Elsie (Sally) Shrigley
1899 to 1987

Veganarchism
late 20th C

Vegetarianism
Vegetarian Society
founded **1847**

Donald Watson
1910 to 2005

Animal Rightism
late 20th C

The West

1700 1800

Mohandas Gandhi
1869 to 1948

1900

**VEGANISM
VEGAN SOCIETY 1944**

2000

— and — ENLIGHTENMENT → ——→ MODERN TIMES ——→

3.

What is an Ethical Vegan?

Tell me who you harm and I will tell you what you are.

We know how the term 'vegan' came about, and how veganism was conceived, sprouted, flourished and finally became a fully fledged concept and socio-political movement based on trying not to harm others (the expression of the idea of *ahimsa*). What about 'ethical vegans'? Are they a 'new' thing, the next step in the evolution of veganism? Not quite.

The definition – the key text to follow

During its initial years, the Vegan Society amended its definition of veganism, but it never abandoned *ahimsa* as its core. In 1988 it was finalised:

> A philosophy and way of living which seeks to exclude – as far as is possible and practicable – all forms of exploitation of, and cruelty to, animals for food, clothing or any other purpose; and by extension, promotes the development and use of animal-free alternatives for the benefit of humans, animals and the environment. In dietary terms it denotes the practice of dispensing with all products derived wholly or partly from animals.

Although this is the official definition of 'veganism' of the Vegan

Society, those who follow this philosophy and way of living as defined by the society are 'ethical vegans'. The term 'ethical' is used today in this context as a synonymous of 'true', 'real' or 'full', meaning the original definition of the Vegan Society. Sometime after the society created the word 'vegan', some people were using this term without adhering to the definition, beginning to dilute its original meaning. In particular, many people only adopted a vegan diet but continued using animal products for clothes, entertainment, cosmetics, etc. 'Proper' vegans needed to add something to the term to preserve the integrity of the concept, especially because those who only followed a vegan diet and not the entire philosophy grew considerably in number. The general public also began assuming a vegan was just someone who follows a vegan diet, so in the last three decades or so it became imperative to add the adjective 'ethical' to distinguish genuine vegans from the rest.

In a way, if veganism had been a religion, we probably would be using the term 'orthodox veganism' instead. Although in the past vegan practices were often part of religions, veganism is not a religion. When the first vegetarian society was created in the 19th century, such a historical connection broke, and it remained broken when the Vegan Society sprouted from the Vegetarian Society. Abstaining from animal products became 'secularised'.

It's easy to prove it is not a religion, because one of the main conditions of joining one is to abandon any previous religion you were part of, and this does not happen when people become vegan. We have vegans who are Christian, Muslim, Jain, Buddhist, pagan, agnostic and atheist. Veganism doesn't have a metaphysical mythology which explains how the world was created or what happens after you die, as many religions have. It does not have sacred books or scriptures. It does not have temples, priests, monks and rituals. It does not require acts of 'faith' or trust in any leader. It does not have common supernatural, transcendental or spiritual elements all vegans share. You don't even have to join the Vegan Society to be a vegan. You don't have to register anywhere, go anywhere, be initiated in any particular way or even tell anyone.

Veganism is not a religion, as pacifism, teetotalism, feminism, patriotism, environmentalism and socialism are not either. However, it is highly ethical, and therefore the term 'ethical' fits very well. As the Vegan Society definition states, veganism is a philosophy *and* way of living. In other words, a philosophy leading to a particular way of living manifested as a rejection of all animal exploitation.

Ethical veganism is a philosophical belief. I know many atheists and anti-religious people out there do not like to use the term 'belief' because they tend to associate it with religion, but not all beliefs are religious. 'Belief' doesn't mean it is not based on facts, it only means you are certain about it (perhaps because of the evidence you analysed), and as such it is synonymous with a 'conviction'.

Therefore, ethical veganism is a philosophical belief, as the certainty of it comes from the evidence of animal suffering at the hands of humanity, the logical conclusion that if all animals suffer you cannot be consistent by avoiding some types of exploitation but not others, and the speculation that all animals (even those we haven't encountered yet) ought to be sentient, and all types of exploitation of animals (even those we haven't invented yet) will either cause suffering to them or deprive them of a fulfilled life.

Because the belief of ethical veganism is based on *ahimsa*, it is based on an action: 'do no harm'. Vegans 'act' on their beliefs, not just reflect on them. Most are no longer the ascetics who forged the concept in the past; they consume many products – however, they only consume those which are 'vegan-friendly', and reject animal products and products connected with animal exploitation in any way.

So, this is how you spot a vegan: someone who rejects the products of animal exploitation and cruelty and embraces their animal-free alternatives. The combination of this particular type of rejection and embracing is what creates a particular 'lifestyle', which manifests itself in the food they eat, the clothes they wear, the products they buy, the places they go, the hobbies they have, etc. So, yes, veganism is also a lifestyle but it is caused by a strong philosophical belief.

V

I had never met a vegan until the end of my second year in the UK. I had no idea what they looked like, but I knew they were more 'committed' than vegetarians as they would not have dairy products or eggs. Those first two summers in Britain, when I hitchhiked through the British Isles, every time I had a lift I asked the drivers if they knew anywhere where they might need a zoologist. I hoped if I kept asking I might find something. The last county I visited was Cornwall, in Britain's south-west, in the summer of 1994. I was not surprised that many people from Cornwall say they are not English, but Cornish. It felt like a different country in many respects. The single-lane high-hedged winding roads are the main cause of surprising stunning sights, which vanish as quickly as they appear, just like the ghosts the Cornish so faithfully believe in. A dramatic rocky shore, an eerie abandoned tin mine, a pastoral minuscule village and ancient smugglers' tavern. All charmingly exotic and evocatively familiar to me, as back home I had avidly watched the original 1975 BBC series *Poldark*, dubbed in Catalan, of course.

Between traditional pasties and the occasional cider – clotted cream teas were beyond my means back then – I asked the usual question to the Cornish drivers who gave me lifts, but one of them gave a different answer: 'Yes, a sanctuary for monkeys in Looe might perhaps need a zoologist.' Finally a result! I made my way there, and when I arrived I had the same feeling I'd had when I first put my foot in this country. *This* was the place.

The Monkey Sanctuary was a paradise for an Anglophile immigrant zoologist such as me. It was located on the south coast of Cornwall, close to Devon, an area which had already lost most of its wildness due to human development. However, the woods around the sanctuary were still quite intact, there were all sorts of trees, shrubs, ferns, mosses and wildflowers. Since the sanctuary was founded in 1964 the people living there had been very respectful to Nature, and as a consequence animals were less afraid of humans than usual. It was like walking into a Disney film – rabbits, birds, butterflies and even monkeys were all around you, without fear.

The house was a listed Gothic Victorian mansion called Murrayton House – haunted, some had said – and the sloped gardens, with wild meadows, ponds, tiny waterfalls and charming woods, ended at a private pebbly beach. The people also looked very friendly. They were generally quite young and British (perfect for improving my English). Although many had a scruffy or hippy look, they sounded very educated and intelligent, which made them pleasantly endearing. They all worked in a co-operative and lived on-site as a community ... with monkeys.

When I first passed the sanctuary's main gate and I saw the house, I knew it would be my home. I looked at one of the windows and knew it would be my room. I looked at all the keepers, and I knew they would be my new family. I chatted with Keith, who was talking to visitors by the monkey enclosure called 'the Gym', and learnt the sanctuary accepted volunteers, although there was a long waiting list. That was fine with me because it would give me time to learn about Amazonian woolly monkeys (*Lagothrix lagothicha*), the only species kept there then. (Today, the sanctuary is called Wild Futures and keeps other species.) I contacted Pam, the always-calm volunteer co-ordinator, and she added me to the list.

As I'd planned, in London I read everything I could find about these monkeys, and a few months later I returned to the sanctuary to volunteer. When I first entered the kitchen I saw Kate, one of the senior keepers. She had very short punky hair and wore denim dungarees over a white T-shirt, if I remember correctly. She was enthusiastically cooking some delicious-smelling food for the communal dinner, without any animal products. She was the first vegan I ever met face to face.

The two weeks' volunteering passed quickly, and during the Sunday meeting when everyone discussed important matters, I made a proposal. I gave a speech about how I knew their dream was returning all the monkeys to the Amazon, where they belonged. They had already attempted this with mixed results, and I said that I could make that dream a reality; that my ethological knowledge could help to teach the monkeys some of the skills they would need to survive in the wild, but had lost in captivity. I said they should let me join their community permanently and employ me. And they did – it seems I managed to persuade them that I had what it takes to help to return the monkeys to their rightful home. I became the research and rehabilitation co-ordinator, and Kate and her Nature-loving boyfriend Nick became my 'trainers' in the complex art of keeping woolly monkeys happy – sanctuary style. Two years later I was a senior keeper and I became one of the joint-directors of the co-operative. I have only worked in animal protection since.

The sanctuary's woolly monkeys were descendants of rescued 'pets'. They are amazing social Neotropical monkeys with a thick prehensile tail (they can hang from it) and thick wool-like grey hair. They are quite big, the second biggest monkey in South America, about 60cm without counting the tail. They have quite a gentle-looking face, a bit squarish in the heavier adult males, and often behave more as controlled apes than hysterical monkeys. Above all, though, woolly monkeys are fluffy; very fluffy indeed.

They are quite vocal too, and we learnt to communicate roughly in their language, greeting them every morning with their polite, '*Eolk!*' It took me a few years to master it, and I also conducted research on their vocalisations and published a peer-reviewed paper about it. They are very social, and at the sanctuary they lived in a single colony of about twenty individuals formed by several family subgroups, who tended to support each other when inter-family feuds arose. As in any human group, individuals had their distinctive character. The mighty Max, the wise Django, the cool Lucy, the cheeky Maya, the shy Tess, the suave Nicky, the diligent Laura, the feisty Ivor, the intrepid Ella, the lusty Chico (who was definitively gay, by the way), and so on. The keepers there told me many stories of the late dominant male of the colony, Charlie, who was supposedly the leader, but while I was there no other male (or female) had replaced him. It was assumed it was the artificial nature of many years of captivity which created such anomaly.

We used to tell visitors that Django, the oldest monkey in the group, should have been the 'alpha male' but his gentle nature made him step aside in favour of his nephew, Charlie. I had not met Charlie, but I met Django, and had a great deal of respect for him, as all keepers did.

We all lived in this Victorian mansion, but the listed building was allowed to be modified internally to convert some of the rooms for monkey living. These rooms were connected by all sorts of passages and ramps to outdoor enclosures of different sizes, which in turn were connected to others. The 'monkey territory' kept growing as more new interconnected enclosures were built.

However, this net of runways, platforms and gates was difficult to maintain. Every morning most of us would wake up very early as we had to clean everything, but to do that each section had to be emptied of monkeys, as the adult males were too dangerous for close contact. Females and youngsters, on the other hand, used to go out with the keepers and forage in the gardens, to the delight of visitors who were much more interested in the relationship these hippies had created with the monkeys, than with the monkeys themselves. You could only clear a section of monkeys with their consent – and bribery involving sunflower seeds or grapes. Only experienced keepers who had been learning about the monkeys for at least two years could form part of such delicate diplomatic negotiations, and when I reached that level of training, I had to do the 'shutting off' (as this morning routine was called) with another keeper two or three days a week.

But if Django did not want to go – well, we accepted that. With others we might try to be more persuasive and imperative. With him, we stepped back; he had too much respect. He normally repaid us with wisdom and kindness, resolving internal conflicts between monkeys by intervening with the right action at the right time, keeping calm and in control in moments of panic. As I've said, this erroneous concept of 'alpha males' first described in wolves had also been used in primates, but by this time it had also been debunked by the research of the Dutch primatologist Frans de Waal, in his book *Chimpanzee Politics*. Now I wonder if the story of Django stepping aside and not wanting to become the alpha male was inaccurate. The idea may never have entered his mind, and it was Charlie who had run an unauthorised dictatorship. When, after generations, the 'ex-pet' monkeys became more 'natural' in their sanctuary's social set up, their true social nature may have emerged. There was no longer room for a fake alpha male.

Living and working with the same people at the sanctuary was difficult, though. Relationships – and aspirations for relationships – often became intertwined, and all sorts of tensions could surface. We easily had more than twenty people in the house, all them carrying their psychological baggage – sometimes leaving it unattended. It was physical work too, hard in winter when we still had to get up early to clean all the monkey territory. Hopelessly seeing monkeys die, sometimes for mysterious reasons, was hard on us, especially if it happened in bouts where we lost several in a short time.

After one of these episodes – I'd been at the sanctuary about three or four years – I had to take off for a week to clear my thoughts. I spent it wistfully wandering through the dramatic landscape of Dartmoor, ending up at the historical prison built for the prisoners of the American War of Independence. The prison reminded me that, after all, I was another type of jailer. Seeing monkeys being born felt like a privilege, but with a bittersweet aftertaste, not knowing if we could give the new members of the colony the freedom and happiness they deserved. Overall, for me, life at the sanctuary was like living in Paradise, but I also had the guilt of living in it undeservedly.

It had not taken long for me to acquire a new nickname, 'the monkey man', because my work with primates went far beyond keeping them at the sanctuary. I had been travelling to Brazil year after year to find the location where we would take the monkeys from Cornwall. For a zoologist like me, wandering through the rainforest was quite an experience. At first, I was a bit apprehensive considering the many ways I could be killed there (from being eaten by an anaconda to being poisoned by a plant) but after a while I began to understand the forest, and merge with it.

One of the most surprising things about the Amazon is the floor. After millions of years of sediment deposited from the Andes and plants decomposing, it is a very soft floor you can comfortably walk on barefoot, with no stones or rocks. It was exciting seeing the many toucans eating dates, I marvelled at huge tarantulas climbing trees, politely greeted the sloths with moss growing on them, and was watched by curious river dolphins. However, for me, the most exciting thing was seeing my first wild woolly monkey.

Manaus, the extremely hot and humid capital of the Amazonas state where I used to stay, is surrounded of hundreds of miles of rainforest. However, much of it is 'secondary' rainforest, named due to the presence of humans and their effect in cutting the largest trees. I wanted to venture into 'primary forest', in particular where no human had yet set foot. For that I had to travel further, so in 1997 I took a plane to Porto Velho, in the state of Rondônia, which borders Bolivia. There I met a PhD student, Simone Iwanaga, of Japanese origin, who was studying monkeys. She had agreed on the phone to take me by boat to the Serra dos Três Irmãos, a primary forest area where a basic state ecological camp had just been built.

My days there were exciting. The forest was ancient and undisturbed; the trees were enormous, and as the animals had probably never seen humans before, some were quite curious and got quite close. For days we were trying to find some woolly monkeys, but although we could hear them, we could not see them. Advancing in the jungle was slow, not only because there were no trails, but also because there were deadly poisonous snakes around, so we had to be very careful. We had to advance in a single line, headed by the most experienced scientist, who was better able to spot danger than the others.

The last day of my stay they allowed me to lead the group, which was quite an honour, but also nerve-wracking. Carefully looking at everything in front of me, I advanced slowly, remembering how the day before the leader had accidentally kneed a very well-camouflaged jararaca, a deadly snake – which made them both jump in opposite directions. I then heard an unmistakable '*Eolk*' of a woolly monkey in the distance, and I decided to go for it. I advanced at a faster pace following the repeated calls, until suddenly we encountered a section of forest that was entirely flooded. After discussing it for a while, the others turned back while Simone and I decided to carry on. We removed our shoes, put them on a couple of branches, marked the position with my handheld

GPS (this well before this technology found its way to phones and cars) and carried on barefoot through the flooded jungle.

Then I saw her. About thirty yards from me, at mid-canopy level, a mother woolly monkey with a baby on her back was purposely cruising the branches. It was brief, but truly magical, because despite the fact I had seen many monkeys moving through the trees when we let the youngest and the females of our Cornish colony use the sanctuary's woods, the grace and dignity of this wild monkey, moving so effortlessly, was astonishing. She stopped for a second, glanced at me from above, wondered which kind of ugly creature I might be, and disappeared into the wilderness. I *eolked* her goodbye with all the respect I could muster. Just a few hours before my departure I had managed to have 'an encounter of the woolly kind', and I was over the moon. I did not mind that a colony of ants had decided to use my shoes for their new home, nor did Simone mind that a colony of termites had done the same with hers. That was a cheap price to pay for the experience.

Eventually, in 1998, after several trips to the Amazon which had allowed me to skip several British winters, I found the right site on some of the islands of Lake Balbina, north of Manaus. I created a partnership with local people who were also rescuing monkeys. The idea was to do a soft release, in which the Cornish monkeys (who were 'socially skilled' and lived in stable multi-aged groups) would join groups of young monkeys rescued from the local pet trade (who were 'habitat skilled' as they had been born in the rainforest), and each group would teach the other the skills the others lacked.

The partnership needed funds for building all the infrastructure on the islands (quarantine facilities, release enclosures, feeding stations, researchers' accommodation), as well as the right permits from the authorities. Funds were coming at a low but steady pace, and in 1998 I helped by giving a sponsored record-breaking unaided, uninterrupted, thirteen-hour lecture at Plymouth University titled 'From Nothing to Everything: The Natural History of the Universe' – yes, sounds crazy, but I did it.

All good things come to an end, and in the year 2000 I left the sanctuary because we had to cancel the rehabilitation project. We discovered some of the Cornish monkeys carried a virus called woolly monkey hepatitis B, which meant we would never get the permission to take the monkeys to Brazil. After that the sanctuary decided to stop allowing the woollies to breed (by using contraceptives), and began keeping monkeys from other species rescued from the pet trade. It changed its name to Wild Futures, and over the years most of the woolly monkeys of the colony I knew died (there are only two woollies left today).

I cut my long hair and shaved my beard, and I moved to Plymouth where I became a British citizen by the process called naturalisation (officialising my condition of being a cultural hybrid). Soon after I was hired by the Born Free Foundation – the anti-zoo wildlife charity founded by the actors Virginia McKenna and Bill Travers – as their zoo check scientific researcher and co-ordinator. I moved to Brighton, the vibrant coastal town in the south-east of England (known for its party atmosphere, its music scene and a large LGBT population), as it was close enough to Horsham, where the charity is still based.

V

My new job was already helping me to acquire vegan traits as ethical vegans do not support zoos. Other traits, though, require more dedication. The second part of the Vegan Society definition is very important in this regard: 'which seeks to exclude – as far as is possible and practicable – all forms of exploitation of, and cruelty to, animals for food, clothing or any other purpose'.

These days avoiding animal ingredients in the diet is relatively easy, as food is often labelled with the list of what is in there, at least in developed countries. However, it's not only about the ingredients, but also the methods of production, which are not normally explained on the labels. For instance, some wines and beers are filtered with animal bones, making them unsuitable for vegans, or some ingredients of foods and toiletries may be tested on animals.

Beyond food, things are much more complicated. Clothes and fashion accessories have labels showing the materials used, but what about financial services (which may invest in animal agriculture or animal testing companies), furniture (which may contain leather, ivory, wool or even animal glues) or appliances (which may have components produced from gelatine derivates)? And then we have the problem of theoretically vegan-friendly products tested on animals (so, no longer vegan) or vegan companies taken over by bigger companies which test on animals, or the issue of medicines and medical procedures developed using animals, or the animals who accidentally perish during the mechanised harvesting of vegetable food or during high-speed transport. The list is endless.

In today's society, it would be practically impossible to avoid all animal exploitation and continue having a normal life as removed from asceticism as the life of an average citizen. Vegans who want to live in the modern world among everyone else have to be pragmatic. They have to try to avoid the exploitation as much as they can but realise sometimes it's not possible, and sometimes it's highly impractical. That's OK; the definition of the Vegan Society allows for this with: 'as far as is possible and practicable'.

What counts are the beliefs, the intention of avoidance and the effort made to achieve the avoidance. In some products, such as food and clothes, most of the time you could expect to be successful in your efforts – and if you live in a modern cosmopolitan city, all the time, to be honest. For some products, you could expect to be unsuccessful most of the time – with banks and medical treatment, for instance. Often, the chance of success varies greatly depending on the country, population, demographic or individual, as circumstances and availability of vegan-friendly options differ a great deal. The products and services people need also vary, and some vegan alternatives cannot always be found. They may be needed for health or work reasons, to keep a relationship, to comply with a legal obligation, to look after others under their care, to help those in need or for their mental well-being – none of us can really know what others truly need.

What unifies all ethical vegans is not their success in avoiding animal exploitation, but their effort in doing it considering their circumstances. However, if you deliberately ignore particular types of exploitation or particular animal species for convenience, tradition or habit, you should no longer call yourself an ethical vegan. We have the 'obstinate' vegetarians for that (as opposed to those who use vegetarianism as a path to veganism), who deliberately ignore the exploitation of cattle, sheep, hens and bees of the dairy, leather, wool, eggs and honey industries. In most cases it's not very difficult to avoid these products, but many don't even try because they believe being vegetarian is enough. Some vegetarians, though, have fallen into the jaws of the dairy and egg industry propaganda and they naively believe cattle and hens do not suffer when farmed, or that organic and free-range methods eliminate that suffering. Cattle and hens always suffer when farmed for dairy and eggs, no matter which methods are used. When these deceived vegetarians discover they are wrong they often swiftly become vegans.

Back when I started working at the Monkey Sanctuary, even I, a zoologist with lots of animal welfare knowledge, did not know male calves and chicks were mass-exterminated soon after birth/hatching. No matter what the farm's size, or whether they are organic or 'high welfare', the dairy and egg industries consider it unprofitable to raise the male animals to adulthood – they will not grow to produce milk or eggs and they are 50 per cent of all animals born in these industries. Being aware of the truth of animal exploitation is essential for living a responsible life, and helping those who don't know about it by providing them with the right information is an integral part of what ethical vegans do. I wish someone had told me earlier.

V

When in February 2018 I sent the email to my colleagues that got me disciplined, it was driven by my moral imperative of providing the right information to people about 'the truth' of animal exploitation. In this case the truth was that, despite what management had told them in October, the pension fund they had been enrolled in by the organisation had not been changed to an ethical fund, and therefore part of their salary was still being invested in companies that hurt animals in all sorts of horrible ways. The truth was also that there were several ethical pension funds they could switch to, not only the one management had sent them, so they could switch themselves to the ethical fund that best suited them.

As an ethical vegan, I had to tell this truth to my vegan colleagues as we rely on each other to find out which products and services are not suitable for us and which vegan-friendly alternatives are available. Without this sharing of information, we would often fail in our attempts to exclude all animal exploitation from all our choices. As an aspiring decent human being, I had to share the info with all the rest of staff, as they should all have the same chance to act responsibly, and I believed most had been misinformed.

I was right – several members of staff replied to me thanking me for my email, including vegans horrified by what they had just discovered.

Then I received the letter inviting me to the disciplinary hearing. I learnt that there was not going to be a formal investigation and the chair of the hearing would be the managing director, my 'accuser'. And I felt something I had never felt before: a profound sense of injustice. After I complained about it, things got worse.

Thursday 1 March 2018 was a cold day. It had been snowing and it was difficult to get to work, so I worked from home as was normal in these circumstances. The only plant I cultivated in my yard that survived the winter was a small bush of sage. Everything else from my first crop had naturally died or had been consumed by either the local wildlife or me, and now the only thing you could see besides the sage were the small shoots of Spanish bluebells. Although it was cold outside, in my flat the temperature was very comfortable, as the gas central heating regulated by a wireless thermostat worked perfectly. I was using my work laptop on the small round table in the living room as I did not want to unplug my personal laptop from the rig I had constructed to be able to use it standing. The room smelled of bananas as I had three in the bowl in the middle of the table, in quite a state of advanced ripeness.

It was four in the afternoon when I received an email from the MD, who had not communicated with me at all since the day I sent the email to all staff. I braced myself and opened it. It only said 'Please read the attached letter and be certain to follow the instructions laid down therein' and it had a PDF attached. I opened it, and my blood froze. It said that I had been suspended from work until further notice pending investigation, that my email account had been suspended, and that I was not allowed to communicate with any employee, trustee or persons associated with the organisation. At least, because I had complained, someone had been appointed to conduct the investigation and the chair changed (to the director of HR), but now I was suspended and an extra charge of 'serious insubordination' had been added by my accusers – this meant that now they could fire me for gross misconduct.

This felt a clear case of victimisation to me. The next day I posted on Facebook a single photo with no text of a small gull standing alone in the middle of a frozen pond, which reflected just what I was feeling.

The period of suspension lasted for about a month, and it was an extremely stressful time. The prohibition of communicating with others meant I had to leave hanging all the people I was working with on several jobs. They kept sending me text messages asking if I was OK, but I couldn't reply. Several research projects I was conducting were now in jeopardy and the blanket gagging order did not allow me to delegate them to anyone. For the first time in more than twenty years I wasn't working trying to protect animals. I was not allowed to work at all, and that was killing me.

A couple of days after the suspension began I submitted my version of events to the investigator, who was another manager in the organisation who had not been involved with the issue at all. Then the only thing I could do was wait. I spent the days in the often snowy park moaning about my misfortune to the ducks and geese, who seemed quite unimpressed, just busy trying to get some warmth.

Eventually, the investigator produced his report, and I was relieved to see that he concluded that there was no case to answer for 'gross misconduct' – which was good, as the remaining charges could only lead to a mild reprimand. However, my relief did not last long, as that conclusion was ignored by the chair of the disciplinary hearing, and on 3 April I went to the office to attend the hearing with the 'gross misconduct' charge intact.

Three days later, when I was lying by a very old oak tree in Greenwich Park, I received a call from the chair, letting me know she would be sending me that afternoon a letter summarily dismissing me with immediate effect. I appealed the decision straight away, hoping that the trustees of the charity would get involved and reverse the draconian decision, but a few days later management denied me any appeal hearing, so the trustees could not intervene. Things couldn't have gone worse.

I was flabbergasted. I was struggling to comprehend what was happening to me. Why summary dismissal rather than any other punishment? Why this determination to fire me to the point of not even allowing me to have an appeal hearing which could reverse the decision? Why did they want me out so badly? I kept reading the dismissal letter and the minutes of the disciplinary. The chair of the disciplinary hearing had said on several occasions through the process that my 'passion' made me biased and my 'ethics' clouded my judgement. This was repeated in my dismissal letter. I finally understood what was going on. It was my ethical veganism, my 'ethics', which had driven my actions, and it seemed it was the same philosophical belief that, in the mind of my employers, would guide me to similar actions in the future. It seemed to me that my employer, now controlled by meat-eating senior staff, did not want to continue offering employment to anyone whose immutable vegan ethics would lead again to the sort of communication I had had with my colleagues, which for them was inappropriate.

I felt offended. I felt harassed. I felt victimised. I felt discriminated against. All that, not for what I chose to do, but what I was compelled to do by being an ethical vegan. Enter the Equality Act 2010.

V

Sentience – the key concept to underpin

When I lived with my parents in the seventh-floor apartment in Mare de Deu de Montserrat avenue in Barcelona, we did not have a garden. We had a balcony completely covered by plants, though, as my mother loved them – a lucky resource for me when I had to think of a present. It was a relatively small apartment. Kitchen, bathroom, living room, three bedrooms (my parents', my sister's and mine), a small room to keep my mother's Tupperware merchandise, and my father's studio where he kept all his cameras and film editing equipment. Not much room for anyone else, and yet, at one point, we shared our home with a goldfish, a green budgerigar, an albino cat and a black dog. One in a small tank, one in a tiny cage and the other two trapped in the same space we all shared. If Nit, the second dog we lived with, needed to go to the toilet, she only had two options. Beg us to take her down for a quick walk around the plane trees (always on the lead as it was a busy road) or do it on the balcony if we all seemed to have more important things to do.

Do ethical vegans have pets? Keeping an animal as a 'pet' can constitute exploitation if the animal is unwilling to be treated as a pet or has been conditioned to tolerate a negative situation in exchange for food. This is particularly clear in cases of exotic wild animals who need to be kept in confinement, whose 'wildness' would inevitably make them unwilling participants. However, most vegans would not consider people sharing their lives with rescued dogs or cats, both domesticated animals, as exploitation. They should not have a traditional owner–pet relationship, but a much more egalitarian 'companionship' relationship, where the animal not only is willing to be in it but clearly wishes to be. In fact, many vegans do share their lives with such companion animals.

Uncontrolled reproduction has created so many unwanted dogs and cats that saving them from being executed is what any ethical vegan able to give them a good life should be doing. The line between giving a tolerable life and a good life is quite fine, though. Developing a properly respectful and mutually fulfilling 'relationship' based on true companionship is not the same as developing a dominant 'petship' in which the 'owner' (or the euphemistically called 'parent') can do whatever they want with their pets. Not everyone can see the difference between the two.

Although relationships with companion animals can be very positive and loving for both parties, sometimes people get dogs or cats as disposable fuss-free emotional partners, acquired to replace or compensate for failed human relationships. As such, these relationships can be parasitical, domineering, co-dependent, inconsiderate, distant, over-protective, suffocating or even toxic, but with the aggravating factor of the legal 'ownership' of the animal and the subsequent entitlement. Domestic violence can even be directly or indirectly channelled towards a companion animal. Therefore, before any human thinks about sharing their life with a rescue animal, they need to ask themselves some serious questions. It should not be taken for granted that anyone can handle an animal properly. I haven't had a companion animal for a long time because I don't think my circumstances (living alone in a small London flat without a garden) would allow me to give them the good life, care and attention they deserve – I grew up with pets living in suboptimal conditions, and I know what it's like.

It's so easy to enjoy the company of friendly, adorable, furry beings that we often omit looking at the experience from their perspective. This may happen in the case of the so-called 'service animals', such as dogs trained to help people with disabilities. Although I think everyone with a disability should be helped to develop fulfilling companionships with domesticated animals if they so wish, I don't think such animals should be bred and trained to become the sentient equivalent of a walking stick or a hearing aid, and although there may be plenty of individual exceptions, I would consider that, in general, the concept of 'service dog' is not suitable for ethical vegans (just as the concept of human 'servants' being reared and trained to help people with disabilities isn't suitable either).

What about riding horses, visiting zoos, killing pests, consuming

honey, etc.? The Vegan Society definition of veganism states that ethical vegans have to avoid 'all forms of animal exploitation'. The question is what constitutes 'animal exploitation'. Animal exploitation is any use of any animal for profit, social gain, ritual, leisure, work or subsistence in which the animal is not a willing participant, or has been physically or psychologically coerced to participate. It is any human action on animals which violates their body autonomy (the right to govern what happens to their body) and their informed consent (permission given after understanding the implications of the action) if the animals are still capable of making positive choices about their lives.

Exploitation carries an inherent element of unfairness, as it can also be defined as the action or fact of treating someone unfairly to benefit from their work or existence. Therefore, seeking to avoid exploitation is an act of social justice, one of the reasons some people become vegan (especially 'intersectional vegans' who make parallels of the exploitation of animals and the exploitation of particular marginalised human groups, including violations of body autonomy and consent). Most acts of animal exploitation are easily identifiable, and the animal agriculture and bioresearch industries cover many of them. Others may be more difficult to recognise, such as keeping of animals in zoos or riding of animals for leisure. I will explain later on more about why these two things are not acceptable to ethical vegans.

It's not only avoiding the exploitation of animals, but also cruelty to animals. Why such a distinction? Is not all exploitation cruel in itself? Most vegans would agree, but be that as it may, not all cruelty is exploitation. Hurting any animal for sadistic purposes, rather than to obtain a particular product or economic gain, is clearly against *ahimsa*, and it should always be avoided. Hunting an unsuspecting wild animal for leisure, even with proficient shooters who may occasionally kill an animal very quickly with a well-placed shot, should never be supported by ethical vegans either, as depriving animals of their life is not only cruel to them, but also to the friends and family members they leave behind.

Think about Cecil for a moment. He was a majestic male African lion who, from about 2005, protected a big pride of lions around the Hwange National Park in Matabeleland North, Zimbabwe. His black-fringed mane and powerful roar were so imposing that all the other lions kept at a distance, and his pride felt very safe when he was around. If hyenas turned up en masse trying to steal a meal, he only needed to stand and walk towards them – that would see them off. If rival prides tried to sneak into his territory, he just roared to the sky and that stopped them in their tracks.

In the evening of 1 July 2015, he was confidently walking around his savannah when he suddenly felt a very sharp pain on one side. A long stick with a sharp end was imbedded deep into his flesh and it would not go away. It had come from the direction of a source of smell he recognised well. The stench of the walking ape. He tried to get away, but those apes continued to follow him. He was losing blood, and every time he moved the stick tore a little bit more of his flesh. After a few hours, in the middle of the night, he tried to rest, but he could not. The apes were still around. He had to carry on moving. Fifteen hours later, he felt another big stick penetrating his body, this time closer to his heart. He could not run anymore. He closed his eyes and never came back. From a distance, a dentist from Minneapolis called Walter J. Palmer jumped in jubilation with his high-powered bow in his hand. The $50,000 he had paid to have fun killing the biggest lion in the land had been well spent. That night, nobody protected Cecil's pride, and the lives of all its lions changed forever.

The 'harm' of 'do no harm' includes causing death as well as suffering. Therefore, chasing, trapping, capturing, chaining, tethering, forcing to work, forcing to breed, forcing to race, genetically modifying them, riding, mutilating, gassing, poisoning, stealing their secretions, stealing their produce, destroying their home, separating them from their family or social group, 'breaking' them, scaring them, stressing them, exhausting them, injuring them and also killing them are all forms of cruelty to animals vegans should seek to avoid – unless done by reputable animal care professionals specifically for the animals' well-being, such as in the case of veterinary treatment.

Which animals? All animals. Any individual of any species belonging to the animal kingdom, both vertebrates and invertebrates. Why? Because they are all sentient beings, and the reason vegans should seek to avoid their exploitation is precisely this sentience which makes them susceptible to suffering.

At its most basic meaning, sentience is the ability to experience positive and negative sensations, which requires two things: firstly, senses to perceive the sensations from stimuli coming from the environment, and, secondly, a nervous system to process such sensations and translate them into experiences which allow the animals to react accordingly, depending on whether they are negative or positive (i.e. fleeing from an adverse environment or moving towards a source of food or a mate). All members of the animal kingdom can do that. They all have senses to perceive their environment, they all have nervous systems (central or otherwise) to process perceptions, and they all can react according to the type of experience. We are yet to discover any living being not belonging to the animal kingdom capable of doing all of that (although there may be borderline cases where some plants have some movement when touched, such as the Latin American *Mimosa pudica*, although we are unable to ascertain if the experience is negative or positive due to the lack of an actual nervous system).

However, some people prefer to use a more complex definition of sentience. For instance, some say the negative experiences should be like 'pain and suffering' and the positive like 'pleasure and comfort'. Some may not accept all animals feel pain or suffering, claiming they need a sophisticated level of cognition or consciousness – they argue some animals they consider 'inferior', such as worms and insects, are not sentient. I disagree with such a view, which I find egotistical and highly human-centric. It doesn't matter whether a negative experience can be classified as 'suffering' or an 'emotion' in the context we use these words in everyday human life. It is negative for the animals, that's what matters, and they can react to avoid the cause or mitigate its negative effects. In 1884 the Canadian–Scottish evolutionary biologist George Romanes wrote:

> Pleasures and Pains must have been evolved as the subjective accompaniment of processes which are respectively beneficial or injurious to the organism, and so evolved for the purpose or to the end that the organism should seek the one and shun the other.

Some species may be capable of more complex thought than others – what some people call 'reasoning' – and some have developed more complex languages and behaviours, but this is irrelevant to define sentience. The British philosopher Jeremy Bentham stated in 1823, 'The question is not, Can they reason? nor, Can they talk? but, Can they suffer?' I would go even further and say the question is 'Can they have a negative experience?'

It makes no sense to focus on concepts such as 'feelings' as they are subjective (available only to the animal experiencing them) and we could never prove any organism (including a human) is sentient if we based it only on that. Fortunately, we do not need to know exactly what an animal is feeling, but only whether it is experiencing something positive or negative, and the behaviour of the animal can tell us that. Experimental methods such as preference testing (giving animals different choices and see which they prefer), motivational testing (in which animals have to overcome obstacles to get what they want) and understanding animal communication (such as alarm calls, screams, chuckling, body language, facial expressions, etc.) can help us to assess whether animals can tell the difference between positive and negative stimuli, and therefore are sentient. These methods can all be done in a non-intrusive way with animals in the wild.

V

When in the year 2000 I began working for the Born Free Foundation, observing the behaviour of captive wild animals in zoos to ascertain if they had a positive or negative experience was an integral part of my job. We set up a project in which we inspected hundreds of zoological collections scattered all over the UK, randomly selecting a sample every year. We visited them unannounced and incognito, recording all the displayed animals, scientifically analysing the recordings, and then producing an annual report titled 'Zoo Healthcheck'. Because of this, I have investigated over 200 zoological collections and observed the behaviour of thousands of captive animals of hundreds of different species.

The more zoos I investigated, the better I became at 'reading' the behaviour of the animals. I was able to more quickly identify which individuals were more likely to express their experience with specific recordable behaviours, and I became better at discreetly recording them to avoid blowing my cover.

I never visited a zoological collection without witnessing animal suffering, which reaffirmed my already-established belief all zoos should be phased out. It did not take me long to realise most of their conservation claims were false. I concluded only 5 per cent of the animals kept in UK zoos belonged to endangered species, only 3 per cent were part of captive breeding programmes, for less than 1 per cent had any attempt been made for them to be rehabilitated back into the wild, and for only a tiny percentage had such rehabilitation been successful.

It was clear to me the 'education' zoos impart was deeply flawed and often counterproductive, as it involved studying unnatural behaviours as if they were normal, observing animal pairings that would never occur in the wild, and learning that sentient beings can be treated as props. Proper scientific research was non-existent in most zoos, and where it did take place it was often misleading due to the captive conditions, hardly ever showing the reality of the species – as with the case of the alpha male wolves.

Even so, only a few of the animals were prisoners of the conservation, education and research industries. The vast majority of wild animals in zoos are captive prisoners of the entertainment industry, kept for profit and entertainment, and discarded when they are no longer profitable.

In zoos, I witnessed many animals showing clear signs of distress, and what could be described as mental disorders caused by their life in captivity (sometimes referred to as 'zoochosis'). The most common way to identify these psychological problems is by observing 'stereotypic behaviour' – abnormal repetitive behaviour with no apparent function.

Some of the cases I witnessed were horrible: the moon bear which developed a 'stereotypia' with his paw and tongue, unable to stop repetitively licking his paw for the rest of his life; the Siberian chipmunk constantly doing summersaults backwards, most likely imprinted in his mind by the past use of a spinning wheel; the llama twisting her neck every a few seconds; the chimp who was bald as he had pulled out all his hair in despair; an elephant bobbing his head up and down non-stop; big cats of all types leaving a visible trace engraved on the ground after endlessly pacing up and down through the same path forever. The examples were endless.

It didn't matter how big or small the zoo was as I always could find cases of animals showing how 'negative' their experience of being kept captive was. So negative it could be recorded from a long distance: I remember lions pacing by the fence of their big enclosures in drive-in safari parks, because for them what mattered was the fence, not the space of the enclosure. I could see the same sort of behaviour in all types of animals, mammals, birds, reptiles and even fish – after an in-depth investigation of aquaria some years later I was the first to describe some specific types of stereotypic behaviour seen in aquarium fish, such as spiralling, flashing and surfacing.

Captivity does three things to any animal: it reduces their available space to move, it reduces the number and quality of stimuli their senses receive, and it reduces the amount of choice they have in their everyday life. Remember what a sentient being is – an organism capable of perceiving the environment, processing the information to assess all choices, and moving as a consequence depending on whether the experience was positive or negative. If you reduce the number or quality of the stimuli below what evolution has shaped its senses to detect, you reduce the choices from what evolution has shaped its nervous system to process, and you reduce the space under what evolution has shaped its body to move around, you will transform the animal's entire life into a negative experience.

Domesticated animals have been genetically modified by selective breeding for generations, and their body and behaviour are no longer the same as those found in the species they come from, so they could conceivably tolerate captivity better if this tolerance was bred in. Wild animals in zoos are still genetically wild, and their bodies and minds face life in captivity as an unnatural situation they cannot cope with, even if they are captive-born.

This is why ethical vegans oppose zoos, aquaria, circuses with wild animals, wild animals kept as pets, and captive wild animals used in the entertainment industry. Fortunately, after a series of campaigns using the information I had uncovered with my investigations, I managed to help close five zoos in the UK (Glasgow Zoo being one of them). Unfortunately, though, I could not save the hundreds of thousands of animals still kept and born in all the remaining zoos, mostly because so many people still bought into their propaganda claims and continued to support them economically.

V

Politically speaking, there has been plenty of resistance to recognising all animals as sentient. As some animal protection laws only affect sentient beings, it is in the interest of the industries exploiting animals that fewer are recognised as such. All jurisdictions in developed countries accept all mammals and birds are sentient, most also include the rest of the vertebrates (reptiles, amphibians and fish), but as far as invertebrates are concerned there is much resistance. However, in the most progressive countries (New Zealand, Norway, Switzerland, Canada and EU nations), species increasingly acknowledged to be legally sentient for legislation purposes include now some invertebrates, in particular cephalopods (a type of mollusc which includes octopus, cuttlefish and squid), and decapods (a type of crustacean which includes crabs and lobsters).

If you observe the behaviour of an octopus it is very difficult not to conclude they are sentient. The nervous system of cephalopods is the most complex of all invertebrates, as they have a well-developed brain, part of it in the head and the rest spread among their tentacles (so it could be said they have nine interconnected brains). Octopus brains have forms of short- and long-term memory, versions of sleep and the ability to recognise people. In experiments, they have managed to solve complex mazes and completed tricky tasks to get food rewards. Octopuses are also considered to have consciousness according to the 2012 Cambridge Declaration of Consciousness – a document written by computational neuroscientist and neurophysiologist Dr Philip Low and signed by an international group of prominent scientists gathered at the University of Cambridge:

> The absence of a neocortex does not appear to preclude an organism from experiencing affective states. Convergent evidence indicates that non-human animals have the neuroanatomical, neurochemical, and neurophysiological substrates of conscious states along with the capacity to exhibit intentional behaviors. Consequently, the weight of evidence indicates that humans are not unique in possessing the neurological substrates that generate consciousness. Non-human animals, including all mammals and birds, and many other creatures, including octopuses, also possess these neurological substrates.

We arrive at similar conclusions when we observe decapod crustaceans such as lobsters, crayfish, prawns and crabs. They also have a brain and one ganglion (cluster of nerve cells) per body segment. Each ganglion receives sensory and movement information via nerves coming from the muscles, body wall and appendages. They can recognise and remember threatening objects or situations and try to avoid them. They most likely feel pain, because they have been shown to have pain relief opioid receptors which respond to analgesics such as morphine in a similar way to vertebrates, and because experiments where pain was inflicted on them (which I consider highly unethical, by the way) showed they react as any other animal would react to pain.

What about all the other invertebrates? Crustaceans, insects, arachnids and myriapods, all arthropods with similar biology. If decapods are sentient the rest of the arthropods should be too, as they have similar anatomy, physiology and behaviour (many social insects actually show much more sophisticated and complex behaviour). We now know you don't need to have all your nervous system in a big lump in your head to have a functional brain. Equally, in the societies of bees, wasps, ants and termites, which have moved to a higher level of organisation, we could argue the brain of the colony is the combination of all the brains of each of its individuals – their combined cognitive ability could even surpass that of certain vertebrates.

We must talk about bivalves (mussels, oysters, clams, etc.) – molluscs characterised by having two shells called valves that can close the animal in. Some people who define themselves as vegans (ostrovegans or bivalvegans) consume bivalves, claiming they are not sentient. I disagree with them, for multiple reasons.

First of all, they are molluscs, and other molluscs have now been recognised as sentient beings. Second, they all have senses. In particular, all have mechanoreceptors (touch) and chemoreceptors (taste). They also have statocysts which help them to sense and correct their orientation, and light-sensitive cells that can detect a shadow (some have actual eyes, such as scallops, who have more complex eyes with a lens, a two-layered retina and a concave mirror). Third, they do have a nervous system, which consists of a nerve network and a series of paired ganglia (they don't have a central nervous system but we know this doesn't matter if they still have enough interconnected neurons spread in different parts of the body). Fourth, research has found endogenous morphine (a natural analgesic) in specific bivalve's tissues appears to be involved in the response to physical trauma. Fifth, they react to negative experiences appropriately, as is the case of blue mussels in an estuary along the coast of Maine – they can somehow sense high-predation areas and develop thicker shells, while attaching to their substrate more strongly. Indeed, all bivalves close their shells when they detect danger and open them when they detect food.

Finally, we have the issue of mobility, probably the main argument of those who want to deny sentience to bivalves. They say the inability of mussels and oysters to remove themselves from hostile environments or go to prosperous ones means they must have lost the ability to have negative and positive experiences, as they cannot do anything about them. But do they really not move at all?

They do move, actually. Sometimes very slowly (as adult marine mussels can attach and detach byssal threads to attain a better position in the subtract), sometimes at mid-speed (as freshwater mussels have a muscular 'foot' that helps them burrow and move small distances), sometimes quite fast (as sea scallops swimming away from immediate danger), sometimes in their larva stages (as in marine mussels where the round microscopic larva drifts for three weeks to six months, before settling on a hard surface), sometimes they move parts of their bodies, which has the same effect of fleeing from a bad situation (such as closing their 'valves' to no longer be 'out there'), as in oysters and others. If we had shells, we could just close them instead of running away from danger too. It is a genuine reaction of a sentient being who has experienced danger approaching, as its senses perceive it and its nervous system correctly processes the information received. Bivalves are sentient, even oysters and mussels.

Do we need to set up experiments where mussels and oysters are electrocuted to convince ostrovegans to return to a plant-based diet? Why keep doing experiments inflicting pain on the animals not everyone agrees feel pain? It is unnecessary cruelty. Every time we do this experiment on a new animal we conclude they do feel pain. Of course they do. In a world where every species competes with others for survival, feeling pain is a very useful tool to avoid injury and death, and the species which does not feel pain would most likely have become extinct. Let's apply the precautionary principle to all animals, even those we have not discovered yet, and assume they all can feel pain and are sentient. This is why the Vegan Society definition does not use the term 'sentient animals', but only 'animals'. There is no need to keep hurting them just to be sure.

An ostrovegan doesn't fully follow the definition of the Vegan Society and so is not an ethical vegan, in the same way a dietary vegan, a hunting vegan, a vegan who eats discarded yard eggs, a vegan who consumes honey or a vegan who visits zoos for leisure isn't either. Widening the respect circle ensures no animal is left unprotected through fuzzy thinking or hasty assumptions. If in doubt about whether a practice is exploitation or if an animal is sentient, we should assume they are. Precaution is a wise response.

Speciesism – the key pitfall to avoid

If you call yourself a vegan but discriminate against bivalves or bees, well, you are a speciesist, which is precisely what ethical vegans desperately try to avoid. In 1971, Richard D. Ryder, the prominent British psychologist and member of the Oxford Group (a group of intellectuals who began to speak out against animal use, in particular, factory farming and animal research), wrote in the book *Animals, Men and Morals*:

> In as much as both 'race' and 'species' are vague terms used in the classification of living creatures according, largely, to physical appearance, an analogy can be made between them. Discrimination on grounds of race, although most universally condoned two centuries ago, is now widely condemned. Similarly, it may come to pass that enlightened minds may one

day abhor 'speciesism' as much as they now detest 'racism'.

Ryder, who is regarded by many as one of the three main academic drivers of animal rights of the 20th century (together with Tom Regan and Peter Singer), was the one who coined the term 'speciesism', a form of discrimination based on species membership, which is a key concept in ethical veganism. By the nature of the definition of veganism, which doesn't exclude any species of any animal or any type of exploitation, ethical vegans are anti-speciesist (I know, it's a mouthful).

People who discriminate against the species *Homo sapiens* would be speciesist too, as the 'do no harm' of *ahimsa* applies to humans as well. Some vegans who dislike others becoming vegan for social justice reasons tend to fall into this speciesism. Humans are primates, and like all other animals are sentient beings capable of being exploited, discriminated against and harmed by other humans. Therefore genuine ethical vegans should not be speciesists, and should not treat humans better or worse than any other species. Regarding humans as something 'special' is what brought animal exploitation in the first place. Treating humans as 'inferior' is as bad as treating them as 'superior', and being anti-human is as speciesist as being anti-cat, anti-rat or anti-bat.

We should never confuse those who fight against people harming animals with those who hate humans or think they are inherently evil. The latter may be cynical misanthropes unlikely to help significantly the animal cause. Also, to be consistent, being anti-speciesist should include being anti-racist, as the difference between races and species is quite arbitrary – you should not be allowed to pick and choose who you want to discriminate against. If we don't put an end to racist behaviour and systemic racial supremacy, how are we going to stop animal abuse and carnism (the systemic indoctrination of meat-eating)?

I often hear vegans saying 'veganism is only about animals, not people'. This is not quite true. Veganism has always been about what people do to animals. It's a human movement directed at humans. Humans are the perpetrators of the exploitation, and sometimes they may be their victims too. If we ignore people or don't understand why they do what they do, we will never be able to stop animal exploitation and eradicate carnism. Animal rights as a socio-political movement will only progress if it focuses on human behaviour, which is what it aims to correct.

Leslie Cross, who succeeded Donald Watson in the leadership of the Vegan Society in 1950, wrote in 1951 about its new 'aims', including this:

> The second broad aspect of the vegan aim is its effect upon human evolution ... Until the present relationship between man and his fellow creatures is replaced by one of companionship on a relatively equal footing, the pursuit of happiness by man is foredoomed to a painful and tragic frustration.

English academic and former ALF press officer Roger Yates states in his blog, On Human Relations with Other Sentient Beings:

> ... yes, veganism has a focus, the relationship between humans and other animals, but the vegan social movement founders never stopped at that limited place – veganism's scope is wider and, indeed, it is true, veganism is about humans too.

Professor Gary L. Francione, an American legal scholar and advocate of 'the abolitionist approach' (who lives with six dogs he calls 'non-human refugees'), has become quite influential within the animal-rights movement. He argues that non-human animals require only one right, the right not to be regarded as property, and that veganism is the moral baseline of the animal-rights movement. He is often controversial because he is very critical of animal protection organisations and single-issue campaigning. He shows that we cannot separate humans from other animals when we deal with veganism, as he writes in his blog, The Abolitionist Approach:

> Veganism is about nonviolence. It is about not engaging in harm to other sentient beings; to oneself; and to the environment upon which all beings depend for life. In my view, the animal-rights movement is, at its core, a movement about ending violence to all sentient beings. It is a movement that seeks fundamental justice for all. It is an emerging peace movement that does not stop at the arbitrary line that separates humans from nonhumans.

You will also be speciesist if you disregard the plight of wild animals and only care about domesticated animals. However, what to do as a response to caring about wild animal suffering is much more complicated. Animals in the wild may indeed suffer a great deal. They may starve to death if they cannot find enough food, they can be eaten alive by parasites, they may fall prey to predators, they may suffer horrible diseases. All this was already happening before humans evolved into *Homo sapiens*, and it has always been part of Nature. Suffering, the ability to have negative experiences to allow an animal to move away from them and therefore more likely survive and reproduce, is a quality intrinsically 'animalist', without which animals would not exist. Suffering (and also happiness, its counterpart) is what makes animals who they are.

Suffering is not intrinsically 'evil'. It is there to maximise survival, to be sure animals can avoid death for long enough to reproduce. Happiness is too, and instead of driving animals away from a situation, it draws them to the right environment for them. Therefore, if we eliminate suffering and pain we would eliminate also happiness and pleasure, as the physiological and psychological mechanisms which create positive and negative experiences are intrinsically intertwined. A world without suffering might become a zombie world.

But if eradicating suffering is not such a good idea, reducing its negative effects could be. If we can find ways to inform the body that it needs to move away from the adverse environment without feeling lots of pain, the function of suffering is preserved without the heavy price. For instance, if we move away from the fire before our flesh has been burnt, we would not need the heat and pain receptors from our skin to tell us to run away. This is all very well with species such as ours that can 'codify' past negative experiences, remember them for the future and then transmit the knowledge to others to spare them the experience. But many animals don't have that luxury. Should we help them?

For instance, wombats are adorable short-legged chubby quadrupedal marsupials from Australia who live in burrows which they dig with their front teeth and powerful claws. They are herbivorous, and the indigestible bits of the plants they eat end up in cubic-shaped faeces they scatter to mark their territory. Unfortunately, though, they don't realise that every time they enter their burrows they can get infected by sarcoptic mange, a skin disease caused by burrowing parasitic mites which seem to hang out in their burrows. Wombats suffer a great deal with this disease, as they lose their hair, their skin becomes crusted, as do their eyes and ears. Sometimes they even die from it. If they could tell when their burrows became infected, they could leave and dig another, but they don't seem to know. Some groups of compassionate volunteers in Tasmania decided to help the wombats and found an ingenious way to do so. Flaps laced with Cydectin, a drug that is used to treat mange, are placed above known pathways or the entrance to their burrow, so every time the wombat touches them, they treat themselves against the disease.

Should we then intervene in Nature and try to reduce the suffering of animals in the wild? Should we pass the knowledge of what we believe are adverse situations to other animals in the hope they don't have to go through a negative experience to learn the lesson? This is a very hot topic within veganism today.

Some say humans have a moral imperative to give wild animals equal consideration as domesticated animals. This means they should take a 'stewardship' attitude regarding Nature, as Nature doesn't care if its animals suffer or not. They say we have a moral obligation to try to reduce, as much as possible, the suffering of all sentient beings of this planet, and they would say 'the wild' is where you can find more cases of such suffering. This could involve interventions in Nature preventing animals from dying of starvation. If too many are all competing for limited resources, we could take them from their habitat and move them elsewhere. It might involve preventing predators from hunting their natural prey by giving them alternative food instead. These vegans say Nature is cruel and we should not have the romanticised view of it many conservationists have.

Other vegans (definitively the majority) say humans are the worst cause of suffering, and any attempt to mess with Nature will end up causing more suffering, as humans have neither the knowledge nor the capacity to intervene in a meaningful way. They believe the best we can do is avoid being the cause of suffering to the animals we have under our control, and letting Mother Nature deal with the rest. They say Nature cannot be cruel. Only humans are, as humans are moral entities who can choose their actions.

You may be wondering which position I take. Well, I take a combination of these two.

I do agree with the conclusion that when humans have tried

to intervene with natural processes, the result tends to be more suffering, even in the cases where the intention was the opposite. We seem to be remarkably bad at dealing with Nature, and we don't seem to learn from our mistakes. On the other hand, humans are already the cause of suffering for many animals in the wild, and if we are morally obliged to care about human-made suffering, we then should intervene to help wild animals every time we harm them. For instance, every time we infect them with pathogens Nature would not have exposed them to; when we cause them starvation because we destroyed their food; when they are eaten because we have forced their predators to move to new areas due to habitat destruction; or when we have messed with their numbers and territories by hunting them. We are ultimately responsible for the current climate emergency, and this is going to affect animals in the wild as well. We are hardly in a position to say parts of the planet are human-free and only Nature operates there.

Therefore, if we want to be consistent and not speciesist, we need to try to help animals in the wild as much as those in our care, because both are now affected by our behaviour, and both are equally sentient and suffer because of it. How can we help, though, when considering the scale of the problem and our history of making things worse every time we try to intervene?

Ethical vegans have a dilemma, then. The concept of what I call 'the ordeal involvement' can help to resolve it. Ethical vegans should stop any ordeal (a very unpleasant and prolonged experience) humans have caused to any animal because of their direct involvement. For the cases of wild animal suffering where humans are not directly responsible, a judgement can be made on a case-by-case basis to decide when to intervene, based on how much we are already involved with their ordeal.

First, we need to assess the degree of the ordeal (how unpleasant and prolonged it is for them) and then the degree of our personal involvement after we suddenly find ourselves part of 'the scene' where the ordeal is taking place (are we in a position to help, both logistically and legally? Do we know how can we help without making things worse?). After this assessment, we need to decide whether we intervene or let Nature take its course, but we should avoid being too anthropocentric. We should not focus on what we are feeling, but rather on what the animals are feeling – sometimes Mother Nature has already helped the animals experiencing the ordeal by 'providing' them with endorphins and/or a 'state of shock', both of which will have reduced the ordeal.

For instance, I was recently walking through London when I happen to see the very moment a wasp became entangled in a spider's web. I then saw a big spider approaching with the clear intention of wrapping the struggling wasp with silk so to immobilise her, and eventually injecting her venom inside the wasp to be able to drink her liquefied insides. That was going to be a clear ordeal for the wasp, who would undoubtedly suffer in the process, so I had to assess quickly whether the spider seemed well fed and if I could intervene to save the wasp without severely compromising the spider. When I noticed the remains of several dead wasps in the spider's web, I concluded that she was properly fed and would have no difficulty in finding other prey, so I helped the wasp to get rid of the silk surrounding their body and fly away. Providence had involved me in this particular wasp ordeal, but not in her less fortunate sisters that had previously been caught.

Natural selection may have also avoided unnecessary 'excess' of suffering. Once a cheetah has taken an impala to the ground, she bites the throat and this leads to a relatively quick death by suffocation. The 'reduction of suffering' in this case probably co-evolved in both species as a prolonged struggle might end up being too costly for both sides in terms of injury and starvation. Cheetahs are solitary hunters, however, and this ability to kill swiftly may not have evolved in a group of hunting predators such as wolves, as losing some of their group in a prolonged struggle might not have reduced enough the chances of survival of the genes of the entire group. Another example of evolution reducing suffering is with the stout-bodied and short-tailed grasshopper mice (*Onychomys*), a rodent native to North America's west. It looks quite similar to European mice, but this mouse happens to be an insectivorous hunter with resistance to the venom of the bark scorpion – it doesn't seem to feel pain when stung by it, and the genetic mutation that allows this has already been identified.

It is possible human-made suffering is more likely to cause worse ordeals for wild animals (more unpleasant and prolonged) as the animals' biology and psychology may not cope with it as well as they cope with the suffering caused by a natural situation. In other words, the 'quality' of human-made suffering may be worse than Nature-made suffering, and this may compensate for the differences in 'quantity'. A turtle lays many eggs in the sand, and from all the baby turtles hatched only a few become an adult and swim the warm seas, while the majority die of starvation. Is that worse than to 'rescue' all the babies and keep them in a tiny tank in a cold aquarium for decades until they all die in their personal ocean of madness? Is longevity more important than well-being?

Those who claim most animals in the wild have a negative net welfare (which means overall they experience more suffering than happiness) may project their own ideas without solid scientific evidence to back them up. Perhaps they are influenced by Nature documentaries, which tend to focus on the most painful moments of life in the wild, such as being killed, and ignore the average life of the average wild animal. I have seen many animals in the wild, and in the immense majority of cases I haven't witnessed any predation or death by disease.

For instance, I have recently been observing the life of a couple of Eurasian coots (*Fulica atra*), the chubby black water bird with a white beak and semi-webbed large feet we often see swimming in city ponds, making very sharp and loud calls which sound like two pebbles hitting each other. They make nests in the middle of shallow water by placing dead branches and other vegetation in such a way that the nest surfaces and provides a dry spot in the middle. I came across a recently built nest in my local park's pond, so decided to follow the couple who built it. They laid several eggs, and after the proper incubation by both parents, four coot chicks hatched. This was the problem, though: the nest was not totally surrounded by water, because two fallen metal poles touched it. Therefore, these four chicks were exposed to the dangers of predation from foxes, rats, crows, herons and even dogs off the lead, all of whom frequent the park. I became concerned, especially when I saw many rats hanging around the metal poles close to the nest, so I decided to check the coots out daily.

Was the net welfare of these chicks negative because of all these threats? No, it wasn't. I have yet to see a moment where they seemed bothered at all. Both parents defended them impeccably every time a potential predator approached, and all potential attacks I witnessed were immediately aborted once the predators realised the parents were nearby. Most of the day the chicks spent their time eating food, which is quite abundant at the pond, as they eat vegetation that grows in it. When they were young, they only had to call a couple of times if they were hungry and the closest parent provided them with a bit of freshly picked salad. When they grew a bit, they quickly learnt how to get their food themselves. When they woke up in the morning, they spent some time cleaning themselves, and off they went to explore with mum or dad, learning how to dive, how to get the more tricky leaves and how to deal with the moorhens, ducks and other coots that might get too close (only by using warnings, there was no real fighting). When it rained and was cold, they all huddled together in the nest under the warmth of one of the parents and let it pass. They didn't seem to be bothered by any insects. They didn't seem to get ill from any disease the nearby rats could pass to them. Two years from now, I expect they will be making their own nests.

Now, think about their life and compare it to a chicken born in a factory.

Those 'negative net welfare' believers tend to be quite anthropocentric in the way they interpret suffering and happiness, possibly overestimating the former and underestimating the latter. For instance, they assume prey are in a constant state of fear, worrying about whether a predator may be around the corner, but such 'anxiety' is a very human trait often based on over-analysing information and pathological paranoia. It is unlikely to be experienced in prey animals who tend to live in the moment, and who have evolved to successfully detect and evade their natural predators most of the time. Finally, these people tend to be 'prey-centric', ignoring how 'happy' hungry predators might become when they finally catch something to eat and to feed to their offspring. In fact, it is possible that, on average, the suffering of prey may be compensated for by the happiness of predators.

So if human-induced suffering may be worse, is this a good excuse not to intervene when wild animals suffer in Nature? I don't think it always is, because for each animal the experience will be different, and in some cases the ordeal is so unpleasant and prolonged we can't ignore it. If we have become somehow 'involved', if we are part of the scene, in the sense we could intervene if we wanted to, and if we decide not to help, our detachment may cause suffering by omission, and therefore it could be said we have been cruel.

If you think about it, the way I deal with the dilemma is to take a dual ethical approach. On one hand I take a deontological approach (the ethical school which states some things are intrinsically bad or good and some behaviours should always be avoided), terminating my activities that harm Nature, addressing this globally and collectively. But then I also take a utilitarian approach (the school which quantifies the outcome of our actions and states the right action is the one which produces more benefits) about the ways I can help individual wild animals in 'natural' ordeals, on a case-by-case basis based on my personal involvement, while still avoiding collective human interventions due to their likelihood of backfiring.

This seemingly complicated compromise is intended to give Nature the chance to still select the fittest and create balanced ecosystems where the net amount of suffering overall is likely to be below unbalanced habitats, and at the same time fulfil our moral obligations as ethical vegans when we find ourselves involved. For this to work, though, we should not deliberately venture far into Nature specifically seeking involvement, because that is when we will become overwhelmed by ordeals we cannot successfully handle.

I believe we should leave the most isolated relatively virgin parts of Nature alone as much as we can, and try to re-wild the areas close to them, 'reconnecting' all the patches of wildness left. Once we have put an end to humanity's major negative interventions against the natural habitat (hunting, pollution, pesticides, etc.) we should let Nature do its thing without us. However, at the same time, in an individual capacity, we should never ignore any wild animal's ordeal providence has placed in our way. I am in favour of rescuing stranded animals we encounter, healing injured wildlife that can be rehabilitated back into the wild, putting out of its misery an agonised wild animal who cannot be saved, or even giving to a prey animal an extra chance to escape if the predator seems well fed and it's unlikely to be hunting food for others.

It's not about numbers, but about experiences; it's not about eradicating suffering, but about minimising the harm we do; it's not about fighting Nature, but about avoiding breaking its balance; it's not about destroying ecosystems to reduce the overall amount of unhappiness, but about preserving them to remove the added suffering caused by humans in them. However, it's not about closing our eyes and looking away either, but about helping when we are already involved, because the morality of ethical veganism is personal, and only you can make the right call based on applying the principle of *ahimsa* in the situation you are in. Always remember you can 'do harm' if you are already involved and choose not to help, and always give equal consideration to everyone, big or small, domesticated or wild, but also prey or predator. An ethical vegan should try to avoid any sort of speciesism. From the blue whale to the marine mussel; from the African elephant to the harvest mouse; from the black cat to the white shark; from the human to the mosquito. It's easier said than done, but worth striving for.

V

Donald Watson might not have had the luxury to consider the plight of wild animals in Nature because he was too busy trying to help other vegans, whose 'ordeals' in an unsympathetic wartime and post-war world were significant. He had contacted the UK government requesting vegans be given a fat ration suitable for them (instead of lard or butter), and additional rationing points to enable them to buy foods such as lentils and dried fruits in place of the meat, cheese, milk and egg coupons. The government refused, and this was probably the first institutionalised official act of discrimination against vegans in modern times.

Since 2010 the UK has had a powerful piece of legislation dealing with discrimination, the Equality Act. Had this law been in place when Donald Watson wrote to the government, he could have taken them to court. This law made it unlawful to harass, victimise or discriminate against anyone for holding certain personal characteristics, to increase equality of opportunity. It affects the workplace (employers', employees' and contractors' conduct), but also the provision of services, both private (such as hotels, pubs or housing) and public (such as hospitals, schools or care homes). The Act established the nine 'protected characteristics': age, disability, gender reassignment, marriage and civil partnership, pregnancy and maternity, race, religion or belief, sex, and sexual orientation. On 'religion or belief', the Act explains 'belief means any religious or philosophical belief and a reference to belief includes a reference to a lack of belief'. Therefore, philosophical beliefs such as ethical veganism should be covered.

When I was fired in April 2018 I did not know much about the Equality Act. I had a rough idea that veganism should be covered by it, but I did not know the details. I knew of a case where a vegan gardener called Joe Hashman had managed to win a discrimination claim at an Employment Tribunal after he had been fired for his anti-hunting beliefs and his belief in the sanctity of life, which prevented him killing pigeons as instructed by his employer, but this was before the Equality Act had been passed, and I did not know how much of a precedent it represented for future cases. I was sure my dismissal was unlawful, and that I had been discriminated against for being a vegan, but I did not know enough about employment law to know if I had a strong case.

The first problem I identified was that I had been employed by the charity for less than two years, and the UK law stipulates you need at least two years of employment to be allowed to claim unfair dismissal (my first employment with them ten years prior did not count for this). I then learnt there were exceptions to this two-year rule. One was discrimination and the other whistleblowing. I definitely felt my case was a discrimination case but was it also whistleblowing? After all, what got me fired was the email I sent to my colleagues about something they needed to know about what our employer had done, or rather not done. In the UK, the Disclosure Act 1998 (PIDA) amended the Employment Rights Act 1996 to protect employees who blow the whistle about wrongdoing committed by their employers. The way the law defined the conditions for that protection to apply seemed to fit my case. Therefore, having a potential double case of discrimination and whistleblowing would allow me to launch a claim against the charity at the tribunal even if I had not worked there for more than two years, but I only had a window of three months to do so. It was time to get help from those who know more about this sort of thing.

Joe Hashman, the gardener who won the landmark legal case, gave up a career as a professional tennis coach to get close to Nature and help animals. He is a lifelong member of the Hunt Saboteurs Association and became an investigator who uncovered all sorts of cruelty to foxes, deer and hares caused by the hunting and coursing fraternities (in 2009 his evidence helped to convict TV chef Clarissa Dickson Wright for attending a hare coursing event). He is also the founder of Hounds Off, an organisation helping landowners opposed to hunting, and author of several organic gardening books and blogs under the name 'Dirty Nails'. This red-bearded, robust-bodied, gentle-faced, country-dressed, dirty-nailed compassionate vegan man happens to be a dear friend of mine. I met him when we worked together at International Fund for Animal Welfare (IFAW) on several anti-hunting investigations. As I needed some emotional support and a fresh set of eyes to look at my case, I went to Dorset to visit him.

It was lovely to see a friendly face and relax a little bit in a warm environment. Joe is a very down-to-earth and wise man – as you would expect of a seasoned vegan organic gardener – and I desperately needed his opinion. Having a cup of tea while sitting at the very end of his beautiful meandering rustic wild garden, close to where every evening he feeds a cete of intrepid badgers, I gave him a detailed account of my case.

It was so liberating. I felt the pressure escape from my gut with every word, and the dark heavy cloud of injustice hovering over me began to thin. Joe agreed I had a good chance of winning. More crucially, he clarified for me that in his case he did not claim 'veganism' as his belief but 'the sanctity of life' – he told me I would need a separate pre-hearing for the Employment Tribunal to accept a new belief as protected, based on a series of criteria set up by the Employment Appeals Tribunal in the Grainger Plc v. Nicholson 2010 case, as it appeared there had not been a case where veganism had been tested.

I realised something very important. I might be the first person in the UK to go to court with a claim of 'veganism' as a protected belief. My case had become something bigger. It had become 'our case', the case for all UK ethical vegans, perhaps the case for all vegans in Europe or in the entire world. With it, a judge could either confirm veganism is indeed protected under the Equality Act (to our delight) or rule it is not (to our dismay). My shoulders felt heavy with the unexpected weight of responsibility. This case could make history, or ruin it for others who came later.

My mood and attitude changed. Since the day I received the first disciplinary letter I had been in survival mode, carrying a defensive attitude. Now I had a new cause to fight for. I could fight for the rights of all vegans and grow something important from the seeds of my misfortune. My mood became combative and my attitude determined. Time to step up the game and hire an employment lawyer with expertise in discrimination and whistleblowing.

Joe had advised me to approach the legal firm who succeeded in his case, and that made good sense to me. I called Bindmans LLP, and a few days later I went to their London offices, close to the Charles Dickens Museum in Clerkenwell. I had an hour's meeting booked with one of their principal solicitors, Peter Daly. I liked him straight away. He was relatively young but very knowledgeable and straightforward. He reminded me of the 1960s actor Sir Dirk Bogarde – slim, composed, elegantly dressed, gentle features and substantial loosely combed brown hair parted from the left – and I later found out he is of Irish descent. I have met many lawyers before and a considerable proportion of them tended to look down on me, assuming someone with my accent would not have any idea about how British law works. Peter wasn't like that. He got me immediately and treated me as someone who knew what he was doing. He was very respectful of my opinions and accepted my approach to the case. Before the meeting, I had sent him the summary of a chronology of events I had meticulously compiled, as I had managed to save the key emails before I was suspended and lost access to my email account. I could see he liked that. I think he realised that someone producing this before the first meeting could have gathered the evidence required to win a case. Our minds met.

That meeting did for me what it was supposed to do, and placed me right in the real world. It moved me away from speculation and fantasy and brought me down to earth. On the one hand, it showed me I wasn't imagining it, that I indeed had a good discrimination and whistleblowing case. It confirmed too that I would indeed be the first vegan attempting this. However, it also showed me how complex and difficult these sorts of cases are, and that only the best legal experts on these issues are likely to win. I learnt how long these litigations can take, and how much they can cost. I learnt Peter was an expert who could win the case for me ... but I could not afford him.

I had enough savings to allow me to survive for a year or so, but not enough to cover my subsistence *and* the legal fees. However, I did not qualify for Legal Aid as I had too much money. I did not belong to any union – I know, I should have joined one. I had no insurance of any sort which would cover legal fees either. As generally speaking employment cases do not award the legal costs to the winner, Bindmans could not offer me a 'no-win-no-fee' deal, and I would need to cover all legal fees of solicitors and barristers. I did have a good case, and an expert lawyer who could win it, but I could definitely not afford him nor a nasty lengthy legal battle which could well last a year or more. Not while being unemployed as I was. Not with a 'gross misconduct' stain on my CV. I seemed to be stuck in an unsurmountable impasse with no resolution in sight. It was not a good place to be.

V

The environment – the key reason to remember

Gabrielle Matthaei was an English plant physiologist who in 1905 married Albert Howard, an English botanist who had worked for the government of India and brought the Vedic Indian techniques of sustainable agriculture to the West. Together, in 1921, concerned about the growth of artificial fertilisers and inspired by the traditional Indian way to cultivate food, they pioneered what we know today as 'organic farming', defined by the use of fertilisers of organic origin (such as compost manure, green manure and bone meal) and by use of 'natural' techniques such as crop rotation, companion planting and biological pest control. However, their visionary ideas did not become mainstream, and most crops in the West continued to be grown with all sorts of nasty chemicals that were damaging the environment, which only increased in the 1940s when chemical pesticides were added to the equation.

In the 1950s, concerns for the environment, and the possibility of addressing them via organic farming, became more prominent among those who tried to follow an ethical lifestyle. This included, of course, the vegan community. However, for vegans, 'organic farming' was an incomplete solution as it used products from animal agriculture. Something better was needed, and members of the Vegan Society came up with it. In 1960, in Rosa Dalziel O'Brien's gardening column of the society's magazine, we first see the term 'veganic farming' used. This is the organic cultivation and production of crops with a minimal amount of exploitation or harm to any animal (for instance, no use of manure or bone meal, no pesticides and no use of animals to plough fields). Since then, many vegans – including me – have been using this method as a way to address both the problems of animal exploitation and the destruction of the environment.

We can find evidence from the early years of the Vegan Society that the environment was something vegans were concerned about, and they realised making the vegan lifestyle mainstream could significantly help it. In 1962 the Vegan Society's 'statement of purpose' included this environmentalist sentence: 'Veganism remembers man's responsibilities to the earth and its resources and seeks to bring about a healthy soil and plant kingdom and a proper use of the materials of the earth.' The 1988 definition, still used today, also mentions the environment: 'for the benefit of humans, animals and the environment'.

Considering that environment is the home where animals live, if you care about the animals but do not care about the environment, this creates a kind of irrational cognitive dissonance. Many early vegans seemed to have been able to avoid this. At the turn of this millennium, though, I was far from avoiding mine.

V

I had been working in animal protection for some time now, and yet I was still consuming all sorts of animal products. I was at the Born Free Foundation trying to close zoos to prevent wild animals suffering life in captivity, and yet to have some cow's milk in my tea I was paying 'others' to raise cattle and keep them in captivity for life in factory farms. I was campaigning against the killing of zoo animals when they are surplus to requirements, and yet I was paying 'others' to kill pigs and chickens for my lunch. I was protesting about how sea lions were forced to perform in safari parks as if they were props, and yet I was paying 'others' to raise and kill animals for my footwear. I was trying to help 300,000 animals in the UK zoo industry, but I was helping to kill over 10 million pigs, 15 million sheep, 14 million turkeys, 15 million ducks and geese, 982 million broiler chickens, 50 million 'spent hens', 2.6 million cattle, 4.5 billion fish and 2.6 billion shellfish, which are the numbers of animals killed in the UK each year. I was a cognitive dissonance mess, and I knew it.

I had met several vegans by then but I was still building excuses for not becoming a vegan myself, using them to rationalise my reluctance to change. One was that I very much liked cheese, and I felt that if I craved it so much it was because my body was asking me for it, which ignored the concept of addiction – I did not want to listen to those who mentioned casein, a dairy protein which releases casomorphins that make cheese addictive. Another was that I was too old for change and I was too set in my ways – but I was only thirty-seven, and I had proved I could turn my life around if I really wanted to by emigrating to the UK. Another was it would be impossible to draw the line between which types of animal exploitation I should avoid and which I should tolerate – overlooking the fact that I could move the line any time I needed to. Another was that although being a vegan in a community such as the Monkey Sanctuary was more feasible, it would be very difficult in 'the real world' – ignoring the fact I had met Tricia, my colleague at Born Free who dealt with rescued big cats, and she was a perfectly well-adjusted healthy vegan living a normal life in the same 'outside' world I was in. My rationalisations were weak and, frankly, ridiculous, but this is what happens with cognitive dissonances. You avoid looking at them, and therefore you don't see how ridiculous they can be.

There was much conflict and guilt in my mind, and to force me to deal with it something drastic was needed. For instance, a blow to my head. Without planning it, this is precisely what happened. On a 2001 summer afternoon, I was going up and down the stairs in the office in Horsham when I tripped. I was going to fall hard on my front but somehow I propelled myself upwards in an attempt to land on my feet. I was successful, but managed to hit my head on the low ceiling. It hurt. I went back upstairs vigorously rubbing the sore spot, and when I sat down I passed out.

I didn't know this, but when you are unconscious due to trauma you can dream. I had an amazing dream in the few minutes I was out, which I forgot after I complied with the instructions of the paramedics who woke me up. Nothing medically dramatic happened after that. I only had a concussion, and after some monitoring overnight, when I had to be awakened every couple of hours or so, everything went back to normal ... or did it? I could not shake off the dream I had forgotten, as it seemed to be quite important. I wanted to remember it, but my busy life didn't allow me to even try.

At that time I didn't take holidays. I was a workaholic. Living alone and not having a relationship often leads to this – to fill the void. My managers had repeatedly told me I had to take breaks and use my allocated leave, but I had ignored them. Perhaps this time, I thought, I should listen. Perhaps this time I should take a break and try to remember the dream. If I did that, though, I knew I would feel very guilty afterwards. I would feel I should have spent my break trying to help animals, not lying down on a beach wasting my life. If I only could work and have a break from work at the same time. Relax but still be productive. I eventually found the solution. I could go to a quiet place and try to write a book about animal rights. That was it. Find a remote place where I could try to remember the dream and write a book in the process.

I had twenty-three days left of leave, which I would lose the following January, and I decided to find somewhere isolated to spend the Christmas period writing the book. I found it on 7 December 2001, during the office Christmas party held at Virginia McKenna's house (the famous 1950s actress who co-founded Born Free). During the casual small talk over delicious vegetarian canapes, I mentioned my idea to several colleagues, and eventually to the ever-elegant Virginia. She told me she had a friend who owned a small cottage on the Isle of Skye, the largest of the Inner Hebrides islands off the west coast of Scotland. She would not be using it during such a cold and dark time of the year. Perfect, I thought.

Three days later, I left my tiny flat in Brighton to begin my slow journey to the beautiful island. It was a very lovely cottage with a corrugated iron roof, isolated from civilisation and with the minimum facilities. I took all the provisions I needed for twenty-three days and buckled up for my new adventure.

It all worked as if it was a plot from an old gothic film. All sorts of fantastic things happened to me in that magical place, with breathtaking sunsets and mesmerising night skies. The days became shorter and darker and the weather increasingly more dramatic. The complete isolation played many tricks on my workaholic mind, and eventually I remembered my dream and I wrote my book. It turned out to be a novel, which I titled *The Demon's Trial*, and I published it in 2006 under the name J.C. Costa. It's the story of an animal welfare campaigner put on trial by the ghosts of all the animals he had failed in the past – autobiographical, of course. A psychological exploration of guilt and conflict.

Most importantly, my experience writing the book in those unusual dramatic conditions emptied my brain of all my memories, thoughts and rationalisations. I laid them down in front of me and then had to choose which I would put back in and which I would discard. Now that I could see them for what they were,

I threw away all those ridiculous rationalisations. On 2 January 2002 I left the island to return to the world down below, and when I arrived back home in Brighton I was an ethical vegan. I had finally made the step from meat-eater to ethical vegan, with no transition between. It seems I required a notch in the head to go all the way.

V

I wonder if Donald Watson or Sally Shrigley had experienced some sort of 'epiphany' similar to what I went through in Scotland. We will never know, but it is remarkable the Vegan Society pioneers were already talking about the environment well before we all knew about climate change and how animal agriculture is a major contributor. According to the United Nations' Food and Agriculture Organization, in 2017 livestock generated 14.5 per cent of global greenhouse gas emissions, the second-highest source of emissions and greater than all transportation combined. This is not only by the amount of CO_2 produced by the vast number of farm animals when they breathe but also by the methane cattle and sheep gift to the air from their rears, which has an even more powerful greenhouse effect. *The Global Methane Budget 2000– 2017* by the Global Carbon Project showed methane traps twenty- eight times more heat than carbon dioxide.

According to the environmental journalist George Monbiot in his 2017 article 'The Meat of the Matter', animal agriculture also uses about 70 per cent of agricultural land, and if we replaced the meat in our diets with soya alternatives, the land area required per kilo of protein would be reduced by 70 per cent in the case of chicken, 89 per cent for pork and 97 per cent for beef. Not to forget animal agriculture is the leading cause of deforestation, loss of biodiversity and water pollution. The World Wildlife Fund found, in 2017, that 60 per cent of biodiversity loss can be attributed to the crops produced to feed farm animals. The 2019 IPBES *Global Assessment Report on Biodiversity and Ecosystem Services* found overfishing and industrial agriculture are the primary drivers of the current extinction of animal species.

We all know this now, but before it was common knowledge the vegan pioneers were already warning everyone about the negative effects of animal agriculture on the environment. Therefore, despite what some claim these days about ethical veganism being 'only about animals', from the very beginning of the vegan movement the concerns for the environment were already there.

I think you can be an ethical vegan for the animals and for the environment. I agree that the so-called 'health vegans', those who only follow a vegan diet to improve their health, can hardly be called ethical (if health is their only reason, and they stubbornly stick to it), but those who do it for the environment or the animals, and not for themselves, fit well into the concept of being ethical. The principle of not wanting to damage the environment is a moral principle, and the philosophical belief we should minimise the negative impact on their environment by avoiding certain products or practices is certainly integral to environmentalism.

There are several gateways to the world of veganism, but once you are in you will end up being a vegan for more than one reason. Those who still claim they are only vegan for the environment are perhaps just across the threshold (yes, they are already vegans) but are still hanging out at the vestibule, not having explored yet all the rooms of the vegan mansion. Give them time, and they will hopefully embrace *ahimsa* too.

V

In June 2018, a headline in *The Independent* read 'Veganism is the "single biggest" way to reduce our environmental impact on the planet, study finds'. That's a classic 21st-century headline and explains why so many people become vegan 'for the environment' these days, even before they have the chance to learn about animal exploitation and abuse. The article draws on research by Oxford University which found that cutting meat and dairy products from one's diet could reduce an individual's carbon footprint from food by up to 73 per cent (imagine how much more reduction this person could attain by cutting out animal fibres in clothes). The study also found that meat and dairy production was responsible for 60 per cent of greenhouse gas emissions from agriculture, while the products of these industries would provide only 18 per cent of calories and 37 per cent of protein produced around the globe. In other words, a big price to pay for very little benefit.

We are all familiar with the term carbon footprint (the total greenhouse gas emissions caused, expressed as carbon dioxide equivalent). What if we use a similar concept for veganism: 'blood footprint', or the total amount of suffering caused to other sentient beings by an individual, event, organisation or product? This is, of course, only a theoretical concept, as we cannot measure suffering, but it is useful to help us understand what ethical veganism is.

Ethical vegans are people who try to minimise as much as possible their blood footprint. Just as we don't go out and criticise companies with 'green credentials' for not having achieved an absolute zero carbon footprint, we shouldn't brand ethical vegans as 'hypocrites' when it turns out some insects were crushed during the harvesting of the vegetables on their dinner plate, or they paid for it by using a credit card from a bank which invests in wool production. Ethical vegans are not 'absolutists' who pretend they have already attained the 'enlightenment' of a cruelty-free life. They are regular people who try to reduce their blood footprint, in whatever ways they can manage.

An ethical vegan is someone who tries, and tries hard; is someone who doesn't want to leave anyone behind; is someone who tries to be as consistent and inclusive as possible; is someone who cares about the little guy, the very little guy; is someone who doesn't want to harm anyone or anything. However, is still a human with all the contradictions, flaws, imperfections and shortcomings all other humans have. An ethical vegan is somebody like me, but is also someone like you, whoever you are, if you care about others.

We can all be ethical vegans.

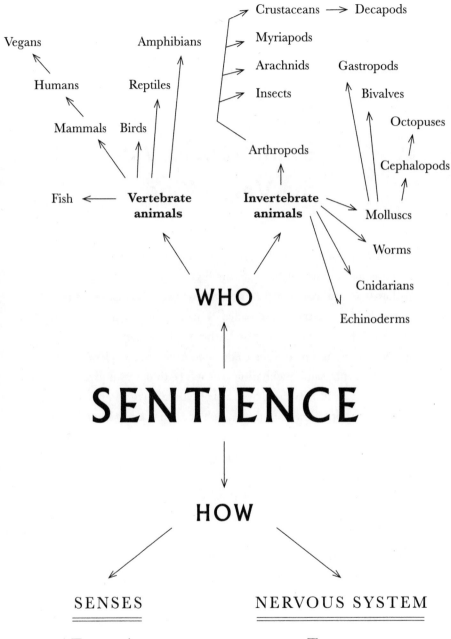

Vegans

Humans

Mammals   Birds

Fish ← Vertebrate animals

Amphibians

Reptiles

Crustaceans → Decapods

Myriapods

Arachnids   Gastropods

Insects   Bivalves

                Octopuses

Arthropods   Cephalopods

Invertebrate animals   Molluscs

                Worms

                Cnidarians

                Echinoderms

WHO

SENTIENCE

HOW

SENSES

To perceive
sensations from
stimuli

NERVOUS SYSTEM

To process
sensations and create
experiences
from them

4.

The Anthropology of
the Vegan Kind

Two dozen assorted vegans will do, thank you very much.

This will be fun. Imagine an intelligent alien civilisation sends to Earth an anthropologist (a scientist whose specialism is *Homo sapiens*) to research the so-called 'vegans' initial explorers had reported about. Imagine that on his home planet they have similar genders to us, and he is a male educated in their equivalent of our West, with the same inclination to classify things and give them names. Let's call him Prof. Spock. He would have to answer the basic anthropological questions, such as: What kind of creatures are vegans? Are there different types? How can you tell them apart? How old are they? How many are there? Do they get along with each other?

If he visited us in 2020, what conclusions would this intrepid scientist include in his final report?

The nature of the vegan primate

Vegans are human, but are humans herbivores? Many vegans would say we are anatomically and physiologically adapted to eating plant material. Others say we are omnivores, as we can digest food from animal origin too (and most do eat animal products and survive to old age). What is quite clear is that humans are not carnivores, as we do not have any of the adaptations carnivores have (in mammals, long canines, big gaps between sharp teeth, short intestines, predatory adaptations such as claws, powerful jaws, etc.).

Humans are frugivores, a type of herbivore or omnivore where fruit and nuts are the preferred food type. As we are primates and most primates are frugivores, our biological adaptations neatly fit this type of diet. If we look closer at the great apes, the group of primates we belong to, the gorilla is definitively a folivore (a type of herbivore which mostly eats leaves), the orangutans, the bonobos and the chimpanzees are frugivores, mostly eating fruit. All the great apes occasionally eat insects and eggs – and 2 per cent of the diet of some populations of chimps is meat that includes the flesh of hunted monkeys (although female chimps hardly eat them).

Therefore, we are somewhere on the spectrum between omnivore and herbivore. It is possible that through evolution some types of now-extinct 'humans' may have moved more towards the herbivore or the omnivore side. For instance, a yet-to-be-debunked 1979 study of the microwear of teeth suggested the *Australopithecus* species, our upright African ancestors who lived between 4.2 and 1.9 million years ago, were still mainly frugivores, with an increased adaptation to eating grains.

For some time it was believed that when *Australopithecus* evolved into early species of *Homo*, around 2.8 million years ago, the diet shifted towards meat-eating as the new stone tools they manufactured made it possible to cut meat, but recent studies involving carbon isotopes suggest there was no such shift then, but much later – the earliest evidence of meat-eating in hominins dates to about 2.5 million years ago.

Homo erectus, the first hominid who left Africa, started eating cooked food as early as 1.9 million years ago, which would give them access to tubers and roots otherwise not edible. They probably evolved the ability to digest starch better, as these hominids were the first to venture into the temperate latitudes of the planet where plants produce more starch (to store energy in habitats with less sun and rain). Enzymes called amylases aid in breaking starch into glucose with the help of water, and modern humans produce them in the saliva. Chimpanzees have only two copies of the salivary amylase gene while humans have an average of six. Perhaps this difference began with *Australopithecus* when they started to eat grains, and became more pronounced with *Homo erectus* when they moved into starch-rich Eurasia.

Homo neanderthalensis (or *Homo sapiens neanderthalensis*), the now-extinct big-nosed archaic humans who lived in Eurasia from several hundred thousand years ago until about 40,000 years ago, clearly ate meat, with steppe-dwelling communities in colder latitudes possibly subsisting primarily on meat. However, it is not known whether the early *Homo sapiens sapiens*, who came to Eurasia from Africa again and coexisted with Neanderthals for a while, ate as much meat as was previously thought. Research from Eaton and Konner in 1985 and Cordain et al. in 2000 estimated that about 65 per cent of the diets of pre-agricultural Palaeolithic humans may still have come from plants – far more than only your recommended five fruit and veg a day, I would say. Interestingly, anatomically modern humans are believed to have more copies of the starch-digesting genes than the Neanderthals and the Denisovans (another extinct species or subspecies of archaic human that ranged across Asia during the Lower and Middle Palaeolithic), suggesting that the ability to digest starch has been a continuous driver through human evolution as much as walking upright, having big brains and articulate speech – perhaps being a baker may be the oldest profession after all.

In any event, looking at this evolutionary history, it does seem meat-eating habits in human-like primates are relatively recent, and most of our anatomy and physiology evolved to make the hominoid lineage mostly plant-based. For an ethical vegan it doesn't matter when we started eating meat and for how long, as animal exploitation is not avoided because this is the 'natural' thing to do, but the 'moral' thing to do. However, human biology helps vegans to thrive, rather than hinders them, which explains all the health benefits reported when people switch to a vegan diet.

Experts on dietetics (the study of diet and its health effects) are finally recognising that balanced vegan diets are healthy. The British Dietary Association has stated well-planned vegan diets can support healthy living in people of all ages, and other similar professional bodies all over the world agree. On the other side, the World Health Organization has classified processed meat as carcinogenic, and there is increasing evidence that eating lots of meat and dairy increases blood pressure and blood cholesterol, which leads to heart disease, and that cutting them out can significantly reduce your risk of type 2 diabetes, a disease which is affecting an increasing number of people in developed nations. What would you expect if you fed a lifetime of scrambled eggs, fried bacon, cheeseburgers and hot dogs to a frugivore?

If, before the trip to Earth, Prof. Spock had examined human 'specimens' comparing them with others species, he would have easily concluded that all humans are frugivores. Yet if, when he landed, he found the majority of humans to be following a non-frugivore diet that appeared to be associated with an epidemic of obesity, heart disease and diabetes, to make sense of it all he would have to study them too.

Collecting vegan types may keep you busy

Systematics is the branch of biology dealing with classification and nomenclature of living organisms. It creates categories and subcategories based on features shared. More often than not, different scientists come up with different classifications which are justifiable by the characteristics they choose to consider. Let's see which systematics of vegans Prof. Spock might come up with after visiting Earth today.

First, the major groups. Prof. Spock could pay attention to the general attitude people have to the exploitation of other animals, and class humans in three main groups: carnists, omnivorous and vegetarians.

He could define **carnists** as people who not only don't care about such exploitation but think it is important (essential, really) that humans exploit animals in any way they see fit. The term 'carnism' was first coined by the American social psychologist Dr Melanie Joy in 2001 (popularised by her book *Why We Love Dogs, Eat Pigs, and Wear Cows*) and it was defined as the prevailing ideology in which people support the use and consumption of animal products. She wrote:

> We don't see meat-eating as we do vegetarianism – as a choice based on a set of assumptions about animals, our world, and ourselves. Rather, we see it as a given, the 'natural' thing to do, the way things have always been and the way things will always be. We eat animals without thinking about what we are doing and why because the belief system that underlies this behavior is invisible. This invisible belief is what I call carnism.

Vegetarians are people who do not like such exploitation and think at the very least we should avoid eating animals killed for food.

Omnivorous are those in between, people who do care a bit about such exploitation, but not enough to avoid eating animals killed for food. (This term should not be confused with 'biological omnivores', which refers to a particular natural food adaptation – I am still using the term here as it has become common usage to describe this particular 'choice' of diet in humans.)

Prof. Spock could look deeper and try to find the next level of classification, with the following subcategories:

1. Carnists
   a. Vegan-ignorant
   b. Vegan-deniers
   c. Veganphobes
2. Omnivorous
   a. Reducetarians
   b. Pescatarians
   c. Flexitarians
3. Vegetarians
   a. Typical vegetarians
   b. Pre-vegans
   c. 'Vegans'
   d. Post-vegans

A **vegan-ignorant** (Prof. Spock's term) would be a carnist who doesn't know about veganism at all, and follows carnism only by habit or tradition, without ever questioning it (I would say the majority of humans on the planet fall into this category). I remember a classic Monty Python-esque incident with a vegan-ignorant waiter I am sure many vegans can relate to. I was in a bar in Malaga, about fifteen years ago, where I was trying to find something to eat during an investigation I was conducting on lion cubs used as photo props on beaches. I told the waiter – in fluent Spanish, of course – that I was a vegan and asked if there was anything suitable for me on their menu. With a confused expression, he said:

'We have chicken.'

'No, I am vegan, we vegans don't eat anything that comes from animals,' I replied politely. 'Ah, OK, what about some sardines?' he suggested, having thought for a few seconds.

'No, fish are animals too. I don't eat anything that comes from animals. No pork, no fish, no eggs, no milk,' I clarified, trying to keep a calm voice.

'No meat, I see, a vegetarian. Why didn't you say so? We have some lovely potato omelettes!' he replied with a satisfied look.

'No, I am vegan, not vegetarian. An omelette has eggs and we vegans don't eat eggs either. Don't you have a salad or something?' I asked, trying not to show my increasing frustration.

'Ah, yes, we have an excellent Russian salad,' he offered with satisfaction.

'Doesn't the Russian salad have egg in it?' I asked with a slightly patronising tone.

'No, it has potatoes and peas in mayonnaise,' he confidently explained.

'Isn't mayonnaise made of eggs?' I check-mated, tilting my head to one side to soften the blow.

'Well, only one or two. Can't you eat that either?'

A **vegan-denier** is a carnist who knows about the existence of veganism but mistrusts any of its claims, assuming it is only a transient fashion and 'not a real thing'. Some of them seem to be triggered by the increasing growth of veganism and are constantly trying to put vegans down or accusing us of being hypocrites. A classic example would be the English TV presenter and journalist Piers Morgan, who seems to 'lose it' every time he interviews vegans on his ITV breakfast programme *Good Morning Britain*. He once said on that programme:

> The vegans don't care about the little guys, the bees that get killed. The billions of bees that get killed every year, the billions of insects that get killed in the pollination process, and they don't care ... billions of those little things are killed every year so that these

vegans and vegetarians can have their avocados and almonds flown on jets.

He also had a public rant on his show about my litigation, stating:

> If I get discriminated against for being a meat-eater, is that a breach of my ethical beliefs? If my belief is eating meat is good for the planet and sustainability – and a strict vegan diet is bad for you – if I was to storm a vegan restaurant and demand meat, would they discriminate against me. Am I allowed to go to court?

Other vegan-deniers take a more respectful attitude and they just feel uncomfortable with veganism, wishing that it would go away, as it constantly makes them feel bad about their choices. A good example is the actor and writer David Mitchell – who I very much like, I find him hilarious in his many appearances on panel shows – who wrote in his *Guardian* column (and in his latest book *Dishonesty is the Second-Best Policy*) the following as a reaction to my case:

> I think what I find annoying, deep down – and, again, some meat-eaters, you don't have to own up to this, but it might interest you to discover whether you feel it – is the very fact that I can't discount vegans any more. The thing that's annoying about there suddenly being lots of them is the nagging suspicion that they might be right. When there were hardly any vegans, I hardly ever had to think about that.

A **veganphobe** deeply dislikes veganism and hates vegans, as a homophobe does with gay people. These people often try to publicly mock, insult or ridicule vegans they encounter, spread anti-vegan propaganda (sometimes they falsely claim they were vegan before, and it almost killed them) or provoke vegans by eating animal products in front of their faces (sometimes raw meat). In 2020, *The Times* reported that in the previous five years a total of 172 crimes where vegans were the victims because of their veganism had been recorded by thirty-three UK police forces (crimes have increased over time; in 2015 only nine were recorded compared with fifty-five in 2019). Unfortunately, I have encountered several veganphobes in my life, as in the case of an infamous Latvian anti-vegan protester who, a couple of years ago, was convicted for disorderly behaviour likely to cause harassment, alarm or distress by eating a raw dead squirrel in front of a vegan food stall in London's Piccadilly Circus. (He is quite a dangerous guy. It has been reported that in 2006 he stabbed four of his classmates.)

A **reducetarian** is an omnivorous who may care enough about animal exploitation to commit themselves to reducing their consumption of meat, dairy and eggs, but not enough to avoid the consumption altogether. The Reducetarian Foundation was founded in 2015 by the American Brian Kateman, who stated in an interview with Forbes.com:

> A reducetarian describes a person who is mindfully eating less meat – red meat, poultry, and seafood, as well as less dairy and fewer eggs – regardless of the degree of reduction or motivation for cutting back. They play around with Meatless Mondays, veggie-heavy lunches, smaller protein portions, vegetarianism, and veganism to see what works best for them. This concept is appealing because not everyone is willing or able to follow an 'all-or-nothing' diet.

According to RSPCA research, red meat (especially beef burgers, sausages and steaks) is the most common food stripped back from a reducetarian's diet, followed by dairy.

Some theoretically vegan organisations are now using reducetarian messaging, possibly because they believe reducing the consumption of animal products is a more realistic goal. I am not sure this is a good tactic, as 'reduction' is an elusive concept to quantify, and because I think persuading someone young to become an ethical vegan for life is bound to be more feasible – and they are predisposed to learn new things, have endured fewer years of carnist indoctrination and they may have their natural empathy towards animals still quite intact – and help many more animals. However, I can see the merit in persuading public bodies or institutions to reduce their use of animal products in their catering and food production for a particular amount by a particular date, as long as when the target is achieved the campaign continues until those institutions are persuaded to reduce it 100 per cent. Tobias Leenaert writes in his book *How to Create a Vegan World*:

> I see a reducetarian call to action as complementary to a vegan call to action. I'm not suggesting we *never* ask people to 'Go Vegan'. Nor am I claiming we should never use the word *vegan*, as it is useful and becoming more widely known. What I *do* suggest is we use both 'Go Vegan' and reducetarian messages and select which one to use depending on our audience.

A **pescatarian** is an omnivorous who avoids consuming the meat of mammals and birds but consumes the meat of fish and shellfish. Robbie Marsland, my first director when I worked at IFAW UK – one of the best managers I ever had, as I loved his informal one-to-ones at the Portuguese café in the Vauxhall 'charity building' where we were based – was then a pescatarian, but we never discussed it as he never ate fish in front of me. It seems that the American TV personality Ellen DeGeneres became one too, and Plant Based News reports that in 2018 she said:

> I was vegan for eight years and I really believe that it's great for you. I was healthier than I'd ever been, I loved being vegan. But in the last year or two for no real reason, I started eating a piece of fish once in a while. Or I'll eat eggs from chickens I know – if they are in someone's backyard or are happy.

Many pescatarians may think fish do not suffer as other vertebrates, but they could not be more wrong. All reputable studies show fish are capable of feeling pain as they possess a suitable nervous system and senses: when noxious stimuli are administered physiological changes occur in their bodies, they have opioid receptors which show a reduced response when then given local anaesthetics and analgesics, they display protective motor reactions against danger and they exhibit avoidance learning, and so on. I find it incredible when people see fish violently gasping and thrashing while suffocating out of the water and don't see in this behaviour a clear expression of suffering.

The scale of the harm humans inflict on fish is unprecedented. Between 0.97 and 2.7 trillion fish are estimated to be killed globally every year, without counting those farmed. Two-thirds of the species of fish taken from the wild are 'overfished', and therefore at risk of disappearing altogether. A 2006 global survey in the journal *Science* estimated that if the rate of fishing didn't decrease we could see all sea animals people suffocate to death for food vanish altogether by 2048.

The ridiculous 'they don't suffer' excuse, coupled with the belief eating fish is healthy as they provide omega-3 fatty acids often lacking in modern diets, are the two main excuses of pescatarians. Although it is true fish obtain such healthy fats from eating sea algae (we vegans can get omega-3 directly from the algae), they also accumulate all sorts of toxins that we pour in the oceans (the most notorious of these being mercury, which fish and shellfish concentrate in their bodies in the form of the even more toxic methylmercury).

Farmed fish is even worse. A 2004 global study published by the American Association for the Advancement of Science found the flesh of farmed salmon had thirteen persistent organic pollutants, and European-raised salmon had significantly greater contaminant loads than those raised in America. The authors concluded: 'risk analysis indicates that consumption of farmed Atlantic salmon may pose health risks that detract from the beneficial effects of fish consumption'.

Prof. Spock may class a **flexitarian** (also known as 'semi-vegetarian' or 'flegan') as an omnivorous who may care enough about animal exploitation to often avoid consuming animal products, but not enough to avoid them all the time. Many flexitarians often eat vegetarian and vegan food, but because they don't want to 'ban' any food from their plates they eat animal products (including red meat) occasionally. It is more about adding new foods to your diet as opposed to excluding any. Annabelle Randles writes in her blog The Flexitarian:

> Living in France I never gave much thought to not eating meat. It was just something I and everyone else around me did. Nothing better than a steak to get you back on track. I discovered vegetarianism when I lived abroad. Slowly but surely my attitude towards what I ate evolved. My 'eco' husband was a big influence. I started looking at the issues around animal welfare, modern farming and the impact of

meat on the environment. Today I hardly ever eat meat and I do not miss it. I truly believe that the future of food lies in a plant-based diet. As we all need to change our eating habits, I feel the flexitarian diet is a great solution for many people who do not want to give up meat entirely yet feel that for health, ethics and/or environmental reasons have to eat less of it.

Flexitarians sometimes make a point of being selective about which type of animal product they consume, perhaps being more likely to use 'free-range' eggs, 'high-welfare' meat or 'organic' milk, under the false impression these supposedly more 'humane' versions of animal agriculture have eliminated the suffering of the animals involved. Thanks to the work of many undercover investigations and exposés (such as the 2008 Animal Aid exposé of an RSPCA-approved 'Freedom Food' chicken farm in Somerset, or the 2016 Norfolk's Hillside Animal Sanctuary exposé of 16,000 'free-range' hens crammed into a shed on another RSPCA-approved farm), we now know that the suffering of their animals has not been reduced in any significant way.

Animals on typical organic and 'free-range' farms often spend much of their time confined to crowded sheds or pens, with the only difference to conventional farming being they may not have individual cages for each. They often endure the same cruel mutilations, such as dehorning, debeaking and castration without painkillers. Male chicks from most free-range egg farms will still be killed soon after hatching, and cows in most organic farms will still be artificially impregnated every year as well, and calves taken from their mothers soon after birth. It doesn't matter if you are from a factory farm or a small 'high-welfare' organic farm, the animals will ultimately be taken to the same abattoir, and there they all will receive the same hellish treatment. 'Humane' slaughter doesn't exist anyway, as it all leads to the forced death of all its unwilling victims.

People belonging to any of these omnivorous subgroups may not care at all about animal exploitation but still restrict their diet in the forms described for other reasons (such as health, environment or religion). In fact, most vegans started their life as carnist or omnivorous, and we all remember what it was like – how little we thought about what we were consuming, and how much the status quo seemed immutable.

V

In May 2018, I was already a fully fledged ethical vegan, having been previously omnivorous for at least seven years (technically a flexitarian when I was living at the Monkey Sanctuary, I suppose), and a carnist for the first thirty years of my life (most of them being vegan-ignorant). I was unemployed and unable to pay for the cost of litigation against my former employer, but my ethical beliefs were a strong motivation to keep me going, and gave me a drive towards not giving up.

Luckily, Peter Daly, the solicitor I had approached, suggested a way out of my impasse: crowdfunding. A new company called CrowdJustice.com had been created for crowdfunding legal fees for court cases, and when I contacted them they agreed to help.

On 3 June 2018 I launched my CrowdJustice page. Titled 'Help an Ethical Vegan who was dismissed by an Animal Welfare charity', I chose as a cover photo an image of me holding an anti-hunting banner alongside Joe Hashman, my friend who was supporting me all the way. The response of the vegan community was quite good. A quarter of the initial £5,000 target needed to start proceedings was achieved five hours after launch and the full amount in a month. My 'extended target' to be able to carry on with the case became far more difficult to achieve.

My former employer denied that ethical veganism was a protected philosophical belief under the Equality Act 2010 and demanded a separate pre-hearing for the tribunal to look into this (and – they hoped – dismiss my claim). We accepted the pre-hearing, as we knew it was important to secure the protection of all ethical vegans. On 3 December 2018 the tribunal agreed, and the pre-hearing was set up for 14 and 15 March 2019, in Reading, Berkshire.

Our task now was to gather all the evidence we would need and for me to write my witness statement and prove two things: ethical veganism does fulfil all the conditions necessary to be a protected philosophical belief under the Equality Act, and that I was a person who genuinely held such a belief. We knew the exact conditions a philosophical belief had to fulfil as they had been set up by the Employment Appeals Tribunal in the Grainger plc v Nicholson 2010 case Joe had told me about.

These were the following: the belief must be genuinely held; must be a belief and not an opinion based on presently available information; must be a belief as to a weighty or substantial aspect of human life and behaviour; must have a level of cogency, seriousness, cohesion and importance; and must be worthy of respect in a democratic society as well as being not incompatible with human dignity or in conflict with the rights of others. We produced more than 1,200 pages of evidence to prove this, and sent them to the other side (the 'Respondent') as part of the process called 'disclosure', in which each side sends the other side all the evidence they are planning to use.

I was still unemployed, and when my former employer published a statement about my case in June 2018 as a reaction to my CrowdJustice page, my prospects of finding work decreased. Their statement said I had been fired for gross misconduct, not for the reasons I claimed on my page, but that they could not reveal exactly what the gross misconduct was about. This could have made potential future employers think that I had done something very bad, and that it would be better to wait until litigation finished before they considered offering me a job.

All the information made public about my case polarised the anti-hunting movement, as some sided with me (mostly the Hunt Saboteurs and those anti-hunting campaigners and animal-rights activist who knew me well), while others assumed my former employer must have had a good reason to fire me (perhaps I was one of those annoying pushy vegans) and took their side.

Eventually, the BBC approached me. A crew of four (a producer, a TV cameraman, a social media camerawoman and the legal correspondent Clive Coleman) joined me at a vegan outreach event in Camden called the Cube of Truth. They interviewed me while I was wearing my black beanie with the large word 'Vegan' in white letters across the front. On 3 December 2018, the BBC broadcasted on all its platforms a piece about the vegan angle of my story, beanie and all.

This attracted a great deal of attention from media all over the globe, from China to Canada. With headlines such as 'Vegans demand same legal rights as religions in landmark case to protect themselves from discrimination' (*The Sun*), 'This British man says he was fired for being vegan, which he believes was discrimination' (*Washington Post*) and 'The vegan debate has taken another absurd turn' (*The Spectator*), my story was being discussed at great length and even appeared in topical satirical panel shows such as *Have I Got News for You*. Overnight, I became 'the vegan-rights man', and selfie-hungry mobile phones began flying my way.

People reacted in different ways. Most vegans were very supportive, and my crowdfunding soon surpassed several hundreds of donors. Anti-hunting activists still expressed mixed feelings, some supported me, while others criticised the fact that I was litigating against a group they worked with. The vegan-ignorants scratched their heads. The vegan-deniers laughed at me and dismissed my chances of winning. The veganphobes had a field day posting abuse, branding me 'the moron of the month'.

Not long after the explosion of publicity, the first spanner was cast into the works. A few days before the pre-hearing the Respondent wrote to us saying they now conceded ethical veganism was a protected belief, and there was no longer a need to proceed with the pre-hearing. It was good they conceded that point, but all the hundreds of vegan donors supporting me were hoping I would obtain a written judgement which would effectively seal the protection of all ethical vegans from discrimination, and it seemed I would not be able to do that any longer. I was hugely disappointed, but there was nothing I could do.

However, luck came to my rescue, because the judge from Reading sent a note to both sides effectively stating the concession on the veganism point was not sufficient, and the tribunal still had to look at the issue to assess if ethical veganism was indeed a protected belief. The pre-hearing on the vegan question was back on the table, with the promised written judgement, but it had to be postponed to 17 and 18 October 2019, and it had to be moved to Norwich in Norfolk, as it was the only available court for the dates both sides could make it. Spanner retrieved!

The second spanner landed in the works again a few days before the October pre-hearing, when the judge wrote to both parties stating it had to be postponed again, apparently because there were not enough staff available on the day. I got the news when Peter texted me while I was walking to the Slater and Gordon offices (the new firm he'd moved to) to be interviewed by the online Veggie Channel from Italy. The interview went OK, but I was constantly distracted by thoughts about what the postponement would mean.

After the two-hour interview, I walked to the nearest park, and from Victoria Embankment Gardens I recorded a short piece to camera for social media commenting on how devastated I was. This postponement wasn't good at all for me.

First, delays meant more cost, and I had not managed to secure all my funds for the entire case yet. The Vegan Society donated a considerable amount to, my lawyers to cover the cost of the pre-hearing (where only the issue of the protection of veganism would be discussed) I could not cover with my new CrowdJustice page (when Peter changed legal firms, I had to create a new page – the money raised from the first had already been used), but they could not donate to my full merits hearing (where my full discrimination and whistleblowing case would be heard) set for February 2020.

Second, if we could not find a replacement date for the pre-hearing soon, quite possibly we would have to postpone the full merits hearing too, as there would not be time for the judge to produce the written judgement that would determine whether the discrimination part of my claim was still possible. If we had to postpone the full merits hearing it would be a nightmare, as it would almost be impossible to find other ten available days in 2020, and we might need to move the whole thing to 2021! Since my dismissal in April 2018 I had managed to work for three months at PETA UK as a senior campaigns manager – it was nice to work for a fully vegan organisation for a change – but that was it. If we had to postpone the full merits hearing I would run out of savings and not only not afford my legal fees, but also my rent! That wasn't good.

V

I don't know how useful the Prof. Spock classifications I have been imagining are, but let's carry on with them and look at the subsets of vegetarians (also sometimes referred to as 'veggies'). He could have identified a **typical vegetarian** as a vegetarian who avoids eating any meat (including fish), but who eats other animal products such as eggs or milk, or consumes products from other non-food-related forms of animal exploitation. And a **pre-vegan** as a vegetarian who is transitioning towards veganism and therefore is gradually phasing out the consumption of other animal products.

A **'vegan'** is a vegetarian who may care enough about animal exploitation to at least avoid consuming any animal product as food. I have added the inverted commas to highlight the fact not everyone in this category adheres fully to the definition of veganism by the Vegan Society. A **post-vegan** is a vegetarian who has at least avoided at some point in their life consuming any animal product as food, but who later decided to reintroduce a small number of animal products for any reason (such as believing there was no exploitation in those cases, or the animals in question are not sentient enough).

Let's move to the next level of subcategories:

3. Vegetarians
   a. Typical vegetarians
      i. Lacto-ovo-vegetarians
      ii. Ovo-vegetarians
      iii. Lacto-vegetarians
      iv. Jain vegetarians
   b. Pre-vegans
      i. Pre-dietary-vegans
      ii. Pre-ethical-vegans
   c. 'Vegans'
      i. Dietary vegans
      ii. Ethical vegans
   d. Post-vegans
      i. Ostrovegans
      ii. Backyard-vegans

Lacto-ovo-vegetarians are typical vegetarians who eat both dairy products and eggs – these are the most common vegetarians in the West. Perhaps one of the most well-known lacto-ovo-vegetarians is the former Beatle Sir Paul McCartney, who in a 2013 Huffington Post Blog titled 'My Life as a Vegetarian – Supporting Linda's Legacy' wrote:

> Growing up in Liverpool, I would have thought of a vegetarian as a wimp. We could be a prejudiced bunch at times but I'm not sure people would automatically think like that these days. I've been a vegetarian for a long time now and over the years I've seen how the attitudes have changed around the world, so I'm not surprised when I see new research that shows more and more people are increasingly adopting 'meat free eating'. Even 20 years ago, it could sometimes be difficult to find vegetarian options in good restaurants. Now it's great to see more and more choice with some brilliant creative dishes in restaurants, cafés and supermarkets. There is definitely now an overall greater acceptance of being vegetarian.

Ovo-vegetarians eat eggs but not dairy products, which is more common in countries with no dairy tradition, such as Japan. Jolinda Hackett writes on The Spruce Eats website:

> You might choose an ovo-vegetarian diet for health reasons. One common reason is that you want to be a vegetarian but you are lactose-intolerant or are otherwise allergic to or sensitive to dairy products. You might find it difficult to get enough protein from a strict vegan diet, so you include humanely-produced eggs to supplement your protein needs.

Lacto-vegetarians eat dairy products but not eggs, and these are the most common vegetarians in India. In a *Washington Post* blog, Roger Piantadosi writes:

> Like a few million Hindus and many others who attend less formal Karma-Enders classes, I am a lacto-vegetarian, meaning I consume milk, yogurt, cheese (if it's not curdled with animal rennet, but don't get me started on that) and other dairy products. And I eschew eggs for the same reason I try to avoid having the lives of other edible animals filed away with my account number on them. (Simplified: Milk is produced to feed offspring; eggs are produced to, like, be offspring.)

Devotees of the Hare Krishna movement are also lacto-vegetarian, but they also avoid eating garlic and onion. Chef and author Kurma Dasa explains it on his website Kurma.net:

> According to Ayurveda, India's classic medical science, foods are grouped into three categories – sattvic, rajasic and tamasic – foods in the modes of goodness, passion and ignorance. Onions and garlic, and the other alliaceous plants are classified as rajasic and tamasic, which means that they increase passion and ignorance. Those that subscribe to pure brahmana-style cooking of India, including myself, and Vaishnavas – followers of Lord Vishnu, Rama and Krishna – like to only cook with foods from the sattvic category. These foods include fresh fruits, vegetables and herbs, dairy products, grains and legumes, and so on. Specifically, Vaisnavas do not like to cook with rajasic or tamasic foods because they are unfit to offer to the Deity.

Jain vegetarians eat dairy products too but exclude eggs and underground vegetables (uprooting them not only kills the plant, but also many creatures in the soil), as well as figs (because of their symbiotic relationship with wasps) and aubergines (because it's difficult to ascertain if they have any insects inside). Members of the Jain religion practise other diet restrictions, always based on the concept of *ahimsa* applicable to all living things (including microbes). For instance, honey is forbidden, food items that have started to decay are prohibited, traditionally cooking or eating at night is discouraged because insects are attracted to lamps or fire at night, and they do not consume fermented foods (i.e. beer and wine) to avoid the killing of the yeast.

One of the most well-known Jains in the UK is Satish Kumar, an Indian–British activist and editor. He was initially a Jain monk, became a nuclear disarmament advocate, founded the entirely vegetarian Schumacher College in Totnes – where I once had the privilege to give a talk about British wildlife – and currently is the editor of *Resurgence & Ecologist* magazine. Vegetarian all his life, he once said on resurgence.org:

> A vegetarian diet is a healthy one and that human beings have no need of meat. I'm 72 and have no lack of energy. We should have no fears about nutrition and lack of protein and is concerned that agri-business uses its economic power to perpetuate these myths simply to bolster their profits. ... Vegetarianism is not so reductionist as to be just about what's on our plates – it is a holistic philosophy, a nonviolent way of life and of thinking. And if we do not go vegetarian then the planet will be in peril.

Pre-dietary-vegans and **pre-ethical-vegans** are vegetarians voluntarily transitioning towards becoming dietary or ethical vegans respectively. It is not unusual for typical vegetarians to encounter an outreach team or watch a documentary and realise they should be vegan, but then find it difficult to change habits overnight and decide to make the change gradually. My very dear friend Nicky, a sparkling hobbit-loving woman with a life as colourful as her hairstyle, was working at the Born Free Foundation in my team when I became vegan. She left soon after me and went on to do all sorts of important jobs (NHS nurse, probation officer, registrar, etc.). She was a pre-ethical-vegan for many years, remaining vegetarian 'on her way there' until attaining veganhood in 2014. I recently asked her what kept her from making the final step, and she replied:

> Cheese is the short answer, and now I think how truly terrible it was that I felt like that, but I know many others use the same reason. I had already phased out anything containing gelatine, I hadn't bought eggs or milk for years and had moved on to plant milks for quite a long time when I finally made the break. I'd also not bought leather or products tested on animals for a long time. My sister worked on a dairy farm and she would come home and say how the mothers were crying for their babies when they were taken. It never registered until years later. I'm so ashamed that I did not make the connection sooner.

I totally understand, as I also share the same shame and experienced the same cheesy addiction. You learn you can give up things only when you have tried to. You may be initially scared of giving up something you think you definitively need, but then when you don't use it any longer you realise you didn't need it after all. For most people it takes a few months to learn this, but for some it takes so long it is justifiable to assign them the term pre-vegan, as they seem to linger in the transition unnecessarily. The hesitation to make the big step is what stretches people's transition, and it makes them rationalise that gradual change is better than abrupt change, but this comes from fear and trepidation not from evidence. Baby steps don't always work – sometimes the best way to overcome a big obstacle is to run and jump over it, even if you are uncertain about how solid the ground is that you are going to land on.

In my case, my abrupt jump from an omnivorous diet to veganism was very smooth. I believe this is for four reasons: first, the abrupt change is clearer to the body and mind, which recognises better the new status quo and adapts faster to it (physiologically and psychologically); second, pre-vegans may remove items from their life and replace them with others not good for their health (for instance, the classic new vegetarian overeating cheese to compensate for the absence of meat) and the body doesn't react positively; third, it is easier to forget you decided to change a habit when you make the change gradually, and that might make it more likely you'll fall off the wagon as you'll have a looser sense of compulsion; fourth, if you are aware you are still causing animal suffering, your 'sacrifice' doesn't feel good, it feels insufficient, and therefore you experience losing things but without gaining anything (whereas the jump to ethical veganism feels very good, as you go to bed thinking you have done your best in trying not to hurt anyone today, and for me this constant positive feedback trumps any feeling of loss).

To be honest, I find it difficult to understand how obstinate non-vegan vegetarians who chose vegetarianism for animal welfare reasons decide not to move towards veganism once they have learnt the truth about the dairy and egg industries. How can people, especially women with children, remain indifferent to the plight of the dairy cow? When the calf is born, it is separated from the mother between a few hours and ten days from birth, causing distress to both – they keep calling to each other in vain while they suffer this traumatic experience.

If the calf is male, he will most likely be shot straight away (as he will not grow up to produce milk), or will be kept alone for six months, often being fed an iron-deficient diet to make his flesh paler, and then killed to be sold as veal.

If the calf is a female, she will be allowed to suckle milk from her mother for the first day of her life, but most are then separated from their mothers and fed on commercial milk replacer. She may then be housed in individual stalls until she is eight weeks old, and her horns, and sometimes her tail too, are often removed to reduce injury. After she reaches one year of age, the farmer inserts his or her arm in the cow's rectum to facilitate the insertion of sperm with a device through the vagina – a forced artificial insemination procedure to make the cow pregnant (you may find other words to describe this act). She will give birth to her first calf nine months later, which will also be removed. The new mother may desperately attempt to get to her calf, but most of the time this will be in vain.

As she was born from a genetically modified cow who, through artificial selection, has unnaturally big udders producing an unnatural amount of milk, she will inherit these deformities and suffer distress because of them. While she is still lactating and her milk stolen, she will be impregnated again, and most will spend about seven months of the year simultaneously lactating and being pregnant, which causes their bodies a lot of stress. Hormones may be administered to them to synchronise better the pregnancies and to make them more efficient milk-producing machines.

The cows will spend about six months of the year indoors (often in disease-brewing conditions), if not more – some will be kept captive indoors for life. The whole thing will be repeated four or five times, and then the cow will be sent to the slaughterhouse and killed. This happens when she is about four to six years old, when her body cannot take this torture any longer and the milk production decreases. A free cow can live well up to twenty years of age, and their premature deaths happen when they are young, at an age equivalent to twenty if they were women. People have been doing this to cattle for hundreds of years.

Some people care about the cow's plight, but not about the suffering of other animals, and some of them are post-vegans. When vegans have 'reconsidered' their veganism and decided they would no longer adhere to the full definition because they no longer want to avoid a particular type of exploitation (one particular practice, or any exploitation of one particular animal), they became **post-vegans**. We already met the **ostrovegans** in chapter 2, who are the post-vegans eating some bivalves (mussels and oysters) because they consider they are not sentient beings. I have met two, Nathan, a colleague from IFAW headquarters in the US, and Diana Fleischman, an American evolutionary psychologist and senior lecturer at the University of Portsmouth. Fleischman wrote in her blog dianaverse.com:

> In May of 2008 I became vegan or ... well, ostrovegan. In this blog I officially come out of the closet, err, shell. I am almost sure that cultivated mussels and oysters are ethical to eat. I argue eating these animals is completely consistent with the spirit if not the letter of ethical veganism and the tenet of causing less harm with our consumer choices.

An interesting group is what Prof. Spock could call **backyard-vegans**, post-vegans who started consuming some animal products because they obtained them in low numbers in their backyards from sources supposedly no longer connected with the animal agriculture industries (such as using wool from rescued backyard sheep, non-commercial beekeeping or eating roadkill). These technically ex-vegans may consider they are still vegan even if they consume the occasional animal products under their 'exception' justifications, but most vegans – including me – object to this. The epitome of this type would be **'beegans'**, post-vegans who keep bees and consume their honey, and **'veggans'** (double 'g'), post-vegans who started eating eggs produced by hens (sometimes rescued) in their backyards, claiming that otherwise they would be wasted. Candice writes in her blog theedgyveg.com:

> I am not technically a VEGAN, I am a BEEGAN – a vegan that uses or consumes honey. I am not one for labels, but most of you are so here I am, labelling myself once again. I believe in the power of bees and their honey. I have had many health issues in the past that were healed by its natural occurring antibiotics and I will continue to use it to keep my body strong. I am open to all opinions, and this just happens to be mine.

In 2016 the LA-based Reiki master veggan Kristin Deiss is quoted in a CNN Health article saying this about eating eggs: 'I just like the taste of them. I'll make the exception when I know it's from a company or person that takes care of their animals.'

If we aim to ultimately achieve a compassionate world, allowing this consumption would be, tactically, the wrong message to send. In the case of eggs, it is wrong because it says that eggs from other animals are legitimate food humans can sometimes consume. It is wrong because it ignores how the industry promoting this idea shreds millions of live male chicks to death and genetically modifies hens to produce between 300 and 500 eggs a year rather than 20, as their wild counterparts lay. It is also wrong as it supports something fundamentally unethical for convenience – stealing an egg from a hen whose instinct is to protect it, as she doesn't know if it is fertile or not. It is also wrong because taking the eggs induces the hen to produce more eggs, causing her physiological stress due to the demand of calcium (on top of the psychological stress of having her egg stolen). It is also wrong as the message says eating cholesterol-filled eggs is a healthy food for human consumption (a medium-sized egg contains 186 mg of cholesterol, 62 per cent of the recommended maximum daily allowance). It is also wrong for giving entitlement to those who free 'prisoners' to then benefit from them and their work. It is so wrong that this is the message you would expect carnists would use in their propaganda, not the message of someone claiming to be 'vegan'.

Finally, we now can move to the subcategories within veganism. Despite the fact some vegans say their type is the only type, I believe there are many kinds (as I would expect from a growing movement). Whether or not you agree about how many subsets of vegans there are and how they should all be named, Prof. Spock could have arrived at the following classification based on how vegans behave (rather than how they identify themselves):

    c.   'Vegans'
        i.   Dietary vegans
           a.   Health vegans
               i.   Raw vegans
               ii.   Wholefood vegans (WFPB)
               iii.   High-carb-low-fat vegans (HCLF)
               iv.   Macrobiotic vegans
           b.   Junk-food vegans
        ii.   Ethical vegans
           a.   Animal-rights vegans
           b.   Ecovegans

    c.   Religious vegans

    d.   Intersectional vegans

    e.   Ethical fruitarians

    f.   Straight edge vegans (abstinent vegans)

A **dietary vegan** (a.k.a. **strict vegetarian**) is a vegetarian who avoids consuming any animal product as food but does not avoid other forms of animal exploitation. Most dietary vegans may have a plant-based diet only for health reasons, and not for any ethical considerations concerning animals or the environment, and when that is the case they are also sometimes called **health vegans.**

The number of this type of vegan has increased over time as the evidence most vegan diets are healthier than other diets has also increased. A 2019 study by Fayth L. Miles et al., published in *The Journal of Nutrition*, found that of 840 people following five different diets (vegans, vegetarians, pescatarians, flexitarians and meat-eaters) consumers with a high intake of fruit and vegetables had more carotenoids in their bodies (an antioxidant indicator of good health), and the vegan participants showing the highest level. They also had the highest levels of other indicators of good health, such as anti-carcinogenic enterolactone and omega-3 fatty acids (interestingly, the levels in flexitarians were not too different from those in meat-eaters).

This surge of people choosing vegan diets for health reasons may also be explained by more eminent physicians now publicly advocating plant-based diets. Two of the most well known are Dr Neal Barnard, who founded the Physicians Committee for Responsible Medicine in Washington DC in 1985, and Dr Dean Ornish, founder of the Preventive Medicine Research Institute based in California. Other very influential doctors are Dr Joel Kahn, Dr Brooke Goldner, Dr Kim Williams, Dr Michelle McMacken, Dr Ellsworth Wareham, Dr Milton Mills, and others I will mention later when talking about specific vegan diets.

It has become increasingly common for athletes and competitive sportspeople to become dietary vegans or at least follow a plant-based diet while training. Scott Jurek, an ultramarathoner, has been competing on a plant-based diet since 1999. The top tennis players Venus and Serena Williams also follow this diet, beginning after Venus was diagnosed with an incurable autoimmune disease called Sjogren's syndrome in 2011. The nine Olympic gold medal winner Carl Lewis credits his 1991 result in the 100 metres sprint at the world championships to the vegan diet he adopted in 1990. Novak Djokovic, considered one of the world's best male tennis players, is so committed to his plant-based diet that he opened a vegan restaurant in Monte Carlo in 2016.

Many of these health vegans prefer not to use the word 'vegan' and say only they follow a plant-based diet – an incomplete description as fungi are also an important part of their food. However, many dietary vegans refer to themselves as 'vegan' even if they don't follow to the full the definition of the Vegan Society, which has caused criticism from other vegans who do follow the definition and object to the term being used by those who don't (ultimately leading to the need to add the adjective 'ethical' to differentiate them). It's not uncommon to hear arguments starting with 'you are not vegan, you are just plant-based'.

Lindsay S. Nixon (a.k.a. Happy Herbivore) posted a blog titled 'Vegans For Health Are Still Vegans' in which she says:

> Just as the vegan community was starting to heal from the ex-vegan manifestos (claiming vegan diets made them sick) a number of vegans took to twitter and their blogs to berate anyone who is a 'vegan for health' and go so far as to suggest you're doing a disservice to veganism if you 'convert' people based on health claims rather than animal rights.

In an interview in *The Vegan Review*, the Londoner Paulina Utnik said:

> I like saying I am plant-based because it's an easy way to generalise my eating habits without defining myself as a core member of a community. I find that as soon as you make a statement of being vegetarian or vegan, you're placed under a microscope. I do not consume any direct animal products and try to stay away from processed goods such as things in plastic or ready meals.

The tennis player Novak Djokovic doesn't call himself 'vegan', and totallyveganbuzz.com reports that in 2019, after winning the Wimbledon tournament, he stated to the press:

> I don't like the labels, to be honest. I do eat plant-based, for quite a few years already, but because of the misinterpretations of labels and misuse of labels, I just don't like that kind of name. I do eat plant-based. I think that's one of the reasons why I recover well. I don't have allergies that I used to have any more. And I like it.

The subcategories within dietary vegans vary depending on which food they eat, rather than which food they avoid. **Raw vegans** eat mostly a plant-based diet where at least 75 per cent of food has not been heated to temperatures above 48°C. This diet is rich in fruit, vegetables, nuts, seeds, sprouted grains and legumes, and is low in processed foods. The reasoning behind this diet is the claim that high temperatures eliminate some of the key nutrients, including vitamins and enzymes. Presbyterian minister and dietary reformer Sylvester Graham pioneered this idea in the

19th century and the world's first known raw vegan (or 'Graham diet') restaurant was opened in 1918 in Los Angeles by John and Vera Richter. The Oscar-nominated actor Woody Harrelson has been raw for over thirty years. He said in an interview with *InStyle*:

> I eat vegan, but I mostly eat raw. If I have a cooked meal, I feel my energy drop. So when I first started shifting my diet, it wasn't as much a moral or an ethical pursuit but an energetic pursuit.

A **wholefood vegan (WFPB)** is a dietary vegan who mainly eats unprocessed and unrefined vegan food (such as whole grains, legumes, berries, seeds, nuts, fruits, greens, colourful vegetables, etc.), and is the diet suggested by prominent vegan physicians and scientists such as Dr Michael Greger (author of the influential 2015 book *How Not to Die*, and his popular evidence-based website NutritionFacts.org), Dr T. Colin Campbell (who coined the term WFPB, whole-food plant-based, and who wrote with his son Thomas M. Campbell II the influential 2005 book *The China Study*), and Dr Michael Klaper (who for forty years has helped thousands of people on their journey to reclaim health through proper nutrition and a balanced lifestyle). Dr T. Colin Campbell said in a 1440 Multiversity interview:

> Whole means we eat the food whole. Instead of taking a vitamin C supplement or drinking orange juice, eat the orange. We choose vegetables, fruits, nuts, legumes, and whole grains. Oil in food like nuts, avocado, and coconut are fine when left in the food, but avoid using it if it's been extracted from the food. In that case it's calorie-dense and nutrient-poor and is a plant fragment, as opposed to a whole food.

The WFPB diet (which some refer to as 'plant-based vegan' diet for short, not to be confused with a 'plant-based person') is credited with preventing – and often reversing – the most common diseases of the modern Western world, such as cardiovascular diseases (high blood pressure, heart attacks, etc.), obesity and type 2 diabetes. We know why. Not only is it a cholesterol-free diet that is rich in vitamins (although it requires vitamin B12 supplementation, like any other vegan diet), but it is also high in fibre, antioxidants and helpful phytochemicals, which help the digestive and circulatory systems (or at least this is what leading scientists say). It is also a very accessible, diverse and filling diet, with fewer restrictions than others, which explains why it is so popular among vegans who care about their health. Dr Greger stated in an interview with *Vegan Food and Living*:

> The reversal of heart disease is by far the biggest nutritional finding linking lifestyle to health. It's the USA's number-one killer and the UK's number two. Since it was researched in 1990, no one needs to die or be diagnosed with it! But yet hundreds of thousands of people continue to do so from a preventable disease.

Because for me it makes no sense to exclude oneself in 'doing no harm' (as I am also a sentient being who is as deserving of a good healthy life as any) I have been trying to follow this dietary approach in the last eight years or so. During my first ten years of veganism, I did not pay much attention to my health. I was eating all sorts of vegan junk food (chips, vegan cheese, fake meats, white bread, chocolate, etc.), and getting too fat in the process. I thought it would be better to move towards the WFPB diet (with the occasional junk-food treat) and stop drinking alcohol or adding salt when I cooked. That was a good move, as I became much more energetic and healthier, and I discovered all sorts of new exciting dishes to play with. This culminated with my attempt to grow in my yard my vegetables in the veganic way, which I thoroughly enjoy.

There are other 'health-oriented' vegan diets out there, though. A **high-carb-low-fat vegan** (HCLF) is a dietary vegan who, as the name suggests, has a diet high in carbohydrates and low in fats. This diet is supported by the physicians Dr John McDougall and Dr Caldwell Esselstyn. One of the supposed benefits of this diet is experiencing less hunger, which can lead to greater weight loss compared to other diets, and better control of diabetes, insulin resistance and blood pressure. This diet has been prescribed by some doctors as a treatment for several chronic disorders, including arthritis, atherosclerosis, some cancers, diabetes, hypertension and osteoporosis. It has become quite fashionable among people who want to lose weight, and many vegans are experimenting with it (especially the part about removing oils from food). Dr McDougall stated in an interview with Vegan Richa:

> People are starch-eaters or 'starchivores'. We are not designed to live well off of meat, dairy and other animal products. Meat is for carnivores (cats), and dairy is the ideal for a young calf. These wrong foods consumed in usual quantities make people fat and sick ... Nuts and seeds are about 80 per cent fat. The fat you eat is the fat you wear. These are often the very rich foods that are the downfall for many fat vegans. Too much fruit can mean too much simple sugar for some people. I recommend about 3 fruits a day.

Other vegan diets take it to another level. A **macrobiotic vegan** takes a less scientific approach, as they follow a macrobiotic diet (based on Japanese Zen Buddhism) but removing all animal products from it. Macrobiotics emphasises locally grown whole grain cereals, legumes, vegetables, edible seaweed, fermented soy products and fruit combined into meals according to the ancient Chinese principle of Yin and Yang. It avoids sugar, refined oils, fruit juice, coffee, alcohol, white flour, white rice and all food additives/preservatives. It also prescribes how the food should be eaten: only eating when hungry and only drinking when thirsty; chewing food thoroughly until it liquefies before swallowing; only using natural materials such as wood, glass and china to cook and store food; avoiding microwave ovens and electric hobs; and purifying water before cooking with it or drinking it.

Because this involves eating locally grown food in season and consuming meals in moderation, this is not only a health-oriented diet but also environmentally sound. This diet was popularised by Japanese George Ohsawa in the 1930s and subsequently developed by his disciple Michio Kush, although some small amounts of animal products such as fish were included (so, macrobiotics as such is a type of pescatarian diet). Doubts about whether it is healthy enough due to being too restrictive have pushed it out of fashion, but it is reported the singer Ariana Grande is a macrobiotic vegan. Bill Tara, a pioneer in the modern macrobiotic movement in both America and Europe, writes on the Macrobiotic Association website:

> Leaving animal products out of the diet is completely congruent with our philosophy. If making balance with nature is a goal of our practice, killing sentient creatures simply for our pleasure or to fulfil an imagined tradition is a great mistake. Ohsawa and Kushi both claimed that eating a diet with no animal products was the best way to achieve mental and spiritual health.

At the other end of the spectrum, a **junk-food vegan** eats lots of processed, refined and high-calorie food (such as vegan burgers, cheese and cakes), almost as a reaction against the 'health freaks' fad, but also for 'comfort'. These are the only dietary vegans who have not chosen a particular diet for health reasons. Despite the fact even they do not consume any cholesterol in their diet, they do consume a high proportion of plant-based saturated fats (palm oil, coconut oil, margarine), as well as sugar, salt, and many preservatives and additives. Therefore they are not exempted from the health problems found in the omnivorous population. When I asked members of the Facebook group 'London Drooling Vegans' if anyone identified as junk-food vegan, Sam Lindsay replied:

> I would only describe myself as a junk-food vegan in an oppositional sense. I don't affirmatively consider myself that, but would articulate it to differentiate myself from 'health vegans'. The motive to do so is twofold. Firstly, because my veganism is not contingent on its health benefits. Not only is it not my key reason for being vegan, but I would be vegan even if it was unhealthy to be so. I think emphasising this illustrates the importance of ethical considerations, or environmental. Secondly, to dispel the stereotype that vegans are naturally preoccupied with healthy eating. I find this detrimental as it can lead to the impression that veganism is a health fad, or to the assumption that vegans are healthy by default, or to the provision of 'healthy' food for vegans that I do not enjoy.

We can move away from 'food' now. As we have seen in chapter 3, an **ethical vegan** is a vegetarian who fully follows the definition of veganism of the Vegan Society, and therefore is a 'true vegan' as they avoid all forms of animal exploitation and cruelty. However, different types of ethical vegans hold the belief for different reasons (which are not mutually exclusive).

An **animal-rights vegan** is the typical ethical vegan, avoiding all animal exploitation mainly for *ahimsa* reasons, and therefore believing all animals have the right to not be exploited. They often share the philosophies of animal rights and abolitionism, but this does not mean all those who follow these beliefs are also vegan, as some may have become 'non-vegan-vegans' and may no longer identify as vegan.

My friend Kim Stallwood, a decade older than me and with whom I share hair and beard style but perhaps not his somewhat dour expression (which may explain why he chose 'The Grumpy Vegan' as the title of his blog even though he is a very kind and compassionate human being), could be a good example of an animal-rights vegan. His pedigree is impressive. Vegan since 1976, he started his career as the national organiser for Compassion in World Farming in the UK, then he became the campaigns officer for the British Union for the Abolition of Vivisection until 1985, then the national director of PETA in the US from 1987 to 1992, and later he was one of the founders of the animal-rights think tank Animal Rights Network, now called the Animals and Society Institute. In his 2014 book *Growl: Life Lessons, Hard Truths, and Bold Strategies from an Animal Advocate* he wrote:

> Compassionate veganism can inspire others to follow a lifestyle where self-knowledge and deep concern for others are united in not only what we eat or wear, but in what we say, think, and do. That's why the thoughts we have, the words we speak, and the way we behave are as important as the food we eat and the products and services we use.

An **ecovegan** (Prof. Spock's term) would avoid all animal exploitation mainly for environmental reasons, and many new vegans today started their journey into veganism from this perspective. Known ecovegans are Roger Hallam, co-founder of Extinction Rebellion and vegan for more than thirty years; Greta Thunberg, the young Swedish environmentalist who also persuaded her parents to go vegan; and Paul Watson, captain of the *Sea Shepherd*, which successfully sabotages whaling operations, with an all-vegan crew since 2002. Watson wrote in the *Huffington Post* in 2016 the following:

> I instituted a policy of vegetarianism in 1978 when we outfitted our first ship. We changed that policy in 1998 when the ships converted to veganism ... A person has to be in wilful denial to not see the connections and the reality is that you can't really be a credible environmentalist if you consume products from the animal agriculture industry ... Animal agriculture is the largest source of groundwater pollution and dead zones in the Ocean.

As discussed in the previous chapter, most ethical vegans – including me – are vegan both for the animals and for the environment.

A **religious vegan** is an ethical vegan who avoids all animal exploitation mainly for religious or spiritual reasons, and the best example would be a **Jain vegan** (someone going beyond Jain vegetarianism by avoiding consuming dairy products to adhere better to the concept of *ahimsa*). The vegan movement within the Jain community started in the US and the UK but is gradually spreading in India where six million of the eight million Jains live. Within Jainism, the 11,000 monks and nuns go further than anyone else in applying the main principles of the religion. They only possess four objects: their simple clothes, a bowl for eating, a stand for books and a brush to brush away insects while they walk, to avoid accidentally stepping on them (their only method of transportation is to walk).

My New Zealand friend Lucy Verde Roze (slim, nimble, with a fresh hippy look and very smiley eyes) could be a good example of a spiritual vegan, embracing what are commonly known as 'New Age' philosophies, rather than established religions. She has been living a nomadic life for some time now, moving from country to country, and she runs Paradise Rizing, a group of heart-centred vegan artists who 'through self-love, self-expression & self-liberation amplify animal voices & support humans to create conscious change for all beings.' When I asked her about the spiritual side of her veganism, she said:

> I used to say that my first Vipassana meditation retreat saved my life and going vegan shortly afterwards gave me a second chance. Now I know they were steps of free-will along my soul's ever-evolving path. The connections with animals' rights started forming after watching *Earthlings*. I was already vegetarian, having spent time with Hare Krishnas, but had no idea about the cruelty involved in dairy, or eggs, or honey. Once I was aware of it I couldn't turn away. Once I woke up to the spiritual power we all have, I couldn't ignore that either. I began the journey of internal exploration to understand the Universe, my place in it, and how I could help as many beings as possible. It all comes back to love. The core of Vipassana as one spiritual or self-care tool is about moving ourselves out of suffering for greater self-love, and by extension, love for the All. A loving and kind world doesn't cultivate unnecessary suffering for anyone. The world we are co-creating as the old

paradigm crumbles is of a very different frequency, and the energy I want to take with me is one of freedom.

Intersectional vegans are one of the most interesting relatively new additions to the vegan family (although the concept has been around for quite some time, but without the name). They come from an ethical angle which could substantially increase the number of people subscribing to the vegan philosophy from more diverse backgrounds. Intersectionality is a theoretical framework for understanding how aspects of social and political identities (race, gender, sexuality, class, ability, etc.) might combine to create unique modes of discrimination. It was initially used in the context of feminism to highlight how other factors (such as race or sexuality) may intersection with it, and was first coined in 1989 by Kimberlé Crenshaw, a civil rights activist and legal scholar, in a paper for the *University of Chicago Legal Forum* titled 'Demarginalizing the Intersection of Race and Sex: A Black Feminist Critique of Antidiscrimination Doctrine, Feminist Theory and Antiracist Politics'. She wrote:

> Because the intersectional experience is greater than the sum of racism and sexism, any analysis that does not take intersectionality into account cannot sufficiently address the particular manner in which Black women are subordinated.

Intersectionals believe sexism, racism, homophobia, ableism, classism, etc., interconnect through what is known as 'the matrix of domination', which will never be dismantled by addressing all these issues separately.

As you should not ignore the intersection between racism and sexism, you should not ignore the intersection between speciesism and any other cause of discrimination, prejudice and oppression. Therefore, an **intersectional vegan** is an ethical vegan who avoids all animal exploitation mainly for the social justice reason of all animals being the victims of oppression, which is as important as the oppression of humans. For an intersectional vegan, fighting for the rights of marginalised groups of humans and fighting for the rights of animals are fights that intersect, and therefore it is consistent to fight them together.

Through history we can find many people with an intersectional approach, such as the vegetarians of the French Revolution, the anti-slavery William Wilberforce MP and the 19th-century anti-vivisection pioneers. Some current prominent intersectional vegans are Marti Kheel, who in 1982 founded Feminists for Animal Rights and who authored *Nature Ethics: An Ecofeminist Perspective*; the feminist-vegan advocate Carol J. Adams, author of the influential 1990 book *The Sexual Politics of Meat: A Feminist-Vegetarian Critical Theory*; Angela Davis, author of the 1981 book *Women, Race & Class*; Aph Ko, anti-racist activist and founder of Black Vegans Rock; Dr Breeze Harper, author of the 2010 anthology *Sistah Vegan: Black Female Vegans Speak on Food, Identity, Health and Society*; and the animal-rights activist Mark Hawthorne, author of the 2016 book *A Vegan Ethic: Embracing A Life Of Compassion Toward All*.

Becoming vegan for intersectional reasons is also an ethical approach which combines *ahimsa* (in this case applying the 'do no harm' to marginalised humans as well as animals) and social justice (the fair distribution of wealth, opportunities and privileges within a society), in which all non-human animals could be considered a wider part of the earthlings' society. Therefore, in addition to religion, health, animal rights and the environment, social justice has now become another gateway into veganism.

Different intersectional vegans would approach the issue differently depending on which intersections they focus on the most. For instance, Carol J. Adam's wrote on her website caroljadams.com:

> I coined the term feminized protein for eggs and dairy products: plant protein produced through the abuse of the reproductive cycle of female animals. Feminized protein is taken from living female animals, whose reproductive capacity is manipulated for human needs. The unique situation of domesticated female animals required its own term: a sexual slavery with chickens in battery cages and dairy cows hooked up to milking machines. Even though the animals are alive, dairy products and eggs are not victimless foods. This is why vegan-feminist rather than vegetarian-feminist.

Angela Davis wrote in the Vegans of Color blog:

> I think there is a connection between, and I can't go further than this, the way we treat animals and the way we treat people who are at the bottom of the hierarchy. Look at the ways in which people who commit such violence on other human beings have often learned how to enjoy that by enacting violence on animals. So there are a lot of ways we can talk about this.

An interesting philosophical tenet of intersectional veganism is the belief the subjugation of animals is inextricably linked to the subjugation of other humans, and one cannot be solved without advocating against the other. However, this approach is also the source of controversy within the vegan movement as it suggests a vegan revolution not embracing intersectionality will fail. Some vegans have become anti-intersectionals as they don't like seeing the focus of attention being removed from the animals, and they see the most vocal militant intersectionals as too divisive and disruptive. In turn, some intersectional vegans have become anti-mainstream-veganism, because they see it as led by the dominating oppressive demographics (mostly, privileged heterosexual able cisgender white men), and they see it as far too tolerant of oppressive voices and inequality.

Many vegans have been left confused in the crossfire between these two, not quite understanding what intersectionality is really about, and tending to lean towards the position of whoever is closest to them. It did not help either when some intersectionals, or people who are assumed to be but may be only fighting for their human causes, attacked veganism by saying it is classist and not everyone can follow this philosophy. It does not help either some vegans branding as 'intersectionals' (almost as a slur word) anyone they don't like who happens to fight for feminism, human rights, gay rights or similar (sometimes, ironically, even 'vegans' rights'), regardless of whether they truly follow an intersectional approach.

In any event, intersectionality has opened an interesting debate and has allowed many people to become vegan when in the past they might have felt they could never belong to the vegan community because they were the 'wrong type of human'. Intersectionality is a good antidote against unintended speciesism by reminding everyone discrimination against humans, in general, is also a form of speciesism, and the 'do no harm' of *ahimsa* is not restricted to non-human animals.

The intersectional approach may sometimes complicate things, and, in many respects, it may still be finding its feet with many vegans (and organisations) who have begun considering it, but once embraced I think it will be acknowledged as a fundamentally healthy approach for the vegan movement. It can encourage you to reflect on your actions (not all products labelled as 'vegan' may end up being 'cruelty free' if they are the direct fruit of the oppression of marginalised groups), it can expand your understanding about how others see the world (people from colonised nations or who have been victims of sexual assault may have a very different way of interpreting servitude or violence), it can help you to untangle all the causes you are already fighting for (animal rights and human rights), it can address some of your remaining cognitive dissonances and blind-spot biases (humans are sentient beings too), it can facilitate the debunking of unhelpful myths (remember 'alpha males'?), it can help to resolve identity conflicts (being vegan doesn't prevent you from being Muslim or transgender, for instance), and it can open veganism up to new cultures and demographics.

My Australian friend Sean O'Callaghan, a pre-Instagram vegan influencer who used to organise very successful vegan potlucks in London before he moved to Mexico, wrote in his book *Fat Gay Vegan: Eat, Drink and Live like you Give a Sh!t*:

> Once of my favourite throwaway lines that I love to bandy about is 'people don't need to limit their acts of compassion to just one area of caring'. You can be all about the animals AND want to resist other forms of oppression such as racism, homophobia, sexism, transphobia, wealth disparity, ableism, colonialism and body shaming.

For what it's worth, as an atheist conscientious objector immigrant of Catalan origin, I consider myself a non-militant intersectional vegan, but as I am also a cisgender heterosexual able middle-aged white man aware of my many privileges, I would gladly relinquish this label if those who may better represent intersectionalism thought I should do so.

V

One can be both the oppressed and the oppressor at the same time, and live a Jekyll and Hyde existence not easy to negotiate. No better example of this can be found than the life of the undercover investigator. In 2006 I travelled to South America to investigate the bullfighting industry and meet with the local anti-bullfighting groups, and part of my job was pretending to be a bullfighting aficionado. By then I was a professional investigator and I knew the techniques well. My speciality was what I call 'shallow cover' operations. In 'deep cover' operations you have to spend years in character before you can produce useful information for your handler, and it involves serious 'method' acting and sophisticated persuasion skills. In 'shallow cover', on the other hand, you go in and out very quickly and rely more on misdirection techniques (such as being able to video record with a camera without looking at the viewer) and nerve. In both styles, though, one skill is essential: the ability to hide your emotions.

The anti-bullfighting movement needed more footage of what happens to the bulls, as what was shown on TV was always sanitised. It glamorised the spectacle by focusing on the 'brave' bullfighters, not the suffering animals. Activists had to attend bullfights and record in detail the abuse the bulls endured, but this was tricky as anyone overtly pointing a camera at the bull being mutilated on the floor when still alive, rather than at the matador parading his prowess with his triumphant walk, would be immediately exposed to the violence of an angry mob. They needed someone with the skills to be able to record under pressure the ordeal of the agonising bull while looking as if he was cheering the matador like everyone else, and I knew I could do that. When I offered my services to the local anti-bullfighting groups many welcomed my offer, so I went from country to country doing this.

It wasn't easy, though. Every time I did it, I returned to my base with a particular part of my body hurting. Every time I did it, I had to prepare myself psychologically before and after to keep my sanity. Every time I did it, I lost a big chunk of my soul.

One of the worst times was 5 November 2006. I was in Lima, the noisy capital of Peru – where drivers are constantly using their car horns to the annoyance of foreign pedestrians – and my objective was to obtain the most graphic footage I could of the bullfight at the Plaza de Toros de Acho scheduled for that afternoon. It would used for a meeting the local activists had planned with some politicians to persuade them to initiate legislative steps towards a ban. I bought the ticket for $50, I ensured that there was nothing in my look that suggested I was from the UK, and I prepared my mental exercises in which I repeatedly told myself that everything would be fine, that paying for these tickets was justified in this case and that if the bulls could have been consulted, they would want me there.

When the time arrived, I entered the bullring and I found my seat (shade area, mid-row, which I specifically selected to have the best view of the bulls, not the matadors). I began talking to people around me, to blend in, pretending to be a Spanish aficionado, a role I could play well with my accent. People bought it, so things were going well. Then, the first of the six bulls condemned to be tortured for twenty minutes and executed entered the arena, and I did my job.

Three matadors – two Spanish and one Peruvian – and their team of three or four assistant bullfighters would be the day's executioners, and the sweaty spectators, children and all, would be the sentencing judges endorsed by the authorities. Still cheering with everyone else, behaving like everyone around me, I was managing to zoom in on the bulls' agony. The lance repeatedly stabbed in their bodies, making a big hole aimed to increase blood loss; the barbed harpoons stabbed in their backs and tearing their flesh every time they turned; the swards piercing their lungs, their livers, their hearts; the daggers stabbed in their necks, cutting their brains; the ears being cut off when the animal was still alive and kicking. I was getting all this, while smiling on the outside and mentally talking to every bull dying in agony, letting them know that today they did not die alone; that it would not be long and all would be over; that they had one friend among the crowd who was witnessing their calvary, and would tell the world what happened to them.

Limeño, the sixth bull, was the most difficult to watch. He was white, so the blood was more visible. The matador, a young Spaniard, was terrible, so when he tried to kill him with the sword he kept stabbing the wrong part, and he had to do it again and again. By his seventh failed attempt, Limeño was no longer white. He was now entirely red.

I left the bullring with everything recorded – three days later we delivered 160 DVDs with the footage to all Peru's Congresspeople – and I took a bus to my hotel, in the Lince district. On my way there through the traffic-clogged streets, I did what I always do. I mentally recited the names of each of the bulls, to honour their memory. Arquipeño, Sonambulo, Celoso, Castellano, Cuzqueño … and when it was Limeño's turn I couldn't contain my emotions anymore, and I started to cry. I spent the evening sobbing in my room, with a painful jaw. A jaw which had smiled against my will for several hours, to match the jaws of hundreds of blind people submerged in an orgy of violence. An orgy I had bought a ticket to attend.

V

It doesn't matter how you get to become compassionate. Animals, environment, social justice, religion and health are all gateways into ethical veganism, and, in my experience, if you start with any of the first four you most likely will end up being an ethical vegan embracing at least the first three. It may take some time, and you may always keep one as your 'main' reason, but if you care about others, whether others are the animals, the planet or human victims of oppression, you will eventually embrace them all. However, if you only care about yourself, if you used the fifth gateway but look nowhere else other than your reflection in your portable magic mirror, or if you seek some sort of personal 'purity' growth, you may fall short of ethical veganism and only stay as a 'health vegan' forever – in the current 'selfie-Instagram-TikTok' era this is bound to happen quite often.

Yet some vegans go even further when trying to expand their circle of respect to 'others'. A **fruitarian** is a vegan who mainly eats fruits and avoids roots, tubers, stems and leaves. In this context, the term 'fruit' means any botanical fruit (the seed-bearing structure in flowering plants), therefore including some vegetables which are technically fruits (i.e. courgettes, bell peppers, tomatoes, bean pods, etc.). The term 'fruitarian' had already been used from the end of the 19th century as synonymous with what we call today 'vegan' (but linked to the Christian belief of returning to the 'utopian' past of Eden), and in the US is today often used as synonymous with 'raw vegan'.

Fruitarians have not agreed on the exact definition of fruitarianism. Some fruitarians don't eat nuts, while some eat nuts as well as seeds. It is reported others will eat only what would fall naturally from a plant, and the plant is harvested without killing it or harming it (although some fruitarians say it is a myth that anyone does this).

Raw vegans and fruitarians cross over, but for me if the main motivation is health I would describe them as raw vegans (even if they may call themselves fruitarians), while if it is ethics then I would call them **ethical fruitarians**. These go beyond the avoidance of exploitation and cruelty to animals into the avoidance of killing any living being. The ethical beliefs of most ethical fruitarians do not necessarily equate to believing plants are sentient and 'suffer' when cut or are uprooted, but rather that they die when we harvest them, and we should avoid the 'harm' caused by their death.

It is reported some fruitarians believe they should eat only plants that naturally spread seeds when the plant is eaten and then defecated. It makes sense to me. Many plants have co-evolved with animals to do this. Some of these co-evolutionary mutualistic relationships may have happened between primates and plants which produce succulent fruits with the right colours and smells – biologist call these traits 'fruit syndromes'.

It is interesting to note that fruitarianism advocates for a human diet closest to what our biology has evolved to be, as it is the diet frugivorous species eat, and strong evidence suggests the human species is anatomically, physiologically and even psychologically frugivore (as our ability to identify and eat edible fruits is quite instinctive, which cannot be said of eating animals or even roots).

The fruitarian author Mango Wodzak writes on fruit-powered. com:

> Unlike most other raw vegans, myself and my partner, Kveta Martinec, have made it a life choice to stick with eating purely fruit. We don't consider ourselves 80/10/10 or low-fat raw vegan as, to the best of our understanding, a calorie is just hot air that should have no part in anyone's diet. We don't obsess over carbohydrates, fats and sugars but instead enjoy eating our fruit, eating when hungry and stopping when full. The real challenge in transitioning to such a diet lies in understanding addiction. The more we ignore it, the less it will chatter. We believe that this world can and will eventually re-embrace the concept of Eden, a place where no harm is done, where

symbiosis has replaced all forms of exploitation and suffering is no more.

Steve Jobs, founder of Apple Inc., and even Mahatma Gandhi tried a fruitarian diet for a while, and the nuns of the Order of St Elizabeth of Hungary, founded in South London in 1916, followed a fruitarian diet as well. From a health point of view, fruitarianism can be a more restrictive diet than raw veganism, and I guess if it is not done carefully and responsibly it may not provide a sufficiently nutritious diet – although bonobos, our closest primate relatives, are almost entirely frugivores, and they are doing well. The perception of being 'more difficult' must be why finding a 100 per cent fruitarian is rare – I don't think I have ever met one – and perhaps ethical fruitarians are more aspirational than real. Personally, the lack of agreed definition and my uncertainty about how feasible a healthy fruitarian life is have prevented me ever attempting to become one so far – although, to be honest, I would like to learn more about it, from reputable nutritionists, dieticians and bonobos.

A particularly idiosyncratic social justice vegan group could represent an example of new things to come. A **straight edge vegan** (**xVx**) is an ethical vegan who doesn't consume alcohol, tobacco or any recreational drugs (sometimes including caffeine). Perhaps drawing from early vegan anarchists such as the French *vegetaliens* (they are not devoid of pedigree then), they tend to belong to a subculture of hardcore punk (and therefore share the characteristic aesthetics we associate with them). The name was taken from the 1981 song 'Straight Edge' by the American hardcore punk band Minor Threat, and the triple X which symbolises the movement is sometimes worn as a marking on the back of both hands. Straight edge bands such as Earth Crisis and Vegan Reich sing about animal rights and environmentalism as social justice issues to fight for (therefore they use most of the gateways into veganism).

These are ethical vegans as they tend to follow the full definition of veganism, not seeing it as a matter of health or personal purity, but as a means of personally rejecting the exploitation of animals inbuilt in 'the system'. Their abstinence from alcohol and drugs (and sometimes from promiscuous sex) comes from the idea of rebelling through self-control, as they believe that with the ability to control their actions they would be better suited to standing up against injustice – as genuine anarchists would.

My rocker-looking friend Jeannie (long platinum straight hair, fake-leather tight jeans with bullet-looking belts, wristbands, black shoulderless tops ... you know the look), a talented graphic artist who triples as anarcho-punk vocalist and animal-rights activist, has been vegan for many years but decided to stop drinking alcohol in the last few months. When I asked her why she said:

> Last year a really inspiring vegan straight edge activist friend of mine passed away. They had a t-shirt that said 'vegan straight edge saved my life', it stood out to me. I realised that as well as being vegan all this time and being kind to all living creatures, it was time for me to extend that to being kind to myself. It was a great lesson and positive realisation. Through contemplating the idea of 'self-liberation' I decided to give up alcohol, I realised it was self-destructive and not bringing anything positive to my life.

She put me in touch with Olly Dean, a thirty-seven-year-old bass player and primary school teacher from Sheffield, who sent me this interesting view of his ethical approach:

> I've been straight edge for twenty-one years and vegan for eighteen years (before which I was vegetarian since the 1980s). Like many teenagers, I was angry

and strong-minded. I saw a lot of injustice in the world and I didn't understand why more people didn't seem to care. I embraced hardcore punk and spent my youth playing in bands and later as an animal-rights activist. I felt strongly about certain areas of avoidable suffering, particularly around animal cruelty and drugs (primarily alcohol and cigarettes). I was disturbed by addiction and the idea that a person can be so compelled to consume that they knowingly abuse themselves and others. That is where the philosophies of veganism and straight edge intersect for me – I see them both as paths to reducing harm and living more consciously.

As I've grown older, my feelings about drugs have softened, and although I don't have an impulse to use them myself, I can see that there are positives of certain drugs for some people. The alcohol and tobacco industries are abhorrent to me though, as they operate on a model of addiction and exploitation of vulnerable people, just as the animal foods industries exploit consumers with misinformation, desensitisation and addiction. Veganism and straight edge exist independently of one another, but 'vegan straight edge' exists as a philosophy and a lifestyle in itself. It is a commitment to a countercultural, nonconformist worldview which combines social justice, self and mutual care, compassion and empowerment.

I happen to be a kind of accidental straight edge vegan as I also avoid all the substances they avoid, but I do not qualify as I don't share their aesthetics or music taste. However, it is possible there are many people like me, and I wonder if we need another term to include non-punk straight edge vegans, something like **abstinent**

vegans (with the original meaning of abstaining from intoxicating substances).

We could ask Prof. Spock to keep subcategorising ethical vegans in further subsets based on the style in which they manifest their beliefs. We could talk about the **vegan sceptics** – I am one of them – who are science-based and who often debunk the false claims of some over-enthusiastic vegans, especially regarding particular exaggerated health benefits or unfounded conspiracy theories; or **activist vegans** who regularly participate in outreach or animal-rights activism, including **militant vegans** who participate in the most 'extreme' forms of direct action – whatever that may mean; or **apologist vegans**, their counterpart, who play it very low, never make a fuss and tolerate any deviation from veganism; or **anti-vegan vegans** who spend most of their time criticising other vegans for not being vegan enough, or not doing what they think they should be doing; or **yogi vegans** who, well, they do all sorts of yoga and meditation. I could go on, but I won't.

We now have the entire classification of ethical vegans from Prof. Spock's point of view, which can be seen as an expression of what we could call the 'conceptual evolution of ethical veganism' (that nicely matches the story of veganism we explored in previous chapters). It would look something like this:

carnist→omnivorous→vegetarian→'vegan'→ethical vegan ⟨ ethical fruitarian / intersectional vegan / abstinent vegan

In each stage of this hypothetical evolution, there would be a minority of trailblazers pushing towards the next stage, another minority of reactionaries pushing backwards to the previous stage, and a majority of 'resistors' who'd rather stay where they are (and often think they have done enough already).

The first consequence of consciousness was the idea of identity.

Who am I in this cornucopia of vegdiversity? Who am I really? Looking at my life, from the day my name was forbidden to me to the day I wrote my witness statement for my Employment Tribunal case, who had I turned out to be? I am Jordi, an ethical vegan who subscribes to most types of veganism. An ethical vegan for the animals, the environment and social justice (embracing the intersectional approach), who mostly follows a wholefood plant-based and abstinent diet for health reasons, and who wishes one day he could become an ethical fruitarian. In this regard, as ethical vegans go, I think I am pretty average. A mixed bag of hopes and aspirations.

Counting vegans may help you sleep

How many ethical vegans are out there? This is not an easy question to answer, especially because most polls don't separate ethical vegans from other vegans, or even from vegetarians. A 2016 poll conducted in the UK for the 'Food and You Survey', organised by the Food Standards Agency with the National Centre for Social Science Research, estimated the percentage of people in England, Wales and Northern Ireland who described themselves as vegans was 0.46 per cent (276,000). A clear increase as the same poll had been conducted several times before (in 2010, 2012 and 2014), with values averaging about 0.25 per cent. In 2019, the Vegan Society conducted an Ipsos Mori poll on 10,000 people over fourteen years old and found the vegan population of Great Britain was still growing, with around 1.2 per cent being dietary or ethical vegans (which works out at over 600,000 out of a population of 52 million adults).

Currently, there doesn't seem to be any country where the percentage of vegans surpasses 5 per cent of the population, which is not very high. I believe that in 2020 the percentage of vegans of any type in the UK may have already passed 2 per cent of the population (at least 1.3 million). In total, a conservative estimate

I trust is 15 million vegans of any type in the world (0.5 per cent), the amount Mic the Vegan (a vegan sceptic YouTuber who is very good at crunching these sorts of numbers) estimated in 2018. He also estimated that in 2018 the likely population of vegans in the US would be 4 million and in the UK 1.3 million (we don't know how many of these would be ethical, though).

V

When I returned from the Isle of Skye in 2002, I mentally added myself to the list of UK ethical vegans. I arrived at my home in Brighton and threw away all the food of animal origin from my kitchen. Next thing, clothes. I had several leather shoes and belts, some woolly jumpers and hats, and a long navy blue cashmere coat (I did not own anything made of silk). I threw away the oldest items and kept the newer to use until I wore them out. Luckily, I had no furniture in my flat made of leather or wool.

When I went to the office I told Tricia (my ever-so-affable big-smiled colleague, who still works at Born Free after almost forty years and was the first person to read my novel) that I was now a vegan like her. It was nice to talk to another human being after my self-imposed isolation, but extra nice to 'declare' to another person my new 'identity'. She was, naturally, very happy, a feeling I have experienced many times since when someone has approached me with similar news.

At first, I brought my food to work, but later I got some vegan sandwiches from the catering delivery person who did the rounds in the office at lunchtime. I bought soya milk, the only plant-based milk I knew about, and although I wasn't crazy about it at the beginning it did not take me long to get used to it. On the other hand, I felt the vegan cheeses were horrible – not any longer, by the way – and I resigned myself to never eating cheese again despite it being my favourite food before. A few months later my addiction to cheese vanished completely and I could not believe those clay-looking yellow smelly rotting blocks were at all edible – it's amazing how the brain works.

I gradually learnt where I could buy vegan food. In Brighton it was very easy, as it was a very vegan-friendly city, probably because it had a significant population of hippies and New Age people. The best shop was Infinity Foods, an organic supermarket in The Lanes that had everything I needed. Every Saturday I took my empty backpack and walked the thirty minutes there to get all my week's provisions (including organic veg). The first day I went there as a vegan I bought deodorant, toothpaste, shampoo and washing-up liquid (none of it tested on animals, of course), and when I got home I threw away all the previous toiletries I had.

I carried on investigating zoos for quite a while, but finding vegan food in a new town I had just arrived in was a little bit more challenging. More often than not, noodles and vegetable samosas, available in most corner shops, saved the day – not forgetting the easily accessible chips for the evenings. For quite a while I did something quite quirky when I was shopping for food in a supermarket. Initially, I would read the labels of anything to find out if there were any animal products, but then, even when I already knew the content, I kept doing it. I liked the feeling of 'rejecting' food after reading the label. It made me feel I finally had control about what I was eating. It made me feel empowered. It's good to reject cruelty. It's good, and feels good too.

I did not take any vitamin B12 supplements then, and I was relying on fortified soya milk, and on my new discovery: Marmite, the black sticky spread made from yeast extract invented by the German scientist Justus von Liebig from a by-product of beer brewing (I bet you did not know that). It's naturally high in B12, but its salty taste has divided the nation between (as the adverts put it) those who hate it and those who love it. I was one of the latter, and I never felt more British – although I later switched brands when I discovered it was owned by a company doing many animal tests. Ten years later I checked my blood for B12, and it seems all the soya milk, Marmite and accumulated vitamins I had stored in my body from my pre-vegan days had been enough, as my levels were normal – now I do take supplements, though, as getting older makes you absorb vitamins less efficiently.

A few months later I left Born Free to work for myself as a freelance animal protection investigator, and I managed to convince two organisations, Advocates for Animals (now called One Kind) from Scotland and the Captive Animals' Protection Society (now called Freedom for Animals) from Manchester, to hire my services to investigate public aquaria and their long-forgotten victims, the fish. I was feeling guilty about still having some leather shoes and belts, and I decided to get vegan versions at the shop called Vegetarian Shoes in Brighton (I was lucky as many vegans travelled to Brighton to buy their shoes there, as at the time there wasn't a shop in London selling any).

The only remaining non-vegan item I had was my relatively new cashmere coat, which I bought for when I had to dress up during lobbying. However, after a few months, I still had not used it again and I felt bad about still keeping it in my closet, so I gave it to charity. Between Infinity Foods, the health-food chain Holland & Barrett, Vegetarian Shoes and the Christmas Without Cruelty Fayre organised by Animal Aid every Christmas at London's Kensington Town Hall (at the time the only big vegan fair; now we have loads of VegFests and the like all year round), I now could buy all the vegan-friendly products I needed.

It took me about a year from the moment I became a dietary vegan to when I could confidently say I had managed to exclude most animal products from my life. The excellent *Animal Free Shopper* guide produced by the Vegan Society, which contained detailed lists of which products were suitable for vegans and where to get them, was a great help. Although I was an ethical vegan in my beliefs from day one, I had been a 'novice' for months while getting to grips with the lifestyle my new philosophy brought me. In 2003, I could say I had 'graduated' as a proficient ethical vegan. There would not be a way back to my carnist days.

I worked as a freelance undercover operative for a couple of years doing investigations on issues such as pet shops and the illegal pet trade. I was quite good at it, and because of my job, I changed my appearance often. My selling point to potential clients was that I was a combination of investigator and scientist: not only could I obtain the information they required, but I could process it scientifically and produce a report useful for campaigning. For instance, when Advocates for Animals hired me to investigate what was going on in Scottish pet shops, I drew a sufficiently large random sample of shops to investigate that would be representative of the entire industry. Then I created a 'cover' and a 'script' designed to obtain key information, and I visited them all wearing a concealed body camera to capture all conversations with staff and all the animals kept. Next I analysed all the footage, devising methods to estimate the size of each cage, the mental state of the animals and so on, and I produced a report with all the results that my client was able to use for their lobbying. This dual report – a flashy summary together with a detailed scientific report – became the trademark of many of my investigations.

I became employed again in 2004 when the Hunting Act was passed, and I moved back to London because I was hired (the first time around) by the anti-hunting organisation that dismissed me ten years later. While there I created the Hunt Crimewatch Programme, and I trained hunt monitors all over the country, who gathered evidence of the hunts' deceptions. After the first successful prosecutions against illegal hunters, I started a new campaign against bullfighting, as described above, where I travelled to all the remaining nine countries where there still is a bullfighting industry (Spain, France, Portugal, Peru, Ecuador, Colombia, Venezuela,

Mexico and the US). In all the countries where I investigated this industry, I met with the local anti-bullfighting groups and I shared tactics and strategies with them to create a unified strategic international movement.

The press was very interested in this one guy travelling from country to country, challenging such a powerful industry, and I ended up having hundreds of interviews and gaining another nickname: 'el antitaurino' ('the anti-bullfighting man'). Because of all this, in 2007, together with Marius Kholff from the Dutch anti-bullfighting organisation Comité Anti Stierenvechten (CAS), and Rita Silva and Miguel Moutinho from the Portuguese animal-rights organisation ANIMAL, we founded the International Network for the Abolition of Bullfighting, which is still meeting every year, in a different country each time. It made the movement a truly international force to be reckoned with, responsible for the current demise of the industry (the number of bullfights in Spain has declined 63 per cent since 2007), and the many bans that have been secured since.

My work against this cruel spectacle was so important to me that I figured I should dedicate all my time to it and go to work in the Netherlands for Marius, with the newly renamed CAS International. My role was campaigns co-ordinator, and I worked in Utrecht for a week every month and from London the rest of the time. Representing CAS International, in 2008 I returned to all the countries I had previously visited and resumed the campaigning I had begun.

Marius and I have always got along well. He is blond, friendly faced and older than me, and in many respects I feel he is quite a typical Dutchman. He is quite direct, speaks at least five languages fluently, is liberal and progressive, although he comes from quite a prominent Dutch family. He is always travelling somewhere (he used to be the travel manager at Shell), is very sociable and easy-going, and he is particularly keen on giraffes. Marius's companion then was Lotte, an Alsatian with whom I became a very good friend – she reminded me of Nit, my canine sibling, as they belonged to the same breed and gender. Every time I went to The Hague to meet Marius at the perfectly circular Prins Hendrikplein square (so he could drive us to the Utrecht office every morning), he would let Lotte off the leash and she ran straight to me at full speed and greeted me in an explosive cascade of friendliness. She was so happy that meeting her in the morning was my favourite thing about my entire Dutch experience. I loved to see her playing with all her canine friends every evening in one of the parks, where all their human companions ensured they could see each other.

It was friendship at first sight. I remember very well when we met. I was organising a publicity stunt in Brussels to request that the EU stop subsidising bullfighting, which involved activists from different countries, and Marius brought Lotte with him. After the event, we all went to a café to have some deserved refreshments, and when I sat down Lotte moved through the tables and jumped on my lap – remember, she's a big Alsatian, not a small terrier. I kept talking to other activists as if I didn't notice, but they all laughed. Marius apologised saying she had never done this before, and I replied it was fine, carrying on as if it was perfectly normal. That was so typical of her. She had this surrealist sense of humour that took people by surprise, but I got it. Our strong bond was forged right there in that café, and it was lovely. As she came to the office with us, every few minutes I would leave my desk and play with her. Some weekends I stayed in The Hague and we all visited nice places together – windmills and all. Marius told me that sometimes she seemed to sense the day I was flying to the Netherlands. It was truly special.

In London, all my friends were humans. The percentage of vegans among my friends grew considerably, and I met all types from all over the world. I felt I truly belonged to a community I was able to support as much as it supported me. For instance, I helped my biochemist friend Ian McDonald (a known pro-European vegan sceptic like myself, with a particular interest in boardgames) to fund his excellent podcast *Vegetarianism, The Story So Far* for his channel The Vegan Option, which taught me most of what I have written in the history chapter of this book. My ever-dancing friend Sarah-Jane taught me how to bake nice vegan chocolate cakes and impress my non-vegan work colleagues with them on their birthdays. I became a regular standing audience member at the Shakespearian Globe, which I religiously visited every season with Keri (the teacher) and Bev (the NHS Lab manager), my vegan theatre comrades.

A bit overweight, with increasing baldness and a badger-looking beard, I left CAS in 2009 to be a freelance animal welfare consultant. Unfortunately, I never saw Lotte again, as some months later Marius told me she'd had to be put down. I didn't ask him about the cause. I could not handle it. The idea of her disappointingly waiting for me to return was something I could not bear. I was devastated for Marius too, as they were so close (fortunately, he now has another friend, Simba). This is what happens with canine companions. They go far too soon, leaving such a big void behind that is hard to fill. Their honesty is so pure and their heart so open that once you have experienced sharing a life with them you may never find anything like it again – if you have had any of these magical relationships you know exactly what I mean.

Life had to go on, and I wanted to help as many animals as I could, so after deciding to switch to a healthier wholefood vegan diet (which made me thinner and much fitter) and practically stop drinking alcohol (just the occasional celebratory beer once a year or so when I felt I had achieved something very significant for the animals), I started to offer my services to clients as a consultant. I was soon hired by several organisations from different countries, and I was able to make a living from it for a while. One of them was

Plataforma PROU, in Catalonia, an animal protection organisation specifically created to campaign for a bullfighting ban there, who sought my services as a strategist, spokesperson and ethologist. It was a very interesting and ultimately successful campaign in which rather than persuading politicians to present a bill to ban this cruel spectacle (which had failed in the past), the bill was presented by this organisation directly through a process called ILP (Popular Legislative Initiative), in which 'official' signature gatherers need to be registered by the government, and then gather at least 50,000 actual paper signatures of Catalan residents in a maximum of 120 days. If that is achieved, the bill can be presented to Parliament and it will be processed in the normal way (with three votes). After very impressive campaigning work from vegan activists such as Leonardo Anselmi and Alejandra Garcia, 180,169 signatures were gathered in a third of the available time.

When on 28 July 2010 I was sat in the top gallery of the Catalan Parliament I witnessed sixty-eight Parliamentarians voting 'yes' for the ban (against fifty-five voting 'no'). Afterwards, the 'yes' voters turned around and applauded us, the campaigners who presented the bill – I felt very touched and highly emotional, as I imagined Limeño, the white bull from Peru, smiling at us too. Catalonia, my original country, had banned bullfighting for good, and this was going to have a domino effect all over the world. This was not only achieved by the hard work of grassroots activists following a well-designed strategy but also thanks to the support of brave politicians such as Raül Romeva and Josep Rull (who today are sadly in prison for their roles as ministers of the Catalan Government in the latest bid for Catalonia's independence from Spain, which I wholeheartedly support). There hasn't been a bullfight in Barcelona since January 2012, when the ban came into effect, despite the Spanish Constitutional Court later ruling against it (yet another expression of the constant conflict between the two countries).

As you can see I have been an ethical vegan in many countries where veganism was hardly known by the population, and yet I was never unable to find something to eat nor was forced to abandon temporarily my lifestyle, even in the most remote spots – and believe me, from the Colombian rainforest dodging the guerrillas on my way to meet young activists, to the Mexican deserts investigating the bullfighting mafia, I have been in remote spots. In my experience, with very few exceptions, you can find food suitable for vegans everywhere in the world. It will be hidden somewhere behind the meat, eggs and milk taking most kitchens hostage. The longer it takes for you to find it, the nicer it tastes when you eat it.

In 2012 the UK office of IFAW employed me as their campaigns and enforcement manager. From their big office in the 'charity building' right by the Thames in Vauxhall (very convenient for me as it was walking distance from home, and on my way there every morning I got to say hello to the horses kept on a nearby city farm), I carried on my anti-hunting work, managing a team of professional wildlife crime investigators and successfully prosecuting illegal hunters (that's where the 'enforcement' of my title came from).

The UK office was quite vegan-friendly (which could not be said of their other offices at that time), and I was pleased to be able to help my big-smiled free-spirited petite colleague Vanessa (with her spectacular dark curly hair) become vegan while I worked there. It was during that time that every 1 November (World Vegan Day, established in 1994 by activist and investigator Louise Wallis) I started the habit of anonymously delivering a box of vegan cupcakes to the offices, from either Ms Cupcake in Brixton or Ruby's of London in Greenwich – everyone knew they were from me, but they played along anyway.

My main job at IFAW consisted of recruiting and training investigators so they could monitor the hunts' activities using enhanced sophisticated surveillance methods (involving camouflage, operating from hidden observation posts at long distances with powerful cameras, evasive manoeuvres in hostile conditions, etc.). Despite the ban on hunting people still go out hunting mammals under the cover of 'trail hunting' or 'exempt hunting'. We processed intelligence to select which foxhunts, stag hunts or hare hunts to target and which days we'd deploy a team to monitor them. Next we'd analyse all the evidence produced and decide which cases we'd attempt to prosecute for breaches of the Hunting Act 2004, and then process and prepare all the evidence to persuade prosecutors (private or public) to charge the suspects. At IFAW I also helped train anti-poaching police and customs officers in Mozambique (it's handy to be fluent in Portuguese), co-authored a report on the world's trophy hunting and campaigned against the infamous UK badger cull.

Let's talk a bit about badgers, as they deserve it. European badgers (*Meles meles*) had it quite bad in the British Isles for a long time, but these tolerant, resilient and resourceful black-and-white, wise-looking omnivores have managed to survive, while most of the big mammals sadly disappeared because of the actions of *Homo sapiens*, an invasive species, the true 'foreigners of these lands'. In June 2016 a tiny majority of the UK public, intoxicated with anti-immigration cocktails laced with lies and bigotry, voted to leave the EU, which depressed me, as now I faced 'society' questioning my identity again (some people told me I was not British, others that I was no longer European).

When I was asked to give a talk at Stafford Badger Festival a few days after the referendum, I could not help speaking about who the real 'foreigners' of these Badger Islands are. I mentioned how badgers arrived at the islands at least 100,000 years before any human, how humans left about 25,000 years ago because the planet got very cold but the badgers stayed, how humans returned about 9,000 years ago and soon the wolverines disappeared, then the Romans came and the lynxes disappeared, then the Saxons and Normans came and the bears disappeared, then the Tudors reigned and the wolves disappeared ... but the badgers stayed. The Tudors captured them and tortured them to death with dogs in macabre badger-baiting spectacles, which became almost a national 'sport'. These, together with the hunters and terrier men persecuting them, almost drove the badgers out of existence.

However, badger bating became illegal with the Cruelty to Animals Act 1835, and hunting badgers was banned with the Protection of Badgers Act 1992 – giving them a breather. In 2012 new humans took charge in the islands and began killing badgers again, this time with the excuse they were causing bovine tuberculosis in cattle and that dairy farmers were losing profits. Still today, the UK Government badger cull is taking place all over the west of England – more than 100,000 badgers have lost their lives in vain, as reputable scientific evidence shows the cull does not significantly work.

When I was at IFAW I joined the Team Badger coalition (firmly supported by the famous Queen guitarist and astrophysicist Dr Brian May, who has recently become vegan, by the way), and I helped by training 'Wounded Badger Patrollers' in evidence gathering and supporting badger vaccination projects as a tactic to save some badgers' lives.

After four years, now practically bald and fully white-headed, I left IFAW to re-join the anti-hunting charity (which would fire me a year and a half later). Despite the exciting new job, the Brexit cloud kept casting shadows over the land, and my sadness about it led me to spend the 2016 Christmas break in Dover. There, I endured the cold days watching the ferry I used when I first came to the UK – right after the Maastricht Treaty allowed me to do so – slowly coming and going as in a melancholic Irish song yearning for a time when opportunity was free.

By then, I had become a proficient ethical vegan, every year getting better at detecting and avoiding animal products, every year removing more items from the list I allowed myself to consume, every year with better information and arguments to help people to become vegan. I eventually felt so comfortable promoting veganism that I would carry the word 'vegan' somewhere on my clothing (often in more than one place) practically every day, from a pin on my lapel to my iconic hat, hoping I would still be campaigning for the cause even if I dozed off on my Underground seat. My collection of T-shirts with vegan messages grew enormously; my microwave had a vegan sticker on its door; my metal water bottle … well, you've got the idea. I was now the archetypical ethical vegan.

V

What is the typical ethical vegan, by the way? A 2016 Ipsos Mori survey for the Vegan Society covering a sample of around 10,000 people from Great Britain found 0.7 per cent could be classed as 'ethical vegans'. Analysing their results in detail the following can be concluded: the majority (64 per cent) of ethical vegans were female; the majority (52 per cent) were under thirty-four years of age; the top social grade was equally middle class and lower middle class (33 per cent); the majority (56 per cent) worked; the majority (77 per cent) were white; the UK region with most ethical vegans was the south of England (33 per cent) followed by the Midlands (31 per cent); the majority (52 per cent) lived in suburban areas; the majority (72 per cent) had an education equivalent to A levels or higher; the majority (61 per cent) were married, living together or single; and the majority of ethical vegans (79 per cent) had no children.

In other words, according to this particular relatively small sample study (with margins of error that can easily swing some of the results), the typical UK ethical vegan in 2016 was a white, educated, middle-class female, under thirty-four years of age, who worked and lived in suburban areas in the South East, and who was either single, married or lived together with a partner, with no children. I, on the other hand, was a white, educated, lower-middle-class male over fifty, who worked and lived in urban London, and who was single with no kids. Five out of nine, 55 per cent typical, then.

We can learn something from all these numbers. They change with time, they fluctuate depending on who calculated them, and in most cases, the majorities are quite small, often not reaching more than 70 per cent. We come in all shapes and sizes, and every time a new gateway opens towards veganism, the demographics shift. We are becoming more and more mainstream, and with it more diverse. This diversity also involves different ways to look at things, different points of view and opinions, which explains why there are so many types of vegans, and subsets within them.

By becoming mainstream the movement will end up reflecting the diversity of the general population, with the good and the bad, the tolerant and the bigoted, the wise and the naïve, the privileged and the marginalised. All the trends and divisions we see in today's society, all the tribalism and infighting, all the politics and ideologies, will be found in veganism too, and little can be done to prevent it.

A difference of opinion is healthy for a socio-political movement, but tolerance is a quality not everyone possesses, and in this day and age, when social media bypasses all the behavioural mechanisms evolution has provided us with to avoid conflict, it's not surprising some of the arguments and infighting caused by differences of opinion may be unproductive, debilitating and demoralising for some. This is a price to pay we cannot avoid, but we can learn to cope with it.

Now imagine that Prof. Spock was not a 'Western' male, but an 'Eastern' female. Perhaps her report would be very different. She might focus more on the waves or goo rather than the particles or prickles (to use the dual nature of light and an analogy of 1960s philosopher Alan Watts), and, as the ancient philosopher Lao Tzu put it when he wrote 'the five colours blind the eye, the five tones deafen the ear, the five flavours dull the taste', she might be less inclined to categorise any vegan. Perhaps she would conclude all humans are ethical vegans in the making. She might say they all look like babies of a vegan being. All screaming with unique demanding cries, but when they calm down, they all look very similar. Some are still sleeping, others are beginning to wake up, but they are all growing babies from Mother Nature. Neither omnivorous nor herbivorous; neither carnists nor ethical fruitarians; neither minorities nor majorities.

Who are we, anyway? What is the human identity our cultures are based on? Are we the naked apes? Are we the talking apes? Are we the clever apes? Are we the destructive apes? We are just a collection of gene bags that happened to acquire a particular form in the last few geological instances of the Earth's existence, not too different from most of the other forms that are also quivering around. 'We' are all the vegans, all the humans, all the mammals, all the animals. 'We' are all the earthlings, and when we harm any of us, we are harming ourselves.

Today, watching a crowd, you can no longer tell who is a vegan and who is not. We are an evolving and diverse bunch of people. We all come from different places but are going to the same destination. We all belong to different tribes but sleep under the same stars. We all have different voices but sing the same songs. We are all guided by a very important idea. An ethical principle affecting us all, merging us into a progressive social movement.

An implicit union of explicit diversity.

'VEGANS'

Don't consume animal products, at least in diet

Dietary Vegans
don't consume any
animal products in diet

HEALTH VEGANS
don't consume any animal
products for health reasons

Raw vegans
(mostly eat raw
plant-based food)

Wholefood vegans (WFPB)
(mostly eat wholefood
plant-based food)

High-carb-low-fat vegans (HCLF)
(mostly eat high-carb-low-fat
plant-based food)

Macrobiotic vegans
(mostly eat macrobiotic
plant-based food)

JUNK-FOOD VEGANS
mostly eat junk
plant-based food

Ethical Vegans
don't consume any
animal products in any way

ANIMAL-RIGHTS
VEGANS avoid all forms
of animal exploitation and cruelty
for animal-rights reasons

ECOVEGANS avoid all forms
of animal exploitation and
cruelty for environmental reasons

RELIGIOUS VEGANS avoid
all forms of animal exploitation and
cruelty for religious/spiritual reasons

INTERSECTIONAL
VEGANS avoid all forms
of animal exploitation and cruelty
for social justice reasons

ETHICAL FRUITARIANS
avoid all forms of animal exploitation
and cruelty, and consuming plant products
that kill the plants when harvested

STRAIGHT EDGE
VEGANS (abstinent vegans)
avoid all forms of animal
exploitation and cruelty, and any
intoxicating substance

5.

Being an Ethical Vegan Today

As always, we have arrived in the present

Life as an ethical vegan can be quite easy. It only requires doing a bit of research to identify what products and services are suitable, creating some personal rules for the grey areas, and then developing new routines. Different vegans all do things differently, and it's not up to me to judge them or criticise how they resolve the constant conflicts we face when still living in a predominantly carnist world.

In this chapter I'll explain how my belief in ethical veganism is manifested in my everyday choices, and how I handle the grey areas and controversial issues. I am well aware I am very lucky to be living in one of the most vegan-friendly countries, and in the best city for vegans, but if you are a new ethical vegan in a less fortunate location, don't beat yourself up if you find it difficult.

V

Before I do that, though, I need to finish my last story, and take you through the last steps of my journey towards my present. In October 2019 the Employment Tribunal postponed my pre-hearing to determine if ethical veganism was a protected philosophical belief. We requested a replacement date for a few weeks later, to try to avoid the postponement of the full merits hearing set up for the end of February 2020, but the tribunal rejected our dates and gave us 2 and 3 January. I thought this was far too late, as there might not be enough time for the judge to produce the written judgement needed for the full merits hearing. Also, how on earth would we able to get up to Norwich for 10 a.m. the day after New Year's Day? Peter, my solicitor, reassured me. Although atypical, the judge could produce the judgement very quickly, knowing the consequences if he didn't. He also said the first day of a pre-hearing is normally assigned for the judge to read all the written evidence, and we might not be required to be in Norwich until the 3rd. After a few weeks of uncertainty, the tribunal confirmed Peter was right.

The world was watching. The main media published articles heightening the drama and fuelling the anticipation: 'Worker could make history in a crucial case for ethical vegans' (*Guardian*), 'Law must protect us from veganphobia, says campaigner' (*The Times*), 'Landmark Norwich hearing to decide if veganism is a "philosophical belief"' (*ITV News*), 'Who Is Ethical Vegan Jordi Casamitjana?' (*Vegan Life Magazine*). The scene was set for something big, something that, like the butterfly effect, could create a global ideological hurricane from the flapping of an unemployed vegan in a courtroom in a small city in Norfolk.

The day finally arrived, and I found myself leaving my flat and heading to Liverpool Street Station when it was still dark. I wore my black polyester suit and a black long-neck cotton polo top – I hate ties! I arranged to meet Peter at the station, together with Megan, the press officer of Slater and Gordon assigned to my case. After buying some juice I met Megan in the lobby, but Peter wasn't there. We decided to wait for him on the train. When the train departed without him having joined us I began to get nervous … but a couple of minutes later he appeared walking down the aisle, sweating and out of breath. 'OK, this is how this day was going to be,' I thought. 'I'd better prepare myself for a roller coaster.'

Megan had arranged for the ITV News channel to record Peter and I entering the red Magistrates' Court building, but when we arrived we saw a bunch of cameras all pointing at the wrong street and we had to 'stage' our entrance again. We passed security and waited for the courtroom to open. My friend Jeannie (the one who has recently become an abstinent) and other activists who had come along were already there, as were the legal correspondents for several media outlets.

Chris Milsom, our barrister from Cloisters Chambers who would act as my counsel, had not arrived yet. He is quite an energetic young lawyer, who reminded me a bit of Orson Wells in his early radio career, perhaps because he has a child-like face in a tall sturdy body. He is quite eloquent but approachable, not like those barristers who like to listen to themselves. I remember how impressed I was when once I saw him talking on the phone on the street, pacing up and down, totally focused on the conversation and completely ignoring the fact that it had been raining for quite some time. The waiting hall was soon packed and the clerk told us there would not be room for everyone in the court. He said he would try to find more chairs to fit as many people in as possible.

The next crisis materialised when the clerk also told us some witness statements were missing from the bundle we couriered there before the Christmas break – Peter had to find some copies to hand to the clerk, in the hope the judge would have time to read them in the remaining twenty minutes before the hearing started.

Ten o'clock arrived, but no Chris yet. We texted and called him, but no response. 'Can you be my counsel instead?' I asked Peter. He reassured me with an affirmative word which did not match the expression on his face. Five past ten, and the clerk was pressuring us. A text reply. Chris had gone to the wrong court in Norwich, and he was running to get to ours. Ten past ten, and we told the clerk he was downstairs, stuck in the security queue.

I entered the fully packed room with four crises averted and two sweaty lawyers. Chris and Peter sat in front of me, at the right side of the court, while the Respondent's team sat on the left. A few minutes later it was my turn to give testimony, and I moved to the witness chair to the right of the judge's desk from where I gave my affirmation (as an atheist not keen on monarchies, when I became a British citizen it felt wrong when I had to give an oath of allegiance to the Queen by Almighty God and I have opted for affirmations since). Chris asked me if my twenty-eight-page statement with eighty-seven paragraphs was indeed my testimony, and I said, 'Yes.' Patrick Keith, from St Philips Chambers, the Respondent's counsel, said he had no questions for me. Time for Employment Judge Robin Postle to ask his ... but he said he had none. 'That's weird,' I thought.

When the same happened with our second witness, Dr Jeanette Rowley, from the International Vegan Rights Alliance and the Vegan Society, the fifth crisis emerged. We did not expect things to go so fast, and our third witness, Jeff McMahan, professor of moral philosophy of Oxford University, had not arrived yet, as he was aiming to come later in the afternoon.

Fortunately Judge Postle said we could side-step the third witness for now, and carry on with the case. And then, the big surprise. After Chris eloquently presented our case, the judge told us there was no need for my third witness as he had read his statement and he had no questions for him either. It seems that, having read the previous day the more than 1,200 pages of evidence we'd produced, he had already made up his mind. If both sides agreed, he could give us a verbal summary judgement right there and then, and in a few days he would send us the written judgement. This was unexpected. We talked to each other for a few seconds, and Chris said, 'Yes, please, Sir.' Mr Keith concurred.

The judge spoke calmly but resolutely. He began describing my normal daily routine, reading it directly from my statement. What I do when I wake up, the products I use in the bathroom, what sort of clothes I wear, what I eat for breakfast, what transport I use. For every new paragraph he read, more tears welled up in my eyes. I looked to the left and I could see my friends' eyes flickering too. Here I was, listening to a judge broadcasting to the entire world my private routines, the things I do every day without anybody watching, but which I think are important because every action is an attempt to distance myself from the exploitation of animals and their suffering.

The judge was describing them with such dignity it felt as if a strong subtext of approval was implied. For each thing he said, I could hear an imaginary chorus of animals of all sorts whispering 'thank you', stamping a magic seal which sanctioned every one of my mundane daily decisions. The judge stopped when he thought he had made his point, spoke a bit more about the conditions needed to be fulfilled, and then ended with these solemn words: 'I am satisfied overwhelmingly that ethical veganism does constitute a philosophical belief under the Equality Act 2010.'

We had done it. We had made history. It took us centuries to make *ahimsa* a coherent and tangible philosophy accessible to everyone with a lifestyle easy enough to follow; it took us decades to find out who we are and fully embrace such philosophy; it took us years to build a solid legal case to persuade the authorities veganism ought to be taken seriously, but it only took a few hours for the judge to understand all this, and announce his decision to the entire world. Like a dam giving in to the perseverance of a relentless force, my eyelids finally folded and my emotions poured out. Images of animals being freed flashed through my mind. The monkey in the lab, the sow in the crate, the hen in the cage, the mouse in the trap, the goldfish in the tank, the wasp in the jar.

'Pull yourself together,' I whispered, drying my cheeks. I had to go out and speak to the media, but I couldn't do it in that heightened emotional state. I stood up, and with the best phlegmatic English smile I could muster, I shook Peter's and Chris's hands. That's when Jeff McMahan, looking just like the endearingly eccentric philosophy professor I thought he might be, arrived. He missed the hearing, but luckily for all he could still join us in our anticipated 'walkout'.

I had to go back to my professional self and be sure I did everything I was supposed to do. I told Megan I needed a few minutes. First, I posted on Instagram a single image of a chess piece. Before leaving home that morning I had done the same, but then it was a black pawn, and now this was a black queen. Second, as we did not expect a verdict the same day, the public statement we had prepared earlier was no longer accurate, and so, on the spot, Megan and I composed a new one on her phone and sent it to all the press, some of whom were waiting outside with a row of impatient cameras.

We passed security, and, with me in the front, Jeff on my right, Jeannie, Jeannette, Chris, Peter and others behind, we opened the door. It felt as if we were in a Tarantino film as we walked towards the cameras, holding controlled smiles in what felt an eternal slow-motion progression – only to be broken by Jeannie's fist punching the air above us. Madness ensued.

Radio, TV, newspapers, podcasts … interview after interview which lasted for days, as the news of my first victory travelled fast all over the globe. More than 1,000 websites from dozens of countries were talking about what we had done. In countries where people had never heard the word 'vegan' before, in places where they definitively never heard the adjective 'ethical' attached to it. I was able to explain to so many people, millions of people, what a 'true' vegan is.

This time the immense majority of headlines were positive: 'Jordi Casamitjana vegan tribunal a "victory for animal protection"' (BBC), 'Ethical veganism ruled a "protected belief"' (*The Australian*), '"Ethical Veganism" Is a Philosophical Belief, British Court Rules' (*New York Times*), 'Big win for "ethical vegans" in U.K. work tribunal' (Canadian *CTV News*), 'Ethical vegans celebrate after winning landmark legal case in UK' (*Euronews*), and so on.

It was the first time someone had made it 'official', the recognition of veganism as something very important was now legal: no less important than environmentalism or pacifism; no less important than Christianity or Islam; no less important than sex or gender ... something which deserves as much respect, as much protection, as any of these. And if it had happened in the UK, it could happen everywhere, as ethical veganism is the same in any country (it does not have cultural variations), discrimination occurs in any nation (it's human nature to look at the 'other' with mistrust), and progress in legislation to prevent discrimination is advancing in most countries (sadly, not in all). The story was relevant everywhere, from Jordan to China, from Peru to Norway. It had a face (mine), it had an idea (veganism), it had a struggle (discrimination) and it had a satisfying resolution (historical legal protection) in a David vs Goliath narrative appealing to carnists and vegans alike.

After a few days, the actual impact of my case could already be seen. HR companies advised their clients to change practices to better accommodate their vegan staff, fire brigades automatically issued vegan PPE to their vegan firefighters, schools added vegan options to their dinners, and even the press – some of whose members were inclined to mock vegan interviewees in the past – started taking a much more respectful attitude. This was real. Vegans were being positively affected by this and they were letting me know on social media. This was a paradigm change, not just a note on a piece of paper.

The written judgement arrived a few days later, and it had everything I had hoped for. It clearly explained the reasons for the judgement. It said all the conditions had been overwhelmingly fulfilled, by a long margin. It confirmed everyone following the definition of vegan by the Vegan Society would be an ethical vegan and therefore the protection would apply to them as well.

The judge entirely got the idea of the cogency of ethical veganism coming from its wholeness, as he wrote:

> ... ethical vegans could be said to be moralistically oriented and opposed to *all* forms of exploitation of *all* animals and to embody genuine philosophical concern for *all* sentient life. [emphasis mine]

He ended with this:

> I am therefore satisfied and find it easy to conclude that there is overwhelming evidence before me that ethical veganism is capable of being a philosophical belief and thus a protected characteristic under the Equality Act 2010.

It was such a potent and unambiguous judgement backed by so much evidence that no other Employment Tribunal judge would dare to rule against it in another case. Although it did not set an actual legal precedent as this was only a first instance tribunal, in practice it was clear it would operate as if it had. No legal commentator disagreed with Judge Postle's judgement. There would be no appeal against it. It was truly official now.

Luckily, the prompt verdict allowed me to carry on with my full merit case on the agreed days in February and March. I now had three more things to attain: prepare the rest of the case in the remaining four weeks; raise enough funds to pay for the legal fees for the next stage (I was £25,000 short); and win my discrimination case.

I don't want to dwell too much on how everything went, as

the big historical event had already happened, but on 24 February my full merits hearing began at Watford Employment Tribunal. Because of the strength of our discrimination case, on the first day we replaced our whistleblowing claim with a new victimisation claim, and everything was now under one piece of legislation only, the Equality Act 2010. Employment Judge Hyams seemed to like this move. The eleven witnesses began giving testimony, and I was the first.

Every day went better for my side and worse for the other, thanks to the excellent job Chris did in cross-examination, which dismantled the Respondent's tactics. Every day the press published an article about it which damaged the other side, and I felt public opinion becoming more sympathetic to me by discovering what had actually happened (headlines such as '"Ethical vegan" sacked for complaining about pension contributions' from the *Telegraph*, or 'Jordi Casamitjana tribunal: Charity boss shocked by animal testing claims' and 'Jordi Casamitjana: Carnivores took over at animal charity, sacked vegan claims', both from *The Times*).

We were set to win this one, and at the end of the weekend after the fifth day, the Respondents threw in the towel. We settled the case in my favour and litigation ended. I got the financial compensation I asked for, so I could pay all the legal fees I owed and also carry on paying my rent for a few more months. I got a total vindication as the defendant published a statement on all their media platforms which included:

> The only reason for the dismissal of Mr Casamitjana in 2018 was his communications to his colleagues in relation to our pension arrangements. Having revisited the issue we now accept that Mr Casamitjana did nothing wrong with such communications, which were motivated by his belief in ethical veganism. We are grateful to Mr Casamitjana for having raised the

issue of pensions to us, which allowed us to change our default pension fund to an ethical one closer to our values.

We managed to secure the first positive outcome from a court for an ethical vegan. The protection was real. Any other ethical vegan in the UK could use it. Any other ethical vegan elsewhere could get inspired by it. The extent of the media interest (at one point 1,445 websites from over 65 different countries were talking about it) shows how relevant my story was everywhere, and how many people are talking about veganism these days.

When I first received the introduction email from my pension provider I asked myself 'what is this?', and my ethical veganism made me dig deeper until I discovered the truth. When I learnt I would be forced to contribute to animal suffering against my will, my ethical veganism made me refuse. When I learnt my colleagues did not know what was happening with their pensions, my ethical veganism made me tell them the truth. When I realised many people thought I must have done something very wrong which justified my dismissal for gross misconduct, my ethical veganism made me litigate for two years until the truth came out. It was always about the truth. The truth, and nothing but the truth.

Three questions (who am I? what is this? what should I do?) generated three stories (my life, the pension problem and the history of veganism) which finally coalesced into a single one: the discovery of the true identity of an earthling learning to not harm anyone. A story determining a code of conduct, and manifesting in different ways depending on the choices at hand. A story which creates a specific lifestyle, affecting every aspect of one's life.

Food and drink

Despite what most people think, eating vegan-friendly food is one of the easiest parts of being a vegan. This is because labelling rules make it easy to find out if a food item has an animal ingredient. These are the ingredients I avoid: meat, eggs, milk, cheese, butter, yoghurt, cream, lard, lactose (lactic acid is vegan, though), whey, albumen, honey, propolis, beeswax, royal jelly, casein, cochineal (carmine), shellac, confectioners glaze, food-grade wax, gelatine, aspic, isinglass, rennet, and vitamin D3 (unless labelled as suitable for vegans, as most comes from the lanolin in wool).

E-numbers
Some additives are clearly of animal origin, but the problem is that, sometimes, the label only shows an 'E' number approved by the EU rather than the name. Therefore, if you are a vegan you have to either memorise the numbers or carry a list with you. For instance, E966 is lactitol, produced from lactose and whey from milk, and is used in many baking and confectionery products. Vegans should avoid at least these:

E-numbers to avoid
- E120
- E441
- E469
- E542
- E901
- E904
- E910
- E913
- E921
- E926
- E966
- E1000
- E1105
- E1518

Honey
You may have noticed honey is on the list of ingredients I avoid, and you may think this is controversial because some vegans eat it. It's very straightforward, really. From the very beginning the Vegan Society included honey in the list of substances not suitable for vegans, as it comes from animal exploitation. When bee farmers remove honey from a hive, they replace it with a sugar

substitute significantly worse for the bees' health. In conventional beekeeping, bees are selectively bred to increase productivity – as in any other type of farming – which changes their genes and increases their susceptibility to disease. Hives are also sometimes killed to keep costs down, individual bee workers are often harmed or accidentally killed during the careless process of removing the honey, and queen bees are sometimes mutilated to prevent them leaving.

Bees collect nectar for one reason alone, to feed their colony in winter when no flowers are around. When honey is constantly stolen from their winter reserves (whether by commercial or backyard beekeepers), bees are under stress all the time, trying to get the levels back up. For bees, making honey from nectar is a huge task. They fly to up to 1,500 flowers a day to collect enough nectar to fill their stomachs (they have two), and a bee produces only a twelfth of a teaspoon in their lifetime. Also, when beekeepers use smoke to 'appease' the bees before opening the hive, what they may be doing is actually giving them more stress – the bees think fire is approaching and eat honey in a panic in case they need to escape and find another place to live. Because they are busy doing this, and their sense of smell may be numbed making them less likely to smell an 'alarm' pheromone, they may be less inclined to sting the beekeeper. No ethical vegan can ignore all this, and maple, agave, apple or other syrup are perfectly adequate substitutes for honey.

Palm oil

Some vegans try to avoid palm oil – and I did for a while – but it is quite difficult if you like processed dried food, biscuits, snacks, desserts, cosmetic products and things like that, as it's one of the few oils solid at room temperature. The reason for avoidance is that it normally comes from tropical plantations which destroyed entire rainforests (with all the animals in them) to plant palms for oil. This is particularly bad in Indonesia, where the demise of orangutans is attributed to palm oil cultivation.

In itself, palm oil is a product suitable for vegans as it does not need to involve animals, but the ecological abuses of the palm tree industry may justify its avoidance. However, other crops also rely on similar rainforest clearings. Currently, if I am after a product and there is an option without palm oil in it, I choose that one, but if there isn't (which may happen less often as alternatives are researched), I may still get the product if I really need it, always choosing 'sustainable palm oil' on the label if I can.

Sugar

Some sugar is suitable for vegans, but some is not as makers can use bone char (a.k.a. natural carbon) from cattle as a decolourising filter. Avoiding white sugar is a good way to avoid this, but some brown sugar is just white sugar with added molasses. I don't buy sugar of any type or add it to any of my food or drinks (as it is not healthy anyway), and as I only eat the occasional cake and dessert from vegan makers, I don't have to worry.

Drinks

As far as drinks are concerned, the good news is that all teas and most coffees are suitable for vegans (I take mine decaffeinated, though, as an abstinent vegan). The only coffee that is not is the Indonesian kopi luwak (civet coffee), which consists of partially digested coffee beans eaten and defecated by the Asian palm civet (*Paradoxurus hermaphroditus*). This civet is a long-bodied greyish mammal, who naturally helps to maintain rainforest ecosystems via seed dispersal from eating lots of fruits, but who is sometimes kidnapped and kept captive to provide sophisticated brews to snobbish humans at some urban low-lit trendy coffee shop.

I don't drink alcohol, but for those who do, most alcoholic drinks are suitable for vegans, but in the case of wines, cider and beer, some brands use bones or fish (a kind of fish gelatine called isinglass) to filter and purify their products. If it's not marked as 'vegan' on the label, it's best to contact the company and ask. There are websites and apps that help to identify if a drink is suitable for us, such as Barnivore.com, Vegaholic and VeggieBeers.

Cost

When doing outreach we often hear the argument that following a vegan diet is far too expensive. But it is only those who try to imitate a non-vegan diet (eating vegan food which looks and tastes exactly like the food they used to eat) who may be spending more than before, as they have to contribute to all the research that went into creating their favourite fake meats, spreads and drinks. Yes, the plant-based version of Bailey's is more expensive than the original, as is the vegan alternative to Hellmann's mayonnaise.

However, if you don't want to stick to things that look like meat, eggs and milk, if you base your diet on plants and fungus with little 'engineering', it is likely to be cheaper – and healthier.

Eating out

Every day it becomes easier to find vegan restaurants. I am lucky to live in London, as it has more than a hundred fully vegan eateries. When I travel, I use the invaluable website and app HappyCow, which I can set up to show me the nearest vegan restaurants (with reviews, and directions for how to get to them), or alternatively vegetarian or other restaurants with good vegan options. It works everywhere in the world I have been and it has never failed me (although it is not always fully up to date). When I eat out when travelling I always choose from the fully vegan eateries first, then the vegetarians, and then the rest, and in this way I am sure I am supporting vegan businesses which may be struggling to survive. Remember, though, if you buy chips (a.k.a. 'fries') thinking they will be cooked in vegetable oil, as is normal in England these days, this may not be the case in other countries (for instance, most chips in Belgium are still cooked with goose fat, which was also used when they invented this type of fried potatoes in the late 1600s).

Fake meats and cheeses

This leads me to the 'Impossible Burger' controversy. It transpires that Impossible Foods, Silicon Valley's inventors of this 'bleeding' burger, marketed in 2016 as the closest vegan burger to the 'real thing', tested a key ingredient, soy leghemoglobin, on 188 rats, allegedly to adhere to the Food and Drug Administration food safety standards. It seems they did it not because it was compulsory, but because they wanted to broaden their reach to larger restaurants and stores. For me, the testing makes the burger not suitable for ethical vegans and I would not eat it. The goals do not justify the means, and rats should not be sacrificed to save cows. For me it's that simple, but other vegans have a different view (perhaps a utilitarian view: the best course of action is the one that maximises a positive effect) and choose to consume these burgers anyway.

There are other burgers that claim to be very close to real meat but were produced without any animal testing. For instance, Beyond Burger, made by the Los Angeles-based Beyond Meat company, and made mostly of pea protein isolates, rice protein, mung bean protein, coconut oil and potato starch. Although I think it's suitable for ethical vegans, if it resembles the 'real thing' it's not for me. I don't want to eat any food that reminds me of meat. To enjoy them I like my burgers to feel different. The same goes for sausages and fake 'chicken'. If they are suitable for vegans I will try them, but I will not use them again if they remind me too much of meat.

People transitioning into veganism may need such products at first as a comfort blanket, and perhaps then keep using them because of habit. If they help more people to become and stay vegan, it's good they exist.

I would also never eat any of the so-called 'lab meat' (or *in vitro* meat), which is made of animal cells but grown in a laboratory, rather than on an animal, because I don't consider it suitable for vegans – the initial cell from which the others grew did come from a real animal. Also, I believe the idea that flesh is something humans can eat is fundamentally wrong – it's not a healthy food as it will still be full of damaging cholesterol, it is unnecessary as there are much better alternatives, and it represents a form of animal exploitation humanity should be moving away from, not trying to imitate.

I could take the same attitude and avoid cheese that looks too close to animal versions, but I don't. Perhaps because I used to love cheese so much before I was vegan and then I resigned myself to never eating it again as the vegan cheese at the turn of the century wasn't very good, I can't help now occasionally eating vegan cheese as it has improved so much.

This apparent contradiction in my approach to meat and cheese is a good example of how the psychological attachments to particular products may affect the food choices vegans make, which can become very personal and unique. In my case, the contradiction is real, and I hope to resolve it in the future – once I get over all the excitement of the current innovations I will hopefully say goodbye to vegan cheese forever and stick to food not imitating the products of suffering.

Following the WFPB diet allows one to largely avoid processed food anyway. New vegan products and restaurant dishes are a treat, but at home I try to revert as much as possible to my wholemeal grains (I frequently eat rice and pasta), pulses, beans, nuts, seeds, fruit, berries, greens and a large variety of colourful veg. My breakfast has been the same for years now: porridge made with water, with ground flaxseeds, walnuts, blueberries, fresh ginger, turmeric and pepper (as it maximises the anti-inflammatory properties of turmeric). I love it, and it makes me start the day with long-lasting energy.

Which vegetables?

Many vegan-deniers often ask, hoping to catch us in a fatal contradiction: 'Don't you know many animals are killed in the fields to harvest all the vegetables you vegans eat?' Well, I can't deny many farming methods do kill animals, especially insects with pesticides or by accident when big machines are used during harvesting. Organic farming kills fewer as it doesn't use as many pesticides, and then we have veganic farming, which, if done properly, would kill none, but it is not yet possible or practical for most to only consume veganic produce.

However, the consumption of plant-based crops kills far fewer animals than the consumption of animal products, as animal agriculture also kills the same animals when they harvest crops to feed their cows, chicken, pigs or turkeys (it is estimated 85 per cent of all the soya cultivated in the world goes to feed farm animals), but then they kill all these extra animals as well. Accidental killing and deliberate killing are very different things, and animal farming kills many more animals than vegetable farming. Reducing our 'blood footprint' is what it is all about.

How do I personally resolve this conflict? My priority is to consume the veg I plant in my yard using the veganic method (so far I successfully harvested potatoes, courgettes, lettuces, aubergines, tomatoes, kale, cucumbers, strawberries, runner beans and a variety of herbs – if I had an allotment I would try to grow more) and no animal is killed (if insects or molluscs eat what I plant, I carefully take them and put them all on the same plant, and this way they can eat one and I can eat the other).

Then I'll choose locally produced veganic veg, next remotely produced veganic veg, then locally produced organic, then remotely produced organic, and finally non-organic veg, although I would avoid certain products from this last category. For instance, I would avoid any waxed fruit (often lemons) as they normally use shellac. Shellac is a resin secreted by the female lac bug (*Kerria lacca*), an unpretentious tiny true bug who lives in India and Thailand, and who for discretion and protection secretes a tunnel-like tube as she traverses the branches of a tree. This tube is scraped up by humans to make the wax and she is killed in the process – up to 300,000 females may die to produce a kilogram of shellac.

I would not consume any vegetable grown by farmers who exploit bees in 'migratory beekeeping', which forcibly moves hives from place to place to pollinate their crops (a practice common in California, but not in the UK), as I consider this animal exploitation. In consequence, I avoid eating avocados, almonds and kiwis if I am not sure if the farm that cultivated them doesn't use these methods – this has been my latest New Year resolution, which for me traditionally involves adding a new product to avoid, which makes me research deeper into the products to see if I can get them from acceptable sources. This is why I don't buy fruit-and-nut mixes any longer as I cannot tell where the almonds come from. As Jains also do, I avoid eating figs as they need a tiny symbiotic wasp of the superfamily *Chalcidoidea* to reproduce, the remains of which may still be inside when the figs are sold – as a former 'wasp man' I could not possibly risk it.

Truffles and coconuts

A plant-based diet also includes fungi, not only plants, but I avoid one type of fungus: truffles. It's not a big deal to avoid them as they are very expensive anyway. In most cases, animals are exploited to harvest them. Trained muzzled dogs are used to find truffles, and sometimes trained pigs. As it's hard to know which farms use this common method, I avoid truffles altogether. On the other hand, I don't avoid coconuts despite the fact in some places monkeys may be used to pick them from palm trees, because in the UK most coconut products do not come from places that do that (but if I travel to any of the places that do, such as some areas of Thailand, I would avoid coconuts there).

Supplements

In addition to fortified plant-based milks and yeast products (such as the delicious nutritional yeast flakes, a.k.a. 'Nooch', which give a cheesy flavour to many dishes), I currently get my B12 from the Vegan Society Veg 1 tablets, which also contain other supplements which are particularly tailored for vegans who live in the British Isles (which has its peculiar geological and edaphic limitations which may lead to some deficiencies for anyone, not only vegans), such as iodine, vitamins D3, B2 and B6, folic acid, and selenium.

Omega 3 DHA supplements, which are made from sea algae, are worth considering too. It seems the medical profession is beginning to understand that long-term vegans could fall a bit short of this important fat for brain function and eye health, although Dr Michael Klaper (the physician promoting the Whole Food Plant Based vegan diet) still disagrees. Omegas are essential fats and include omega 6 and omega 3. There are three types of omega 3s: alpha-linolenic acid (ALA), docosahexaenoic acid (DHA) and eicosapentaenoic acid (EPA). ALA is found in flaxseeds, chia seeds and walnuts, and is present in plant oils, such as flaxseed, soybean and rapeseed oils, and it is easily obtainable by vegans if they consume these in food. However, DHA and EPA are difficult to obtain as the body has a very difficult time converting ALA into them (on average, only 1 to 10 per cent of ALA is converted into EPA and 0.5 to 5 per cent into DHA), and this is why some doctors recommend the algae supplements.

My attempts at veganic farming are not perfect, as my education is still in its infancy and my yard is quite small, but hopefully it will improve. In any event, any vegan who only eats plant-based food will always contribute to fewer animal deaths and suffering than a non-vegan. Don't forget the definition includes 'as far as possible and practicable', and what is practical will vary as the circumstances of each vegan (from wealth to location, or from health to psychology) vary too. No vegan dinner table is alike.

Clothes and fashion accessories

Finding clothes suitable for vegans is also one of the easiest parts of our lifestyle, as most carry labels showing what are they made of, and many vegan-friendly fibres already exist. Again, as in food, it is up to each vegan to read the labels and decide whether the garment is suitable.

Materials to avoid

- leather from any animal (including suede)
- the fur of any animal (including wool from sheep and alpacas, cashmere from goats, angora from rabbits, mohair from goats and horsehair)
- feathers of any bird (including down)
- teeth (including elephant ivory)
- silk from invertebrates
- horns
- antlers
- tortoiseshell
- real pearls from oysters

Natural fibres suitable for vegans

- linen
- hemp
- wicker
- palm
- cork
- bamboo
- coconut
- bark and wood

Human-made fabrics suitable for vegans

- acrylic
- batiste
- buckram
- calico
- cambric
- canvas
- chenille
- chino
- chintz
- corduroy
- cretonne
- denim
- dimity
- duck cotton (duck cloth, duck canvas)
- elastane
- elastic
- faux-leather (leatherette, vinyl or polyurethane)
- flannelette
- fustian
- gingham
- khaki
- lamé
- lint
- lyocell
- mackintosh
- madras
- marseille
- microfibre
- modal
- moleskin
- monks cloth
- moquette
- muslin
- nankeen
- nylon
- oilcloth
- organdie
- orlon
- percale
- pilot cloth
- polar fleece
- polyester
- rayon
- sateen
- seacell
- seersucker
- silesia
- spandex
- tapa
- ultrasuede
- vegetable cashmere
- velour
- viscose
- voile

This should cover the four fashion seasons from the Arctic to the Equator.

Wool

The use of wool is a subject often misunderstood, as vegan-deniers often say its production is not cruel as sheep are not killed and need to be sheared anyway. This is not quite true. Domesticated sheep (*Ovis aries*) are very gregarious, good-tempered and clever social animals who can remember up to fifty individuals by their face for years, can self-medicate when they feel ill and can recognise their babies by their calls. They are descendants from the wild mouflon of Europe and Asia (*Ovis orientalis*), who still exist today and do not require shearing as they lose their hair naturally.

Sometime between 9000 and 1000 BCE, humans in Mesopotamia began selectively breeding sheep, effectively altering them genetically over generations to make them produce more and more hair. That led to today's breeds which grow dangerous amounts of hair (as they can overheat and get parasites) and need to be sheared periodically. Their shearing is only needed because the wool industry has genetically manipulated them and they have become so deformed that intervention is required for their welfare. However, the industry could breed sheep to make them have normal amounts of hair, and if they choose not to they are responsible for the suffering of the sheep – there are breeds already that don't need shearing, such as the Katahdin, Dorper, American Blackbelly, St Croix, Romanov, Blackhead Persian, West African Dwarf and Red Maasai.

The shearing itself also causes suffering, as it is normally done very quickly as the shearers are contractors paid per fleece, not per hour working, and therefore are likely to rush the job, treating the animals very roughly and often causing injuries and bleeding. Numerous undercover investigations conducted by PETA have exposed this in several countries, including Australia, where most of the globe's wool comes from – Australians use the breed Merino, which is the most aberrant breed with the highest excess of hair. These exposés have shown to the world what 'mulesing' is – carving out huge chunks of skin from the sheep's backsides to prevent 'flystrike', where flies lay eggs in the folds of the skin and the hatched maggots eat the sheep alive. All this is to produce some fabric easily replicable today with eco-friendly fibres without the need for any animal suffering.

Environmentally speaking, wool is not the natural sustainable fibre the industry's PR departments want us to believe. The 'Pulse of the Fashion Industry Report 2018' published by Global Fashion Agenda and The Boston Consulting Group ranked wool production in 5th place of the fibres with the worst environmental impact (the first being leather followed by silk), and experts now recognise wool is far worse than acrylic, polyester, spandex and rayon fibres for cradle-to-gate environmental impact per kilogram of material.

Silk

Talking about fluffy animals, we also should discuss silk. Silk is not suitable for vegans as it is an animal product obtained from the cocoon of the mulberry silkworm (*Bombyx mori*), a type of domesticated moth created by selective breeding from the wild *Bombyx mandarina*, whose larva weave big cocoons during their pupal stage from a protein fibre they secrete from their saliva. These gentle moths, who are quite chubby and are covered by white hair, are very partial to the aroma of jasmine flowers, and this is what attracts them to the white mulberry (*Morus alba*), which smells similar. They lay their eggs on the tree, and the larvae grow and moult four times before entering the pupae phase in which they build a protected shelter made of silk, and perform inside the miraculous metamorphic transformation into their fluffy selves ... unless a human farmer is watching.

For more than 5,000 years this jasmine-loving creature has been exploited by the silk industry (sericulture), first in China and then spreading to India, Korea and Japan. They are bred in captivity, and those who fail to produce a cocoon are killed or left to die. Those who do make it will be then boiled alive (and sometimes later eaten) and the fibres of the cocoon removed to sell for profit.

In facilities claiming to produce the so-called 'ahimsa silk' (in theory more humane than normal silk production), even if they don't boil the cocoons to obtain the threads, they obtain the eggs from the same breeders. Once the adults get out of the cocoon by themselves, they cannot fly due to the big bodies and small wings created by many generations of inbreeding (so, they cannot free themselves from captivity, and again are left to die). To make a silk shirt 1,000 moths have to perish. Why all this suffering? Many artificial fibres now have very similar properties to silk.

Shoes

Shoes used to be more difficult to source, as not many places sold vegan shoes made of leather substitutes. You could find many online, but it was difficult to find shops selling them. If you wanted to try shoes on, the only option was going to vegan fairs where manufactures would have a stall. Now, however, they can also be found in vegan fashion stores, which are increasing in number in big cities. The good thing about them is that despite not being made of leather they can last a long time (the previous dressing-up shoes I had lasted me for eight years, although not all the substitute leather is equally durable, so it is worth checking with other vegans who may have experimented with different makes). Ah, and if you are an old fashion skinhead, you can find vegan Dr Marten boots too.

Other ethical fashion considerations

Animal exploitation and cruelty are not the only 'unethical' problems of the fashion industry. Poor working conditions, exploitation of children and marginalised groups, fair trade, sustainable production, environmental pollution, high carbon footprint, etc., are all problems the traditional fashion industry has failed to address. It is certainly true that if an ethical vegan chooses to use lots of cheap fast-produced plastic-made clothes, they may be contributing to these problems – including the production of microplastics dislodged from the clothes during washing which will end up polluting the environment.

However, ethical vegans can do many things to avoid this. For instance you can:

- Reduce the number of clothes you buy.
- Try to repair what you already own.
- Use specially designed bags during washing that trap microplastics.
- Buy Fairtrade clothes from reputable companies.
- Buy second-hand clothes.
- Use more clothes from plant-based fabrics rather than synthetics.
- Buy recycled synthetic fibres.

Transport and travel

This one is interesting, especially because transport is an issue many vegans don't think about. Sometimes we don't have that much of a choice regarding the transport we can use to go to our destination (for instance, if you're travelling from London to Sydney), but more often than not we do, and, as yet, many vegans don't approach transport choices as they approach buying clothes or food.

Some forms of transport are more vegan-friendly than others. For instance, if you are an ethical vegan you should avoid any form of transport driven by an animal, whether either this animal pulls some sort of vehicle or you are supposed to ride on them. This one's easy as the animal involvement is clear.

It gets trickier if a vehicle has some animal products inside, such as leather seats or leather straps for passengers to hold on to. If I have no other choice than to use the vehicle I will try to avoid touching these items. I don't make a fuss about it, but I'll try to stand and hold on to something else. I do this to remind myself I am surrounded by parts of a sentient animal who had a family, friends and aspirations just like me, and sadly now has been reduced to a fabric or a decoration. We should never normalise this sort of indignity, but instead make a 'stand' against it (literally).

Then there is the problem of accidental animal killings – often because of speed, and most commonly invertebrates. A 2004 UK study concluded a postcard-sized area of the front of a driven car squashes one insect every five miles. Vegans who acknowledge this problem may all resolve it differently, and I deal with it in the following way: if my destination is in within an hour's walk and the weather permits, I walk if I have enough time. This is the method of transport I can use which most reduces my 'blood footprint'.

When I walk I take a great deal of care to see where I step, always trying to avoid stepping on any snail, worm or insect. I try to walk on stones, concrete or asphalt, as I can see better what is on there, and if I have to walk on grass or soil I may consider what time of the year it is (in winter there are few insects I could crush). In reality, very small insects such as ants are unlikely to be crushed by people walking on the grass – the terrain protects them by giving way to the pressure and creating crevices operating as crush shelters. Small insects are hardly ever at the surface of the grass as this exposes them to predators, and flying insects have faster reaction times than us and they can easily fly away when they see us approaching. On hard surfaces, creepy crawlies are unlikely to be found, and are easily detectable. With a little bit of attention, I can walk for hours without any accidental crush.

If my destination is more than an hour's walk, or if for any reason I need to use transport, this is what I do: I don't own a car or motorbike, and I don't drive (or have a driving licence), because the blame would be entirely on me if I crush or run over an animal while driving. Also, most cars have components manufactured using animal products – tallow, beef or mutton fat is used to toughen tyres and tubing, and steel can be coated with lubricants made from animal products.

If I have a choice to use a bus, train, tram or underground, I choose differently depending on the time of the year, distance, speed, weather and latitude. If it rains (or has rained recently), I avoid travelling on a road during the warmer season, as this increases the chances of worms and snails being on the asphalt. In spring and summer, when many insects are around, underground public transport is my preference.

If I have no choice other than to take overground public transport during these seasons, if available I try to use trams rather than trains, as they normally have a smaller front surface and they travel slower. For longer distances, I try to take journeys when it is colder (at night or after sunrise) as there may be fewer animals. I also tend to choose trains over buses as normally they are more direct, and the straight lines allow the animals a higher chance of successful evading reactions due to the train's better visibility and predictability. Also, the surface of the first set of wheels touching the ground is normally smaller on trains than buses. It is all about giving invertebrates equal consideration, reducing the probabilities of accidents and then hoping for the best.

Personal care and health

Vegan-friendly personal care products such as toiletries and cosmetics are relatively easy to find online, in vegan supermarkets, fairs and cosmetic stores, but also in general stores as they are often labelled with the trademarks of the Vegan Society, 'Certified Vegan', or 'Cruelty Free'. The 'Leaping Bunny' cruelty-free certification was created in 1996 by several animal protection groups, and products holding it cannot be tested on animals in any way, although they may contain animal ingredients. Therefore this certification, or in fact any 'cruelty-free' certification, is not a guarantee of being suitable for vegans.

Personal care ingredients to avoid

- animal fats
- bee wax
- casein
- cochineal (carmine, or red 4, E120)
- collagen
- dairy products
- elastin
- fish compounds
- gelatine
- guanine
- honey
- keratin
- lanolin
- non-vegetable glycerine
- oleic acid (aka oleyl stearate, oleyl oleate or tallow)
- shellac
- squalene
- stearic acid
- anything tested on animals

Panthenol, amino acids and vitamin B, often found in shampoos, can be either from animal or plant sources.

In 1998 the UK banned animal testing for cosmetics and their ingredients, and in 2009 all other European countries did the same, while imported cosmetics ingredients tested on animals were phased out for EU consumer markets in 2013. Naturally, this increased considerably the availability of vegan-friendly cosmetics. Other countries, such as India, Israel, New Zealand, Brazil and Guatemala, have also banned testing on animals since.

However, healthcare is one of the most difficult aspects of veganism, not because it leads to health problems – on the contrary – but because, if we need medical treatment, it is very difficult to find suitable medicines or medical procedures not tested on animals and/or not containing animal ingredients. Many medicines are normally first tested on non-human animals and such tests are compulsory in many jurisdictions, and the pharmaceutical industry uses gelatine from cattle bones for things such as pill casings. For healthcare, the 'possibility' rather than the 'practicability' is what limits our choices.

If you are an ethical vegan, before rejecting any medicine or procedure it is worth talking to your doctor about your concerns and beliefs, not only because perhaps a vegan-friendly solution can be found, but also because it is important the medical profession is aware of the restrictions veganism imposes on some people, and this may fuel research for alternatives.

When I was a teenager I had to undergo an operation to remove my appendix. All the drugs I was administered for it, from the anaesthetics to antibiotics, were tested on animals, and many of the surgical procedures may have been as well. Possibly the doctors involved in the operation were trained using animals too – conducting operations on pigs, for example. Had I been a vegan then and because of that denied all such treatment, I have no doubt I would not have survived, and therefore I would not have been around to help all the animals I've helped since.

Complementary and alternative medicines (CAM) are beginning to be accepted by established conventional medicine in the West, and are sometimes prescribed as complementary therapies working alongside scientifically proven methods. However, some of these therapies will not be suitable for vegans because they use animal products – Chinese medicine, for example, uses compounds from tiger, rhino, deer, bear, snake, pangolin, etc. Additionally, many CAMs do not work as well as conventional medicine does, and some don't work at all – some are not based on anything remotely plausible.

Healthcare is a tricky issue, and in my experience vegans deal with this conflict in very different ways, and I don't want to suggest any is better than any other. I do not think vegans should sacrifice themselves, increasing the chances of not recovering from illness, by rejecting a particular procedure or substance for not being vegan-friendly enough. I take the view the world is better if there are more vegans around, healthy and capable of protecting animals and helping others to become vegan. The 'do no harm' applies to ourselves as well, and although we should all have the right of 'body autonomy', looking after our well-being is morally justifiable.

Sometimes it is easier to deal with this dilemma if the medicine or procedure was tested on animals many years ago and affects only *your* health. But in other instances the issue is far more difficult to resolve – if the tests are happening right now and the procedure affects other people, as is the case with vaccines.

The issue is not of whether vaccines work or not (the anti-vax arguments are beyond veganism and they are often fuelled by irrational conspiracy theories which do not help to address the issue objectively), but the fact they often contain animal products and they are tested on animals. This makes the current vaccines not suitable for ethical vegans, and we should campaign for better alternatives, supporting non-animal research to find them. However, the problem is that refusing vaccination for not being suitable for vegans (based on the available evidence, most vaccines do work as a form of preventative medicine) may cause harm to others, not only us, as it may prevent eradicating pathogens that may kill other people. The reason an ethical vegan rejects products is to stop harming others. If you take the concept of *ahimsa* as a non-speciesist concept in which people must be included, then both accepting and rejecting the vaccine may harm others – a real dilemma. A utilitarian vegan may evaluate the numbers harmed in either case and choose the option with fewer sentient beings harmed, but the problem is you cannot know how many people may be infected if you contract the disease and infect others who in turn infect others. These are hypotheticals difficult to guess.

To be honest, I don't have the answer for this dilemma, and if the time comes where I have to decide on whether or not I should get vaccinated to address a serious public health issue such as Covid-19, I will have to resolve the conflict there and then, with whatever information I have at the time.

Since I have become vegan I haven't been vaccinated, but I haven't been in any situation where a vaccination was advised (all my trips to the South American rainforest where vaccination against tropical diseases was compulsory happened before I was vegan). Currently, if I am in Europe and a mosquito is already on my skin about to sting me, I do not kill it but let her suck all the blood she needs – it is for her offspring, really, and she is only being a good mother. This is because, as Europe is not a malaria area, and as I can anyway identify visually whether the mosquito is from the genus *Anopheles* (which carries the disease), the only bad thing that will happen to me is I will suffer a bit of skin irritation for a few minutes – it's not worth killing the insect to prevent only that. However, if I had to return to a malaria area and all my attempts to prevent mosquitos getting on my skin failed (and there are many ways to prevent them, from nets to chemical repellents), I don't really know how I would react then and what I would do.

In these very conflicting cases, every vegan would have to rely on their common sense and how they interpret their beliefs. This suggests we are unlikely to find a good enough answer all vegans can agree with, considering the uncertainties and the stakes at hand. It doesn't matter if we all agree, though. What matters is we all try to avoid, in our own way, all animal exploitation and cruelty to anyone (including other humans and ourselves), with whatever we have at hand. Personal well-being is also important.

Furniture, appliances and household products

Ethical vegans who have control over the purchasing of the furniture in their homes naturally avoid any fur, suede, leather and wool, which is often seen in carpets and the upholstery of sofas and chairs, but they should not forget that cushions may be filled with down, and decorations may contain animal products such as ivory or horns.

Some furniture will contain horsehair, which is still used in upholstery, and it was also used in old buildings as plaster to cover walls – horsehair was used in the walls of one of the old flats I used to live in, which I discovered to my dismay when I attempted to repair some damage caused by damp. There is very little you can do about it if you happen to be living in such a building.

Mattresses may contain silk, wool or down, and latex mattresses may have been treated with casein from milk, but most memory foam mattresses are suitable for vegans as they are made of synthetic polyurethane.

Animal glues can be an issue too, as they are sometimes present in old wooden furniture. Old-fashioned glues used collagen in animal hides, bones (most nineteenth-century furniture was made with bone glue) and fish, but fortunately most modern glues are suitable for vegans now, as they are made of synthetic adhesives extracted from petroleum, such as polyvinyl acetate (PVA), cyanoacrylates, polyurethane and epoxies. Therefore, unless vegans are into antique furniture they should be fine regarding glues.

There are a few things vegans need to pay attention to when buying household items. Bone china items contain around 50 per cent cattle bone ash (hence the name), but porcelain, sanitary items (sinks, toilets, etc.), mugs and similar affordable ceramics are vegan-friendly. The heads of matches and incense sticks may contain gelatine, and paint may contain casein, beeswax or shellac, or be tested on animals. Rubber gloves and other latex products may have been processed with milk casein, but there are versions suitable for vegans. Believe it or not, toilet paper is not always suitable for us, as some manufacturers use gelatine to hold the paper fibres together. Thin disposable plastic bags (yes, those in supermarkets we are not supposed to use to protect the environment) may be treated with stearic acid, the 'slip agent' which allows them to separate easily from each other, another reason not to use them (I always try to carry with me a fabric bag in case I ever have an impromptu shopping urge).

What about appliances? There has been a good deal of talk from vegan-deniers about whether it is impossible to have 100 per cent vegan-friendly modern electronics and appliances. Most are only made of metal, plastic and ceramics with no animal involvement in the manufacture (as most glues used these days are synthetic). However, some electronic equipment may indeed have some components where animal products may have been used in their processing. In particular, it has been rumoured some LCD screens may contain a derivate from cholesterol, some lithium batteries may contain gelatine, and the rubber components of some devices may have been stabilised with stearic acid. However, it is not clear how common these may be, and I am yet to find a manufacturer confirming they use any of these methods in their components – I wrote to the companies of the electronics I own and most reassured me they don't use them.

Although the life of each vegan is different and some have managed to avoid the use of electronics and be happy about it, for most who want to live in modern society and access the same technological advances as anyone else, it would not be 'practicable' to avoid all electronic devices because of the manufacturing treatment of some of its small parts – each vegan has to decide which of such devices they definitively need.

Ethical veganism should not be about 'sacrificing' or self-handicapping, and living a sheltered life on the fringes of society, because if you isolate from the world you will not be able to stop much of the animal exploitation that goes on. Ethical veganism is about normalising civilisation without animal exploitation. Normalising, not exceptionalising it; living a full life, not a half-life, without exploiting animals. We should show everyone that becoming an ethical vegan is not a 'loss' of anything, but instead we gain something important.

Vegans should not be treated as animals are treated in zoos, kept away from their world, alone and in distress. Vegans should be in the real world, in their 'wild', helping animals and other people until veganism is the norm. Trying to be as 'normal' as possible may be a good way to get there, and in today's society this may well involve interacting with all sorts of technology, even if some hasn't yet reached their 100 per cent vegan-friendly status.

Therefore, when a needed service or a product doesn't have any vegan-friendly options, ethical vegans may not have any other choice than to use them, but innovation may provide a solution in the future. For instance, up until quite recently in the UK, all power and gas companies were not entirely vegan-friendly because they used electricity from the burning of biofuels from the animal agriculture industry. However, in the last couple of years the energy supplier Ecotricity stopped doing so, and because of that it has been certified by the Vegan Society. This company specialises in selling 'green energy', and it was founded in 1995 by the vegan industrialist Dale Vince OBE (also known for being the chairman since 2015 of the world's first fully vegan football club, Forest Green Rovers FC, based in Nailsworth, Gloucestershire). This is the energy provider I use for my electricity and gas, and I was pleased when Dale supported me in my litigation.

As far as household products are concerned, as with cosmetics, they may have been tested on animals or contain animal ingredients, but for each type of product there are always vegan-friendly versions (some with the Vegan Society or the 'Leaping

Bunny' certifications) available in vegan supermarkets, health shops and online, and every year there are more to choose from. These products are beginning to be sold in regular supermarkets too, and some supermarkets produce their own brands suitable for us.

I recently stopped using a vegan-friendly brand when its company was bought by another which tests on animals. When that happens, it is up to each vegan to decide whether they want to stop using the product, even if the brand itself remains vegan. You might want to support the brand to ensure their products continue to be vegan-friendly, but this clashes with not wanting to financially support the parent company. However, the same could be said about a vegan shop in rented premises of a non-vegan landlord, or even a vegan product being delivered to your home by a non-vegan delivery company. Everything is connected. A product is made in one place, by a company that may be owned by another company, using components of another maker, transported by a separate company, regulated by a local government, following the laws of a nation, dictated by the values of a civilisation, inspired by the philosophies of another time. Everything is connected, and it is even said that all humans are related by no more than six degrees of separation. But each degree makes the connection thinner. How thin it needs to be to conclude we are no longer talking about 'the same thing' is something quite subjective. Any vegan may draw the line in different places, and I don't have a specific rule on this to apply to all situations – perhaps I should have one, though. I am still learning.

Entertainment and leisure

The life of a vegan is never boring. Constantly checking what things are made of and thinking about the consequences of our actions keep us entertained. However, if we want a break from this form of entertainment and choose a more traditional way to pass the time, we of course can. We stopped being the austere naysaying ascetic bores in the Renaissance. We vegans now have fun too.

Entertainment activities we reject are, naturally, any which directly involve animal exploitation or cruelty, such as animal racing, and competitions, festivals and sports which use animals. In all these instances the animals are killed, hurt, stressed, exhausted, distressed or coerced to perform against their will. In cases where such activities involve spectators, attending them (and therefore supporting them) is not compatible with ethical veganism (except when done to expose their cruelty, of course).

Other activities undertaken for entertainment purposes including animals may be less obvious forms of exploitation, but vegans still won't support them. One is the use of live animals in films, theatre, television programmes, commercials and other forms of publicity. If the animals are forced to perform against their will, have been trained to perform by coercion or they are already in distress because of their living circumstances (such as wild animals in captivity), then this is unacceptable exploitation for us. When animals are exploited in a publicity context, the normal response from an ethical vegan should be not to purchase the product or use the services advertised.

I participated in a campaign against the UK coffee chain called Costa. Several years ago they ran a TV ad in which they used captive primates of several species, and as a consequence I (and many vegans who campaigned about it) boycotted the brand. After public pressure, the company produced a statement promising not to use primates again, although they would let the publicity run its course. As a response to this, I wrote to the company thanking them for stopping, but let them know that, as a 'penalty' for keeping the ads running, I would boycott their products for five years. True to my word I did it, and when the five years expired, I went to a Costa on Borough High Street, had a decaf soya latte, took a photo of it, and posted it to them on their social media thanking them for having kept their promise.

The good thing about animals in the entertainment industry is that advances in CGI technology make the use of live wild animals close to obsolete, and now we have many films with many realistic-looking animals where no real animal was ever used. The most iconic of these must be *Noah*, the 2014 film where the Biblical character is played by Russell Crowe, and where thousands of animals of all types are seen on the screen, all very realistic computer animations. The story of the film is also very veganish, showing Noah's family as vegans, and the 'bad' people the flood must eliminate as violent meat-eaters. It is not surprising this film turned out this way, as it was produced, written and directed by Darren Aronofsky, a vegan.

Another less obvious form of exploitation of animals within the entertainment field is horse riding for leisure, and it may be a controversial subject because some vegans who own horses (or had them in the past) may have a blind-spot bias in favour of this activity. Although I acknowledge some horses seem to 'enjoy' being ridden by a human, the key issue for me is why that happens. The answer is because they have been 'broken', so they are no longer able to judge the situation in their best interest, or because they want to please the hand who feeds them. I have not used the term 'broken' hyperbolically. This is the actual term used to describe the process of 'taming' wild horses, or horses who do not want to be ridden and eventually give up all resistance (their fighting spirit has been broken, and now they are docile and obedient).

As horses are herd herbivores (who evolved over the last 55 million years to live with many other horses in open spaces with sparse vegetation, not by themselves in stables), they are the natural prey of predators (such as wolves), and they have evolved a series of defence mechanisms to avoid capture. Some of these involve running as far as they can, kicking backwards to expel the incoming attacker, or jumping up and down to dislodge any predator already on them.

Sometime around 5,000 years ago some humans in central Asia began capturing wild horses and jumping on their backs, and the actual instinctive reaction of having people on their back would naturally be to get rid of them as their life might be at stake. Even after all these years of domestication producing many breeds of horses of all shapes and sizes, that defensive instinct is still there.

The process of breaking horses is aimed at eliminating such fear by repeating, again and again, these 'predatory simulations' until the horse realises this 'predator' only bites if you turn left when he wants to go right, or stay still when he wants you to move forward at the precise speed ordered. Therefore, breaking horses is not only a bad thing because the final result is a horse who has lost some of its 'integrity', but it is also wrong as it causes distress to the horse while it is being broken. The whole concept is already telling in that to get the informed 'consent' of the horse, you have to use force or coercion until the natural mental state of the horse has been changed 'permanently'. Therefore, this is indeed animal exploitation, and ethical vegans should not support it.

Those who train horses may not use the same methods used in the past and they may say what they do now is no longer breaking, but a gentler and subtle 'training', but the end result is the same. As I mentioned earlier, there may be a fine line between owning pet dogs or living with dogs as companions, but if part of the relationship with the dogs was to physically and psychologically subjugate them to carry you around to precisely where you instructed them to go, you would see the line more clearly. This is what happens with the relationship riders have forced on their horses, who become conditioned to accept riders on their back when they go for a walk (which they may enjoy doing while not carrying a human around).

Having a human on a horse's back, together with metal bars

(the 'bit') in their mouth (a most sensitive area) and metals spurs poked into their flanks, is not good for them anyway. Horses suffer specific diseases from having the weight of a person on their back, which their bodies have never evolved to accept. The weight of a person on a horse for a long time will compromise circulation by closing down the blood flow in the back, which over time can cause tissue damage, often starting close to the bone. Kissing spines syndrome is also a problem caused by riding, where the spines of the horse's vertebrae start to touch each other and sometimes fuse.

Horses sometimes fall from exhaustion if forced to run too much or under the wrong conditions, or they may fall and break their limbs, which often leads to their euthanasia.

You may be a horse 'lover' – there are many out there – and if you are an ethical vegan who wants to help them, creating a horse sanctuary might be the way to go. However, you can treat your horses with great care and compassion, remove the metal from the riding gear, and even the saddle, and only take out for a walk those who want to go ... but you could do all that without climbing on their back and in doing so exercising your dominion over them, wrongly reinforcing the psychological control which broke them. Surely that is a much better way to love them.

Work and hobbies

Humans are social animals with complex civilisations, and what do they have that less organised animals haven't? They have division of labour and the sum of their work is greater than each individual's part. Some of this work is remunerated with economic recompense, some with satisfaction and praise.

When they are not campaigning for the cause, what work can ethical vegans do? The rule to follow is simple: if you avoid a product or a service, you should not work in producing, providing or promoting it.

However, what happens if you become a vegan while you are

already working in an area you should avoid? Not everyone is privileged enough to be able to afford to quit their job. An ethical vegan in this situation could find comfort in realising their new philosophy might have a positive influence in their workplace and, who knows, this might lead to a drastic change involving a reduction, or even elimination, of their contribution to exploitation. Often this will be wishful thinking, but in some situations it might be plausible.

On a more practical level, vegans might be in a better position to help other people become vegan if they are surrounded by non-vegans at work, rather than living in a 100 per cent vegan bubble isolated from carnists and omnivorous. Opportunities are there to be taken – one of the most effective methods I have used to help people become vegan is to show them I am no different than them, and that I successfully manage my lifestyle in the same world they live in.

Vegans may choose to manifest their beliefs at work in different ways, and in some instances this might involve letting other people know about their philosophy and how it affects their choices. In turn, this might cause them problems because some colleagues and managers may single them out as 'different' and perhaps discriminate against them because of that. If you work in Great Britain and that happens to you, don't worry, you now have a tool to defend your rights that you didn't have before. Because of the success of my litigation now you can prove to them your ethical veganism is a protected philosophical belief, and the conduct of those discriminating against you is unlawful.

My legal case does not give vegans more rights than others, though. It confirms they have equal rights. This protection is not a tool vegans can use to disturb the workplace with impunity, or to 'proselytise' beyond what it is already accepted for other groups. It's a tool to help vegans defend themselves when their work has been disturbed by colleagues or managers (for instance, by not providing them with adequate food or equipment), or they have been bullied by members of one group (veganphobes). It's a leveller, a mechanism to resolve injustice, not a weapon to use for advocacy.

This is why the protection is only given when an employment judge is brought into the picture, who will determine if the vegan is indeed an ethical vegan; if discrimination, victimisation or harassment did indeed take place; and if the main reason it took place was the protected characteristic of ethical veganism, and nothing else – and for judges to rule on that, good and reliable evidence of the events must be presented before them, following the proper lengthy and costly procedure.

By discrimination, the Equality Act 2010 means two things: direct discrimination (a person 'A' discriminates against another 'B' if, because of a protected characteristic, A treats B less favourably than A treats or would treat others), and indirect discrimination (a person 'A' discriminates against another 'B' if A applies to B a provision, criterion or practice which is discriminatory in relation to a relevant protected characteristic of all Bs). For example, in my litigation case, I claimed that providing a non-ethical pension fund as a default auto-enrolling pension (the provision) was indirect discrimination because it affected not only me but also all other ethical vegans as this fund was not suitable for us. I also claimed that firing me was an act of direct discrimination as it only affected me, and no others, vegan or otherwise, were also fired.

The Act also defines harassment as saying a person 'A' harasses another 'B' if A engages in unwanted conduct related to a relevant protected characteristic, and the conduct has the purpose or effect of violating B's dignity, or creating an intimidating, hostile, degrading, humiliating or offensive environment for B. However, it also says that in deciding whether conduct is harassment in the perception of B, other circumstances of the case, and whether it is reasonable for the conduct to have the effects described in the definition, must be taken into account. This means vegans cannot claim harassment if a colleague mocks them at work while he or she is clearly joking in a light-hearted manner and not intending to degrade or intimidate (and any onlookers agree). In my case, I claimed harassment when I was told during my disciplinary process that my ethics clouded my judgement and made me biased and unmanageable.

The Act also defines victimisation as follows: a person 'A' victimises another person 'B' if A subjects B to a detriment because B does a protected act (which means either bringing proceedings under the Equality Act, giving evidence or information in connection with proceedings under this Act, doing any other thing for the purposes of or in connection with this Act, or making an allegation that A or another person has contravened this Act), or A believes that B has done, or may do, a protected act. In other words, when any sort of 'revenge' against a vegan took place after she or he made a complaint. In my case, I also claimed victimisation as when I complained about my disciplinary hearing being chaired by my 'accuser', and no formal investigation had been conducted, an additional charge against me of 'serious insubordination' was added, which made it easier to fire me for 'gross misconduct'.

If ethical vegans are employees or contractors in Great Britain (as Northern Ireland is not covered by the Equality Act yet) who feel they have been the victim of any of these problems, the normal course of action would be to raise an official complaint or grievance to their managers following the complaints procedures set up by the company, and if this does not resolve the issue then a claim can be made at the Employment Tribunal within three months of the events causing the complaint.

In some work scenarios, forcing a vegan employee to undertake a task which would go against ethical veganism may be unlawful and therefore a formal complaint could be made at the Employment Tribunal, but this would be unlikely to succeed if the task is part of the claimant's job description, it is implicit in the work contract and the employer cannot easily reallocate the task to someone else without incurring significant extra cost or a major disruption in the workplace (in these situations pragmatism and common sense will play a major role).

Veganphobia is not a 'hate crime' (in the UK official hate crimes identified under the Protection of Freedoms Act 2012 include religion but not yet philosophical beliefs) and the offences under the Equality Act 2010 are civil offences, not criminal. Therefore, if vegans feel discriminated calling the police is not an option – if no other crime has been committed, that is – but litigation could be (which means they would have to make the claim themselves to the Employment Tribunal or get legal representatives to make it on their behalf).

Vegans feeling discriminated at work are far more common than most people think. In 2013 Lancaster University conducted a small study of vegans and found most of the participants endured a range of unpleasant, unfair and discriminatory experiences at work. In 2017 Go Vegan Scotland conducted a survey and concluded vegans were routinely ignored, dismissed, marginalised and made to feel as though they do not count. In 2019 Crossland Employment Solicitors surveyed 1,000 vegans concluding 45 per cent of them felt discriminated against by their employers, and 31 per cent felt harassed or unfairly treated at work due to their veganism. Therefore, ethical veganism definitely needed to be recognised as a protected characteristic, as many vegans may need this protection. Hopefully, other countries will follow suit and protect them too.

As far as hobbies are concerned, ethical vegans need to be careful in selecting the right products and materials. For instance, horsehair is used in fine arts paintbrushes and instrument bows. Crayons' waxy consistency may come from animal-based stearic acid or beef tallow. High-quality art papers may have casein.

Animal glues may still be used in antique restoration, gummed tapes, glass chipping, paintballs, art canvas or musical instruments. Leather is used in many sports as well (gloves, boots, balls, etc.). However, there are vegan alternatives for all of these.

Money and financial products

In 2017 the Bank of England issued a new type of five-pound note made of polymer plastic, rather than the traditional cotton paper. It contained a transparent section manufactured with the use of tallow, a rendered form of beef or mutton fat often used to make soaps and candles, and in this case as a source of stearic acid that allows the note to be lubricated and not stick to any surface. This not only made them unsuitable for vegans, but also unacceptable to many vegetarians, Hindus, Jains and others. Because of this, an online petition which ended up gathering 138,315 signatures was launched, demanding the cessation of the use of animal products in the production of currency. The Bank of England replied saying it had considered destroying, reprinting and delaying the issue of the new note in response to the backlash, but eventually decided it would not do it as it would be too expensive and would compromise anti-counterfeit measures.

I dealt with this problem by increasing the number of occasions I pay with a credit card, debit card or contactless card (I could choose contactless phone payments too, but I haven't got that function yet), and by asking vendors not to give me a five-pound note as change but coins instead. However, in 2018 the ten-pound notes were also changed to polymer, which made it more difficult as vendors were not always willing to give me so many coins. If they gave me any of the new notes, I immediately tried to find a nearby shop that could exchange them for coins or old notes. In 2019 the new polymer twenty-pound notes were introduced too, making it even harder, and on occasions impossible, to find the equivalent in coins.

Because of this, many vegans have opted to continue using the notes as usual, as the alternatives are not always practicable. This is one of the rare occasions where, seemingly, advances in technology have made the life of ethical vegans harder. I wonder whether, if my litigation had been successful sooner, the Bank of England might have reconsidered, as in effect it was entirely their choice – a form of tallow can be made from coconut or palm oil.

The good news is that it is increasingly possible to pay for goods and services with credit or debit cards, and the number of establishments accepting contactless payments for small amounts is also increasing. Not only that, but some vegan businesses also do not accept cash payments any longer, possibly to avoid the notes, and the new affordable mobile credit card charging devices can now be used with mobile phones and tablets, meaning even vegan stalls can use them – technology may have come to the rescue after all.

Using a bank card may allow us to avoid using vegan-unfriendly notes, but it cannot prevent us using vegan-unfriendly banks. Unfortunately, the banking sector is one of the few sectors very far behind, because it doesn't have any suitable options for ethical vegans yet. Most banks invest in companies incompatible with ethical veganism, and the few that may not do not offer the full range of services normal banks offer (such as current accounts, debit cards, etc.). Naturally, you could decide not to use banks at all and keep all your money under the bed (but if you are a UK ethical vegan you would need a big bed as you would have to keep it in coins), or you may need to resign yourself to using building societies instead as they don't invest in other companies (but they may not offer the full services banks offer).

There is another option, though: virtual currency, which is unregulated digital currency only available in electronic form. One type of virtual currency is called cryptocurrency, where individual digital token coin ownership records are stored using strong cryptography to secure financial transactions, control the creation of additional digital coins and to verify transfers (the most well-known of these currencies is Bitcoin, and one of the more than 18 million of these coins currently in circulation would cost me £6,969.80 if I bought it right now).

All types of developers can create virtual currencies to trade within their communities in exchange for goods and services, and of course the vegan community latched on to the concept, and now we have VeganCoin, a traceable cryptocurrency developed by VeganNation (an organisation which aims to create a vegan economy in which business are 'connected' and can trade with digital currency). Although I believe this cryptocurrency is still in its embryonic state, if it grows sufficiently and embraces most vegan businesses (a big ask!) it might in the future resolve the conflict we have to endure when using money.

Other financial services such as pensions, insurance policies, stock brokers, credit companies or investments providers can all end up investing in companies not suitable for vegans, and more often than not it is very difficult to find these details out. However, as far as pensions are concerned, the situation has improved because for some time now several pension providers have offered pensions labelled as 'ethical', some of which may be suitable for us. One of the consequences of my legal case is that it may 'shake up' the pension industry, which may now be more concerned about other vegans rejecting their pensions, or the general public realising they should check where their pension contributions go (and switch pensions or providers if they go to the wrong firms). This may create a competitive edge which will increase both the number and quality of ethical pensions available. Perhaps the vegan revolution could also spark a financial revolution which ends up washing away all the blood and soot covering our money. I can always dream, right?

Activism and campaigning

In August 2018 Ronnie Lee, one of the founders of the ALF, gave a talk at the Vegan Campout festival in Newark Showground, Nottinghamshire. In it, he proposed a new definition of veganism he created with the campaigner Tony Harris. It was similar to the definition of the Vegan Society, but with two key additions. A more explicit commitment to the environment by adding 'natural habitats' ('seeks to exclude all forms of exploitation of non-human animals, which extends beyond dietary considerations to the avoidance of all forms of animal abuse, including harm to their natural habitats'), and a commitment to do what we generally consider activism and campaigning ('It includes a moral duty to actively oppose all forms of animal exploitation and to encourage and educate others to become vegan, with the core aim being the eradication of speciesism'). The Vegan Society 'rejected' this proposal and decided to keep its agreed definition, but some supported the idea. Nevertheless, this opened the debate about whether genuine vegans need to also be activist or campaign to promote veganism and animal protection.

If you are an ethical person you may find being an ethical vegan is not enough, and you may feel you have to do more. First, because the problem of animal exploitation and suffering can only be solved when a significantly high population of ethical vegans shift the paradigm of consumer demand or successfully lobby for a meaningful political change. Second, because to reduce your blood footprint it's not enough becoming vegan – you have to consider how high it was before.

Most ethical vegans did not follow the philosophy their entire life, and there was a time they were contributing to all kinds of animal exploitation (and still today there may be unwillingly contributing, as most likely they have not managed to find 100 per cent vegan-friendly alternatives in all the products and services they use). There is no shortcut to getting rid of a 'blood debt' (what Eastern philosophers call bad *karma*), but there are ways to gradually pay it back. One is to try to help many other people become vegan as soon as possible, and the other is to try to help others in need to increase your 'positive' contribution to the world, and in doing so not only stop doing 'bad things' but begin doing 'good things'. Therefore, I believe any ethical vegan, at some point, will have to start thinking in which way they can contribute positively to the world beyond getting better at avoiding hurting anyone or anything. They may realise being passive is no longer enough for them, and the next step is being active too, in any way that suits them.

The forms in which they could do this vary, but broadly speaking would fit two basic concepts: activism and campaigning. The former will normally be a grassroots unpaid activity undertaken 'out there' with the general public or where animals are exploited, while the latter would normally be working with an established organisation in a paid job undertaken in offices or political institutions. In reality it doesn't matter whether activists are paid for their activism by an organisation, by donations or are not paid at all, as it is the work they do that counts.

A form of campaigning that everyone can do from home is **letter writing**. Writing to companies either complaining about something related to their products or trying to persuade them to become more vegan-friendly. For instance, in 2012 I corresponded with Virgin Atlantic complaining about the existence of non-vegan items in some of the inflight vegan meals, and next time I flew with them this had been corrected. Most recently I wrote to the hugely successful Swedish oat milk company Oatly letting them know that I had discovered some of their residual oat by-products were sold to local pig farmers. I said I would try to avoid them until they stopped doing so. They were quite understanding and engaging, and when I suggested alternative vegan-friendly uses for their oat by-products the company publicly stated it was now looking into some of these. Organisations hire professional campaigners for this sort of corporate engagement, and several new vegan products were developed on the back of these types of constructive interactions. Many activists (or the general public) can be rallied by professional campaigners to write to a company about a particular issue, and this can produce good results – generally speaking companies care about what their customers think of them.

Pressure campaigning – thinking strategically and applying the right pressure to the weakest point of the animal exploitation companies and industries – is something experienced campaigners, backed by big organisations, can do with considerable success. They can devise effective targeted tactics and co-ordinate grassroots activists to apply them at the right time and place. A career in campaigning can build up the necessary experience and expertise to be effective at this, starting as campaigns assistant and ending as director of campaigns. Some of these professional campaigners may have different degrees of involvement in grassroots, online, policy and lobbying. Within an organisation, they may only cover one particular issue or project, but together with others, especially working in coalitions with other groups, they may all add a piece to the complex puzzle any international movement will inevitably become.

Lobbying is a type of campaigning targeting decision-makers, normally politicians or civil servants. It is a truly specialised job done by professional lobbyists, which many NGOs have on their staff. Networking in the political landscape is crucial for this, and every election may change it. Finding the right political allies, and having a good sense of timing and diplomacy, are skills good lobbyists possess. Although I have done some lobbying myself, mostly in the EU Parliament and in other countries on issues related to bullfighting, this is not something I am particularly good at – I try to reduce the occasions I have to wear a suit!

Moving to the street, the most common form of activism ethical vegans can participate in is **outreach events**, aimed to encourage passers-by to take veganism seriously, and hopefully help them to become vegans sooner rather than later. Many forms of outreach require different levels of knowledge and skill. The simplest consists of handing leaflets or flyers to pedestrians in public places, such as the entrances of Underground stations, which normally doesn't involve speaking to anyone. The next stage is to hold a thought-provoking not-too-graphic sign in a public place which allows this sort of 'protest', and let people pass and read it. The next steps are to hold more poignant signs or a screen showing footage of the reality of exploitation, and engaging people who stop and ask questions in conversation. From here we can move to having a stall with campaign materials and sometimes vegan food, and encourage people to try the food and take the material home – these events require more logistical preparation.

The most complex forms of vegan outreach involve events such as The Earthlings Experience described in chapter 2 (page 76), with devices that show footage of animal exploitation (such as laptops, large screens, projectors or virtual sets) held by immobile activists (often with masks) creating some sort of attention-grabbing performance, while other activists with plenty of knowledge and conversational skills engage in relatively long friendly chats with bystanders who stop to watch.

I have personally participated often in all these sorts of events, many of which are very rewarding as you can experience very emotional transformations in people's attitudes towards animals, and you can give the 'final push' to pre-vegans who need a few answers to dust off their remaining doubts.

Not all street activism is as tension-free as vegan outreach, though. **Protests** by more 'militant' activists, where the emphasis is on a 'negative' message (i.e. highlighting the cruelty of those who are being protested against), are normally more 'passionate'. They may express more openly and loudly their feelings of sadness or anger, which may create hostile reactions. They may be staging a publicity stunt or demonstrating with signs or banners outside a premises or an event, perhaps with megaphones and chanting, or may even involve entering the premises and protesting inside (known as 'disruptions'). The regular protest at the entrance of London's Canada Goose stores, the infamous company which sells winter jackets with coyote's fur and goose's down, might be described as the former. While the latter might be non-violent disruptions in restaurants or supermarkets performed by activists of the grassroots organisation Direct Action Everywhere.

Although this sort of activism is not for me, it might be right for some who feel angrier and prefer a more 'aggressive' but still non-violent outlet to manifest their feelings. I certainly understand the logic behind it: to challenge the normalisation of cruelty by making people think about what they buy or consume while they are doing the buying and eating. The next time they do it they may remember the event, and perhaps pause and think. I am not sure how effective these protests are, or whether they might put too many people off veganism, but I certainly think the experience may suddenly 'wake' some people who otherwise would have never approached a relaxed vegan outreach event.

Another type of disruption is a **vigil**, where for a few minutes activists stop lorries with live animals before they enter a slaughterhouse, to say 'goodbye' to the animals and record videos. This is organised all over the world by the grassroots group The Save Movement. More often than not the lorry driver, knowing it's only for a couple of minutes, will comply and no major incident takes place, but in June 2020 the activist Regan Russell was tragically killed in a vigil when she was run over by a lorry outside a slaughterhouse in Burlington, Ontario. A few days after a newly passed bill 156 criminalised such demonstrations in this Canadian state.

Some more militant activists may go further than this and engage in **resistance activism**, such as blocking roads, buildings or events in protest (always without violence, by the way), often chaining or gluing themselves so the police cannot easily remove them. This last is the speciality of the recently created grassroots group Animal Rebellion, which was inspired by the environmental group Extinction Rebellion. Other activists may 'invade' the inside of farm buildings or slaughterhouses for some hours as a 'sit-in' non-violent protest (often recording the event and broadcasting it on social media), which sometimes includes the rescuing of individual animals in particularly bad shape.

All resistance activism could lead to the activist being arrested and charged with blocking a public road, criminal damage or aggravated trespass, and this is another reason I avoid it as I prefer to operate inside the law. I also avoid any activism likely to raise people's tension to the point of violence erupting, including verbal violence, as I think this would be against my interpretation of the principle of *ahimsa* I follow. When I see in the media acts of vandalism with clear threats to carnists, I often wonder if these were self-inflicted to discredit the vegan movement. For me, it is important to ensure all activism I participate in is peaceful.

At the end of the day, as in any transformative socio-political movement with a non-violent direct action component, nobody knows which tactics work best, as things that work in one context may not work in another. Often positive results are a combination of many tactics, the effect of which is impossible to separate – I find research claiming to have found the main tactic leading to past social justice successes (i.e. anti-slavery or the women's vote) unconvincing and not necessarily transferable. Activists and campaigners will find the activism that works for them, and they should not assume it will work for others too.

I have tried several forms of activism over the years and I know what works for me. I was never involved with any animal liberation group, but I have been very involved with the anti-hunting movement and I often participate in outreach events (so I do qualify as a 'grassroots activist', I suppose). Although I have been employed by many animal welfare organisations (I qualify as a 'professional campaigner' as well), I am an abolitionist, and I mostly worked on abolitionist campaigns. Ethically speaking, I embrace both the deontological and the utilitarian approaches, but the former for 'negative' actions and the latter for 'positive' actions. That is to say, I believe there are some things we should never do (such as exploiting animals) as they are intrinsically wrong, but I also think that for what we should be doing, helping animals in need, we should choose the actions that help more animals, and in a more significant and effective way. With this dual approach, I managed to navigate successfully the ideological and practical maze of the animal protection landscape.

Ethical vegans may have all sorts of emotional responses to the reality of animal exploitation and cruelty they are constantly discovering. If their main reaction is sadness perhaps vigils may provide the right 'mood' to express their activism. If it is 'anger' perhaps a protest or a disruption. If they feel eloquent and cerebral, vegan outreach may be for them (and this is the type of street activism I prefer). If they feel inspired, they may instead write, compose a song or create art. If they feel too intimidated by the idea of doing activism on the streets, or they are unable to do it, online activism is always an option. There is a form of activism for everyone, and I think we should never judge other activists for not choosing the form we chose – as long as they never become violent, both in action or in words (activists should never forget *ahimsa* also applies to any human, as despicable as some can be).

* * *

Although everyone can be a vegan activist and the more people who are the better, in the last two decades, thanks to social media, there has been a new type characterised by standing above the crowd: the so-called 'famous activists' (although they would never define themselves as such, but rather as educators, public speakers or online content creators), such as the American Gary Yourofsky, the Australian James Aspey, the British Ed Winters (Earthling Ed) and the Australian Joey Carbstrong, all ethical vegans with their own styles (although most leaning towards confrontational debating of the 'prove me wrong' type).

However, their success has not been well received by all vegans, some of whom resent the idea of some activists being paid (by donations, fees or online adds) and others not, who disagree with their style or language, who do not like that they are excessively 'idolised' by many vegans or who think they are monopolising the limited available campaign platforms while most of them only represent a particular problematic demographic (young white cisgender heterosexual able males).

Many other activists, campaigners and educators from other demographics have been rising in notability, but they are not so well known yet everywhere (except the young Swedish environmentalist Greta Thunberg, now possibly the most recognisable activist of modern times). For instance, Lauren Ornelas (founder of the Food Empowerment Project), Christopher-Sebastian McJetters (intersectional vegan advocate), Aryenish Birdie (founder of Encompass), Liz Ross (founder of Coalition of Vegan Activists of Color), Genesis Butler (vegan activist), Seb Alex (vegan activist), Fiona Oakes (athlete and animal sanctuary owner), and many more I must have missed, especially from non-Anglo-Saxon nations.

If we could widen the number and diversity of vegan activists and campaigners, and find ways they all could do this as a paid profession, they should all become better at delivering the *ahimsa* message, more people will hear it and everyone from any community will understand it. The animals, the environment and marginalised groups will all benefit because of this.

'Celebrity' or unknown, paid or unpaid, full-time or part-time, online or on the streets, rational or emotional, ethical vegans who decide to become 'active' in promoting veganism and protecting the vulnerable not only can considerably reduce their personal blood footprint, but they can become an inspiration to others, who in turn can also rise and 'do something'. One after the other, they can build a community which, sometime in the future, may reach a critical mass, cracking the carnists' fortress and bringing real hope for a meaningful change capable of making this planet a peaceful home for everyone.

If we build it, more will come.

FOOD & DRINK	Meat, eggs, milk, cheese, butter, yoghurt, cream, lard, lactose, whey, albumen, honey, propolis, beeswax, royal jelly, casein, cochineal (carmine), shellac, confectioners glaze, food-grade wax, gelatine, aspic, isinglass, rennet, vitamin D3 (unless labelled as suitable for vegans), E120, E441, E469, E542, E901, E904, E910, E913, E921, E926, E966, E1000, E1105, E1518, and ingredients tested on animals.
CLOTHES & FASHION ACCESSORIES	Leather (including suede), fur (including wool from sheep and alpacas, cashmere from goats, angora from rabbits, mohair from goats and horsehair), feathers (including down), teeth (including elephant ivory), silk from invertebrates, horns, antlers, tortoiseshell and real pearls from oysters.

WHAT MOST ETHICAL
VEGANS AVOID

PERSONAL CARE & HOUSEHOLD PRODUCTS	Beeswax, honey, gelatine, shellac, animal fats, fish compounds, dairy products, cochineal (carmine), lanolin, non-vegetable glycerine, casein, squalene, guanine, oleic acid (a.k.a. oleyl stearate, oleyl oleate or tallow), stearic acid, collagen, elastin, keratin, horsehair, bone, silk, animal glues and products tested on animals.
ENTERTAINMENT, WORK, HOBBIES, TRANSPORT, FINANCIAL, ETC.	Anything involving chasing, trapping, capturing, chaining, tethering, forcing to work, forcing to breed, forcing to race, genetically modifying, riding, mutilating, gassing, poisoning, keeping captive, stealing secretions, stealing produce, destroying homes, separating from family/ society, 'breaking', distressing, scaring, stressing, exhausting, injuring, killing or harming any individual member of the animal kingdom.

6.

The Future is Vegan

It's a political journey, and it hasn't ended yet.

I don't have a crystal ball, but even if I did it would only distort the light of the present and make me imagine things that might never come to fruition. Nevertheless, without any esoteric divination technique, all humans can process information and make predictions, regardless of how accurate they may be. Speculating about what will happen has become very important to us. Predicting is the main justification for science, the main driver of economics and the main motivation in sport.

We know where ethical veganism has been and kind of know where it is now, but where is it going? To answer that, we need to look at the current socio-political trends blowing the world's sails right now, because wherever they are taking humanity, that's where vegans will be going too.

Human population growth

We have been experiencing this trend for the last 10,000 years when the 'takers' took over the 'leavers' and the agricultural revolution began. However, since the 18th century growth has been exponential. The world population increased from 1 billion in 1800 to 7.7 billion today, and it is estimated that by the end of the century over 11 billion humans will be trampling the Earth. The more people there are on this planet, the more animals will be exploited and the environment damaged, and I think this is the main trend that will slow down the effectiveness of the vegan movement in addressing the animal and environmental problems.

Some people are very concerned about this and are campaigning against human reproduction. I think the intersection between these and ethical vegans will solidify, and not only will more ethical vegans choose not to have biological children – such as myself – but they may try to persuade other vegans to do the same, becoming **anti-natalist vegans**. Politically, there will need to be a change facilitating anti-natalist vegan families to adopt or foster children (as currently some vegans seem to have some difficulties in some jurisdictions in this regard) as otherwise if anti-natalism grows too much within veganism there may be a risk of fewer 'ethical vegans from birth' (potentially the humans with the lowest blood and carbon footprint), who should be the majority.

Flesh consumption

A consequence of the growth of the human population is that more people than ever are consuming flesh from animals – the breeding and slaughter of animals has massively increased since the 1960s. According to Animal Charity Evaluators, in 2016 over 74 billion animals were slaughtered for food (9.93 for each person). The country with the most animals killed was China, with 13 billion kills at 9.77 per capita, followed by the US with 9.3 billion animals at 28.96 per capita – that's more kills than the entire EU.

The organisation Our World in Data has reported the world now produces more than four times the quantity of meat as it did fifty years ago, and although the flesh of pigs is the most popular meat globally, the production of poultry is increasing most rapidly. They found the world now produces around 800 million tonnes of milk each year – more than double the amount fifty years ago – and meat and milk consumption increases when countries become richer, as is happening in China. This is not good news for ethical vegans, as for every person we help to become vegan, many more people are born who fall for the relentless indoctrination of carnism, which makes them swallow more flesh and drink more animal secretions. Carnism still has a firm grip on the world's societies, feeding on economic growth, and the vegan movement will have to tackle this and work harder in developing countries.

Climate change

Despite the annoying persistence of climate change deniers in prominent political positions, there is consensus among experts about the planet experiencing a very serious human-made global warming crisis. More people are agreeing with them, which is a trend that will hopefully lead to real political commitment to address it, rather than just talk about it. We are in the midst of an environmental crisis causing the sixth mass extinction of the Earth's history, with up to 200 species becoming extinct every single day (nearly 1,000 times the 'natural' rate). The 2020 study 'Vertebrates on the brink as indicators of biological annihilation and the sixth mass extinction', published in *PNAS*, found that more than 500 species of land vertebrates are on the brink of extinction and likely to be lost within 20 years. The Intergovernmental Panel on Climate Change should gain political influence if it is finally regarded as the prevailing wisdom.

Carbon dioxide and methane produced by human activities are the major drivers of this crisis, and as the animal agriculture industry is, without any doubt, one of the top contributors of these emissions, political initiatives attempting to reduce them (perhaps co-ordinated by the United Nations Framework Convention on Climate Change, UNFCCC) will eventually have to end up reforming the food and fibre sectors and promoting alternative plant-based industries. Ethical veganism and concern about global warming will grow hand in hand, and, hopefully, more environmentalists will become vegan – or ethical vegans with an even lower carbon footprint – and more vegans will become environmentalists. I can't wait to see an adult Greta Thunberg becoming prime minister of Sweden! Therefore, this trend will create more ethical vegans, and the closer we get to experiencing the real effects of the crises in our everyday lives, the higher the number of people entering veganism via the environmental gateway.

Hunger and poverty

Ironically, while we see an epidemic of obesity spreading through the richest nations, most people in the world live in poverty and many go to bed hungry. The combination of an increase of human population, global warming and unequal distribution of wealth and resources favouring developed nations and a handful of billionaires (according to Oxfam, 1 per cent of people have more than twice as much wealth than the combined wealth of 6.96 billion people) has created a trend that is still going strong: the increase of world hunger and poverty. According to the World Health Organization, global hunger continues to rise, with 821 million undernourished in 2017, or one in every nine people. At one point it seemed this trend was going to slow down, but it seems that hunger has been on the rise over the past few years, returning to levels from a decade ago. The UN found that climate variability, changing rainfall patterns and climate extremes such as droughts and floods are among the key drivers behind this recent rise.

Veganism could substantially help to solve this problem, because one of the top causes of world hunger is the unnecessary focus on the production of animal-based foods. There are enough edible plants cultivated to nourish the entire human population, but most crops are fed to livestock for rich nations. According to the World Animal Foundation, there are millions of tons of soybeans and corn produced globally, but about 40 to 50 per cent of the corn and 80 per cent of the soybeans are directed towards feeding livestock, which is a great waste of food as 13 to 20 pounds of grain is needed to feed cattle to increase muscle mass by 1 pound, but 13 to 20 times more people could be fed if they ate the grain directly. It's the same with all the other animals bred for food: about 7 pounds of grain is needed for one pound of pig's flesh, and 4.5 pounds of grain for one pound of chicken's flesh. Researchers at the University of Minnesota's Institute on the Environment estimated in 2013 that growing crops for direct human consumption increases available food calories by up to 70 per cent, and all the new crops that could be created from stopping animal agriculture would be enough to feed an additional 4 billion people (enough food to cover the estimated increase in the world population of 2 to 3 billion people by 2050). The final impressive figure deduced from this study is that a purely animal-based diet would require 909 per cent more crop growth in comparison to a purely plant-based diet.

Animal agriculture is not only wasting lots of energy and resources to produce insufficient amounts of food that are actually unhealthier than the alternatives, but is selling itself as the 'model' for developing nations to imitate, making the problem of a hungry majority ruled by an obese minority worse. If the world's agriculture policies shifted towards incentivising farming crops for direct human consumption and penalising animal farming and the cultivation of crops to feed livestock, the global hunger trend could be stopped. For that to happen, vegan policymakers and economists may become emerging professions with a prosperous future.

Pandemics

From the moment *Homo erectus* expanded from Africa to Eurasia the Pandora's box of pandemics opened. 'Humans' began to encounter new pathogens carried by animals they hadn't evolved around, and therefore had no natural defences against. These pathogens mixed with others, or with the genetic codes of their hosts, and new diseases emerged that could be passed from non-human animals to humans (known as zoonosis), or the other way around. The more we expand and connect different parts of the globe, and the more we mess with Nature, mixing many species and their pathogens (in animal markets, in zoos, in pet shops, in farms, etc.), the more we will create pandemics which will lead to all sorts of catastrophic effects.

It is believed at least 60 per cent of the emerging infectious diseases are zoonoses. Tuberculosis is thought to have been acquired from the domestication of goats, typhoid from domesticating chickens, whooping cough from domesticated pigs, leprosy from water buffalo, the cold virus from cattle or horses, HIV from apes ... and then there was SARS (2002), MERS (2012) and now Covid-19 (2019), which most scientists agree originated in bats, who may have infected an intermediate animal, and then was passed to humans.

Animal exploitation is intrinsically linked to the appearance of new emerging infectious diseases, and cheap international travel will always transform local epidemics into pandemics. Sooner or later, these two facts will have to be addressed if we want to spare ourselves an increasing number of pandemics hitting the entire world. Because of the current Covid-19 crisis, people and politicians may finally acknowledge the gravity of this trend and try to slow it down. To address the problem, policymakers around the globe will have to consider abolishing the bushmeat trade, the wildlife trade, all web markets and factory farming, which are all hot spots where new zoonoses are likely to emerge.

Then they will have to go further, by abolishing zoos and the keeping of wild animals as pets ... and if they honestly want to eliminate the risk, well, a vegan world would be the answer. Therefore, I expect the narrative of the #3in4 campaign recently run by Viva!, highlighting three in four new or emerging infectious diseases come from non-human animals, will become a strong new argument vegan outreach can add to its arsenal.

False news

We seem to be experiencing a growing trend of another type of 'infectious' social disease caused by the contagion of false news (the infectious agent), spread via uncontrolled social media hot spots and rushed twenty-four-hour news cycles, in a post-truth environment ('the circuitous slippage between facts or alt-facts, knowledge, opinion, belief, and truth', as academic Barbara. A. Biesecker put it in an article published in the journal *Philosophy and Rhetoric*). The common symptoms are belief in conspiracy theories, lack of trust in any authority, paranoia, re-emerging of ridiculous geological anachronisms (yes, you know whom I am talking about), anxiety, miseducation, bigotry and general ignorance. This is not new. Superstition, quackery, religious indoctrination and carnist propaganda have existed since the rise of human civilisations, and they have always rivalled reality and objective truth championed by scientists and enlightened humanists. However, it seems that since 2015, in the lead up to the Brexit referendum and the emergence of the Donald Trump regime (which issued false news and then labelled corrective news as 'fake news'), we have now entered another particularly serious 'pandemic' of this information disease, comparable to the appropriately named 'dark ages' of the medieval period.

This epidemic worries me as it is negatively affecting the vegan movement, and I cannot help but be upset by seeing vegans falling victims of it, and by doing so discrediting the movement. I am not quite sure how we should be dealing with this. As veganism is so easily promoted through critical thinking, rationality, facts, evidence and science, any trend which undermines the importance of these beacons of truth is bound to prevent more people becoming vegan, and lead vegans to start consuming animal products again.

This is because they may fall to any anti-vegan conspiracy theory (including one which could 'reveal' vegans are a secret elite trying to take over the world).

However, as in the Renaissance, I expect in the next few decades a second Enlightenment movement may come to the rescue, and we will return to the 'True-Truth Era', much more fertile soil for the growth of ethical veganism. I expect pathological conspiracy theorists within the vegan movement will eventually be exposed and their shouts fade away. Some signs suggest this may be already starting. In the UK the House of Commons commenced a parliamentary inquiry into the 'growing phenomenon of fake news'; the International Fact-Checking Network was launched in 2015; Facebook and YouTube are beginning to ban the worst offenders (including the most notorious conspiracy theorists); and in March 2018 Google launched Google News Initiative to fight the spread of false news.

Political uncertainty

It's difficult to keep track of politics these days. The old simple models don't seem to work any longer, and the current trend of political uncertainly is likely to keep confusing voters – and keep feeding opportunistic political scavengers. The traditional two-side contests seem a bit obsolete. Yes, we still have left and right, and democracy and dictatorship, but they don't look the same. Communist China seem to be capitalising on capitalism; populist parties are run by totalitarian despots; old European countries leave the continent but don't go anywhere else; immigrants vote against immigration; rebellions use the system instead of breaking it; globalist nations seek independence; poor people vote for rich rulers. It's hard to make any prediction with such a shifting landscape, and I won't even try.

Veganism, which is a socio-political movement in itself, can grow in all political environments but will do so more significantly and effectively if it is firmly supported by a progressive liberal social justice movement. This is why I hope intersectionalism is eventually embraced within the movement, and is no longer faced with the current resistance in certain sections of the vegan community. I don't think we'll see 'anti-intersectional' vegans in the future, as their stand is not a sustainable cogent position (you cannot ask people to become 'woke' to the reality of animal exploitation but then criticise people for being 'woke' to the reality of human exploitation). Unchecked racism and xenophobia will always be an obstacle to a vegan world. It may take a generation to get there, but social progress always takes a long time.

In a different corner of politics, be prepared for a likely political surprise: in the future, anti-establishment people who are currently with the movement campaigning against carnism may turn against veganism if it truly becomes part of 'the system', becoming instead the emblem of receding carnism. In a vegan world, carnist libertarian anarchists might block roads and occupy public buildings in an ironic twist historians will write theses about – we will have to deal with this when we get there.

Equality

As the ruling pig of George Orwell's *Animal Farm* said, 'All animals are equal, but some animals are more equal than others.' For millennia, only privileged groups of particular genders, races, ethnicity or class have received the biggest portion of 'society's cake', but in the last couple of centuries the trend to change towards equal opportunity began, and it's still going strong today. Despite the progress of the civil rights movement, tragic events such as the recent murder of George Floyd by Minneapolis police officers continue to awaken people to the reality of systemic racism, galvanising many into the Black Lives Matter movement and giving further momentum to the equality trend. The more anti-racist society becomes, the easier it will be to argue against speciesism. Intersectional vegans will be crucial to help the vegan movement to address issues such as racism, xenophobia, ableism, antisemitism, misogyny, homophobia, transphobia or Islamophobia, and do it in an appropriate way which maximises the efficiency of the vegan message without marginalising other important social justice causes.

As far as gender equality is concerned, we have an interesting dynamic in the movement. Prominent male vegan activists receive a great deal of media attention, while most vegan organisations are currently led by women (PETA, Animal Aid, Animal Equality UK, Viva!, Go Vegan World, Veganuary and Beyond Carnism spring to mind). I don't think we want to be in either a pendulum of dominance or segregation of roles, but I am not quite sure how and when the right equity balance will be found. A nasty expression of gender inequality, sexual harassment in the workplace, has been highlighted by the recent #metoo campaign, which I expect will continue to make waves and affect all aspects of society. People will become more open and accountable about inappropriate sexual behaviour, and that's definitely a good thing.

Another equality component of veganism will certainly grow: the equal treatment of vegans within society. I expect our legal success securing the protection of ethical vegans from discrimination will be replicated in many other countries, possibly starting with those with common law systems (such as Canada) or EU countries which have the European Convention of Human Rights to draw legal precedent from (will Germany be next?). This will lead to more people becoming vegan, and staying vegan for longer. I also expect equality of vegans in the UK will expand beyond what we have already achieved. We have potent equality laws and precedents, and organisations such as the Vegan Society can push the envelope further. However, notwithstanding the legitimacy of equity tactics, promoting tribal mentality and victimhood as a method to drive equality may not always be a good idea – we don't want to go too far, and rather than reaching equality cross the line towards privilege (hopefully we will be able to prevent this before it happens).

Social media

For a social animal such as *Homo sapiens*, having a way to expand your social circle with a minimum effort is something bound to spread like wildfire. After a few experimental trials, we now have found the social media platforms that work, and more people are using them. This trend will continue to grow, with new forms being created, and new functions being developed. You can of course resist the pressure to join, as in the past some resisted the pressure to learn to read, but today, if you want to be social enough, if you don't want to be handicapped by absence, you have to use the media people around you use to communicate.

What is the price, though? A humongous avalanche of chatter. The YouTube generation broadcasts their opinion without checking anyone else wants to hear it. We live in a world full of unopened bottles with trivial messages drifting around, and this not only makes it more difficult to navigate the already highly polluted information sea, but also gives a false sense of entitlement which inhibits healthy modesty – but I can't complain as I am taking for granted that readers of this book will want to hear what I want to say.

For the vegan movement, though, social media has been great and will continue to be great, as our message thrives on these platforms. 'Go vegan', or its more intellectual grandparent 'do no harm', are clear enough messages, and the debates they generate feed many thoughts. In a world boiling with information, the ideas that survive are simpler, clearer and more coherent. Ideas that can be summarised in a short easily pronounceable word, and explained in no more than five words. Veganism fits the bill: Vegan – against all animal exploitation.

Activism now reaches much bigger audiences too. A demonstration of ten people can be seen by thousands and a clever publicity stunt by millions. The so-called 'vegan influencers' will come and go as their credentials will always eventually be challenged, and infighting will still spring up all over the place, but this is a fair price to pay for having an important message amplified. It doesn't help that we have information overload, echo-chamber ping-ponging and the nastiness of false news ruining it for all, but at least the information is ready to germinate when the conditions are right. The vegan message is out there, floating in virtual clouds raining down on thirsty minds.

Vegdiversity

One of the fundamental concepts of physics is 'entropy', the degree of disorder in a system, which according to the second principle of thermodynamics always increases. Since the big bang, we are constantly moving from uniformity to diversity. This trend is reflected in all forms of evolution, from stellar to cultural. However, where we find diversity as things split into different types, we also see forces lumping things together. Supernova stars explode in a trillion pieces, but from their dust lumps are created, which become bigger lumps, which form into dust clouds, then new stars and then new planets. In this universe, splitting and lumping forces are constantly at play, and while we can see an overall increase of disorder, within it we see many cycles of increase and decrease of diversity.

We have seen how many types of vegans and vegetarians there are today. Are we going to see even more types in the future? I think most good ideas evolve in cycles of alternating maximum and minimum diversity, and although we are certainly in a high-variety moment, I am not sure if we have peaked yet. In the first 'unification' we may see the consolidation of animal-rights vegans and ecovegans as 'ethical vegans'. Abstinents and intersectionals may be the next lump to be formed, and finally dietary vegans may embrace the whole philosophy and the adjective 'ethical' will no longer be needed. In the peak of the next unification, we may have only two groups, omnivorous and vegans, in a final struggle for domination – I can see the Marvel film already.

We may have to go through another cycle or two until the utopian 'vegan world' we dream about could become a reality, and that will be when the infrastructure of animal exploitation could be so severely depleted that in future cycles omnivorous might no longer be in the picture. Perhaps we will then see diversification going in all sorts of interesting directions. One could be true 'ascetic vegans' rejecting all forms of consumerism, evolving from abstinent vegans. These, with the help of technology of this future time, could attain a level of asceticism not even hermits could reach (if a Sramana monk could meet an abstinent neo-punk, it would be an interesting full circle to behold). All of this is, of course, wishful thinking and wild guessing. I may be wrong and we may have a 'big crush' or an infinite expansion towards total dilution, both leading to the end of the most powerful idea ever conceived.

Vegan options

Nobody can dispute that every day, at least in developed nations, it is easier to become vegan because there are more vegan-friendly options everywhere. When I first become vegan, soya milk was the only milk I could regularly find. Now, in my local corner shop, they have twenty-five types of plant-based milk available. With an increase of the number of vegans, but especially because a wider spread of the 'vegan message' can make people question their habits and begin shifting their consumer choices towards plant-based products without necessarily becoming vegan themselves yet, this trend is likely to continue. Mintel reported in 2019 nearly a quarter of people in the UK consumed plant milk, up from 19 per cent in 2018. According to a study by the British Takeaway

Campaign, between 2016 and 2018 plant-based meals became the fastest-growing takeaway choice with a 388 per cent increase. An Opinion Matters study showed in 2017 one in five Brits were considering going vegan. According to Sainsbury's *Future of Food Report*, vegans and vegetarians will make up a quarter of the British population in 2025, and just under half of all UK consumers will be flexitarians. The recent report *Vegan Food Market by Product Type and Distribution Channel: Global Opportunity Analysis and Industry Forecast, 2019–2026* by Research and Markets concluded the global vegan food market was valued at $14.2 billion in 2018 and is expected to reach $31.4 billion by 2026.

This is certainly an impressive trend, but a trend of what? It is not a trend of a reduction of animal exploitation in agriculture, because sadly the number of animals used by the industry continues to increase, year after year, and the current vegan trend is not yet showing any effect on this. It is not a reflection of an increase of the number of ethical vegans either, as we are still a very small percentage of the population, and polls do not show any sign of exponential growth yet (although sometimes it feels this way, when our enthusiasm re-bounces in our echo chambers). It is only an increase of consumption of vegan-friendly products, many consumed by only dietary vegans, many by typical vegetarians, and many by omnivorous – and we are still talking about food products only. This is a commercial trend, not a moral trend, and as such could indeed only be a transient fashion sparked by the novelty factor.

I expect this growth will continue but it will slow down – although we will see a further increase of the number of vegans, it will not grow exponentially but at a much slower pace than many people anticipate. The current explosion of interest in vegan products will make it more likely people will become vegan, for longer, and people in vegan-unfriendly locations may finally find enough suitable products to have a satisfactory lifestyle. However, I expect many reducetarians and flexitarians will slip into their old omnivorous habits without even realising it – or without anyone who is out there counting them even noticing it. The former because at some point they will cease to reduce the consumption of animal products after considering they have 'reduced' enough. The latter because they will not have a moral drive that is strong enough to push them forward. People who put pragmatism above ethics may not be able to resist the pressure of the animal agriculture industry, which, now realising the 'vegan threat' is serious, will begin to fight back with well-funded propaganda programmes, politically supported by a society still run by carnists.

After this 'bubble' of vegan content, many small vegan businesses may fail as now they will be competing with many others (especially considering a Covid-19 recession). Therefore I expect the numbers of vegan eateries in big metropolitan cities such as London, Berlin or New York, which have experienced an increase in recent years, will go down to more stable levels before rising again. However, when the current bubble bursts, we, ethical vegans for life, will be in a much better position to advance the movement, as there will be more of us, and with better logistics to keep us going. As with a tsunami crashing against the harbour, the waters will recede to normal levels, but sea defences will then be weakened and new estuaries will be formed where water dominates the landscape.

Veganism is not becoming mainstream because more people are becoming vegan, but because the concept is penetrating all sections of society in all corners of the globe. This is the first step for the 'vegan revolution', but by no means the last. After the current vegan boom, if we keep going, if we keep being true to the concept of *ahimsa*, others will come, every time eroding more and more the pillars of carnism until, hopefully, they all will crumble.

A vegan world

Having looked at all these trends, what is my prediction? Are we ever going to have a 'vegan world', or not? The threat of global warming and pandemics, the surge of vegan options, the persistence of world hunger, the improvement of equality, the increase of diversity and the spread of social media will all push us towards a vegan world. The growth of human population, the rise of flesh consumption in developing nations, the proliferation of false news and the continuation of political uncertainty will push us in the opposite direction. Who will win? I don't know, but I am an optimist – working in my field I have to be – and I would dare to say the vegan world will indeed come, if humanity survives long enough to build it. And this, sadly, is far from guaranteed. I am an optimist because I trust Mother Nature, and I recognise that we are part of it, that we are not directed by anything external. We just need to find our way back home. It may take a long time, but unless we change to regain the right to be in this world, the planet will eventually cough us out.

Veganism will ultimately win the debate and show it is a viable response to global ill health, climate crisis, famine, pandemics, social injustice, habitat destruction, mass extinction and animal cruelty. Not a luxury or a fad for those privileged enough to indulge in it. Not a theoretical argument or an intellectual proposition to be discussed in elitist academic circles. It is an intelligent social response to all these crises, a coherent practical solution which can address them all with a simple change of attitude. The *ahimsa* approach not only affects every aspect of the lives of ethical vegans; it can affect every aspect of humanity's existence as well. Veganism may turn out to be our essential response to survive. The light at the end of the tunnel.

How will this utopian vegan world come to fruition? This is the realm of pure speculation and fantasy, but let's give it a go anyway. We may see a series of splitting and lumping cycles associated with a succession of increasingly bigger 'bubbles', where the popularity of vegan products will come and go, but through which the number of ethical vegans for life, the bedrock of the movement, will steadily increase until they reach a critical mass making them politically viable. Veganism will become the trading 'currency' all political parties will use to win the next election, while international bodies will finally adopt the vegan agenda to save the increasingly threatened world. Carnism as such will disappear, and without it, the omnivorous will lose.

On the way there, we may see many interesting developments. Veganic farming will gradually replace organic farming, and the first step to phase out animal agriculture would be banning factory farming. Abstinent vegans may become a big thing, and straight edge vegans may end up being a small subset of them. Before the next unifying cycle, we may see ethical fruitarians and abstinent vegans as 'the next ethical level', those who will push the *ahimsa* concept further. If the former is confirmed as a healthy diet both may grow in numbers, but they may always be a minority, carrying the 'moral' standard at the vanguard shifting the average vegans towards the ethical side. It's possible that, well before the vegan world is in sight, all Jains may have become vegan, as they have Mahavira's spirit nagging them. Before merging with the rest of ethical vegans, intersectional vegans will gradually grow in number and soon may become as common as ecovegans, as they will have the backing of entire new demographics which will easily survive without the support of reactionary orthodoxy.

I believe in the next unifying period we will no longer see typical vegetarians, as business and public bodies will only provide vegan options (instead of both vegetarian and vegan), and their ethical position will become more untenable. By then the letter 'V' may be universally interpreted as the symbol of veganism, and the old Churchillian 'victory' hand gesture may only represent vegan identity.

I think flexitarians and possibly reducetarians will disappear relatively soon, when the current bubble bursts, as they are not a cogent group and the only rules they follow are not to follow any rule. I don't think animal-based 'lab meat' will survive either, because the idea of meat will become politically incorrect, and companies will move away from the shapes, colours, textures and smells of animal exploitation.

During this process, several types of animal exploitation will be gradually abolished either by law or from falling out of practice, and the numbers of animals bred in the animal agriculture and bioresearch industry will be gradually reduced. By the time the vegan utopia arrives, only a small controlled population of former farm animals will be kept in sanctuaries, and these, without human selective breeding, will gradually revert to their original 'wild' forms by a phenomenon known as 'atavism' – restoration of ancestral phenotypes by the natural reappearance of traits previously lost but still codified in the gene pool. Sanctuaries will then become protected animal reserves with ex-domesticated animals becoming feral, and the animals we took from Nature may eventually return to it.

Without animal agriculture monopolising the countryside, all the land recovered could now be used to produce food for everyone, with less water and chemicals used. There would be enough land to be able to re-wild part of it, and new forests could now connect old forests, all of them absorbing CO2, which is now produced in lesser quantities. What would the result be? Earth's balance restored, global warming, pandemics, hunger and inequality averted, and a new inclusive non-racist and non-speciesist enlightened political system designed to avoid ever falling back to humanity's past mistakes. In the end, the term 'vegan' will no longer be needed, as *ahimsa* (this embracing Yin force) will have become an integral part of humanity in all its dimensions.

What if the utopian vegan world doesn't come, though? Perhaps it's already too late and global warming will become irreversible and we end our days on Earth in a Mad Max dystopia rather than an Eloi utopia (the fruitarian civilisation in H.G. Wells' *Time Machine*). Who knows? Before that, will veganism disappear to be taken over by the next best thing? Are the forms of the so-called post-veganism we see today that 'next thing'? Perhaps, but I don't think so. When you learn about the story of veganism, the story of *ahimsa*, and how it has moved over centuries, always advancing in the same direction, and how many variations have appeared without eliminating the genuine concept, you may realise there could not be such a thing as post-veganism, or post-human, or post-evolution.

It is all a flowing continuum, a journey with no destination, and even if we remove the adjective 'ethical', or if we replace the word 'vegan' by something else, the idea will prevail. However, these self-defined post-vegans may indeed slow down the advance of veganism, as those becoming vegan without conviction may be seduced by 'the dark side' of convenience, ideological pragmatism and relativism. Those nihilists who do not like to be 'too ethical' may go that way too, as embarrassed omnivorous looking for a quick way out from blame may also. Nevertheless, ethical veganism will prevail because of its simplicity. Black-and-white clear moral imperatives work better than flexible grey-area afterthoughts. Veganism will prevail because it is based on a coherent uncompromising powerful idea made practical and accessible to everyone. As simple as that.

V

What about my future? Last time I was properly 'out' (going somewhere other than exercising around my flat) was 10 March 2020. I took with me my black beanie with the big 'vegan' across its front, the old black jacket adorned with four metal pins – a badger, a fox, a cow and a 'proud vegan' sign – and my almost-empty rucksack only carrying a metal water bottle, a thermal mug and my bamboo cutlery. With all this I walked for about half an hour to the Southbank Centre in Waterloo.

As I arrived a bit early I spent some time wandering around, thinking about what I was going to say. At 10.45 I went to the sixth floor, the members' area, to check if the person I'd arranged to meet was already there. I saw a woman talking on her mobile phone sitting by herself at one of the tables with a distinctive pile of books – the mutually agreed identifier. 'Must be her,' I thought. I approached and she gestured in recognition. I sat on the chair diagonally opposite, so we could avoid facing each other directly – I thought it would be safer. After she finished her call, she greeted me, and when she politely extended her hand, I did not reciprocate. 'We are not supposed to shake hands anymore,' I said. She agreed.

I proceeded to tell her who I was, which was the purpose of the meeting. I talked for hours. I described my childhood in Catalonia. I explained all my adventures hitchhiking to the Monkey Sanctuary. I talked to her about my epiphany on the Isle of Skye. I discussed my legal case, and the prominence it brought me. However, I don't remember if I said it. I don't remember if I said the words 'I am an ethical vegan'. That would have summed everything up. It would have nicely encapsulated the three stories converging into my present. The raising of my awareness of the real world, the discovery of my true identity, and how *ahimsa* became alive for everyone.

I am more than an ethical vegan, though. Veganism isn't everything. It's the bare minimum for me to feel I have a real chance to become a decent human being. I have only dedicated one-third of my life to veganism so far. My veganism will improve further with time, and if I get to live to seventy-four years old, I will have been vegan for most of my life. Still, I would have spent the other half exploiting animals, causing them fear, pain and death.

Being an ethical vegan is not enough for me. No longer doing any harm is not enough. The manifestation of *ahimsa* is only half of who I am, only my Yin. I also have to help others to find out who they are (not to tell them who they are not), to be aware of the real world around them (not to move them from a fantasy world to another), to do what their true nature tells them they should do (not to force them to follow any false doctrine). Above all, I have to keep trying to protect the most forgotten animals and learn to do it better.

I will never stop asking the three questions: Who am I? What is this? What should I do? I will carry on searching for better answers, which with time should become more accurate, more genuine, more real. I will find other obstacles, new dilemmas, different paths. I will battle other contradictions, old demons, different weaknesses. I will persevere and do my best.

Stories may end, but not the reality which inspired them. Life progresses, evolves. Individuals may be born and die, but the best genes that started life on Earth survived, constantly replicating and multiplying. The best ideas do the same. They move from person to person, from culture to culture, from generation to generation. Through millions of years of biological evolution, altruism became a survival tool. Through thousands of years of human civilisation, this tool became the philosophical concept of *ahimsa*. Through hundreds of years of human history, this concept became the moral imperative 'do no harm'. Through decades of human enlightenment, this moral imperative became the belief of veganism. Through years of expansion of veganism, this belief became the identity of 'ethical vegans'. It's not over yet, though. Ideas progress and evolve too. This identity may become the new salvation for humanity, and we can finally share this planet with all the other earthlings in a true, compassionate, non-violent, just world. The future may be vegan after all.

I left the Southbank Centre with a sense of accomplishment.

We said goodbye without shaking hands – the new civility – and I proceeded to walk home. On my way there, I stopped at a coffee shop to get a matcha tea oat milk latte, but I left empty-handed as they no longer accepted customers' own containers – sensible rule, I thought.

A couple of days later I got the email. The meeting had indeed been successful, and now I had a publishing contract to sign. I could now tell everyone. I could now let everyone know how everything went. I could tell them stories of being an ethical vegan. I could explain to them how this personal, social and political journey could certainly change the world.

At the very least, I could try.

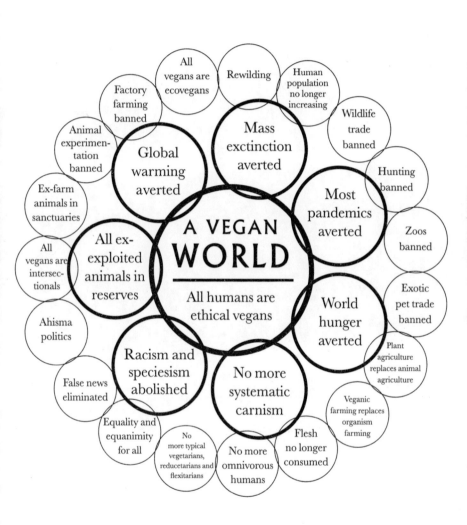

Acknowledgements

I would like to thank all the vegans I met in my life, many of whom have been an inspiration to me to become a better person, and in particular to Joe Hashman for his constant support during the latest milestones of my journey.

About the Author

Originally from Catalonia, and resident in the UK for several decades, Jordi Casamitjana is a vegan zoologist specialising in animal behaviour who has been involved in different aspects of animal protection for many years. In addition to scientific research he has worked as an undercover investigator, animal welfare consultant and animal protection campaigner. His most notable work achievements have been his involvement with the first successful prosecutions under the Hunting Act 2004, the exposé of trail hunting as a false alibi for illegal hunters and his participation in the campaign that led to the ban of bullfighting in Catalonia. Jordi published the novel *The Demon's Trial* under the pen name J. C. Costa, in which he explores many of the dilemmas animal protectionists face.

Jordi has been an ethical vegan for over eighteen years, and recently became well known for securing the legal protection of all ethical vegans in Great Britain from discrimination, a landmark case that was discussed all over the world.